COMPUTER PROGRAMMING

FOR BEGINNERS

AND CYBERSECURITY

4 MANUSCRIPTS IN 1:
THE ULTIMATE MANUAL TO LEARN
STEP BY STEP HOW TO
PROFESSIONALLY CODE AND
PROTECT YOUR DATA. THIS BOOK
INCLUDES: PYTHON, JAVA, C ++ AND
CYBERSECURITY

ALAN GRID

THIS BOOK INCLUDES

BOOK 1: 12 (PAGE)

PYTHON PROGRAMMING

THE EASIEST PYTHON CRASH COURSE TO GO DEEP THROUGH THE MAIN
APPLICATIONS AS WEB DEVELOPMENT, DATA ANALYSIS AND
DATA SCIENCE
INCLUDING MACHINE LEARNING

BOOK 2: 130 (PAGE)

JAVA PROGRAMMING

LEARN HOW TO CODE WITH AN OBJECT-ORIENTED PROGRAM TO
IMPROVE YOUR SOFTWARE ENGINEERING SKILLS. GET FAMILIAR WITH
VIRTUAL MACHINE, JAVASCRIPT AND MACHINE CODE

BOOK 3: 286 (PAGE)

C++ PROGRAMMING

A STEP-BY-STEP BEGINNER'S GUIDE TO LEARN THE FUNDAMENTALS OF A
MULTI-PARADIGM PROGRAMMING LANGUAGE AND
BEGIN TO MANAGE DATA
INCLUDING HOW TO WORK ON YOUR FIRST PROGRAM

BOOK 4: 454 (PAGE)

CYBERSECURITY

LEARN INFORMATION TECHNOLOGY SECURITY: HOW TO PROTECT YOUR
ELECTRONIC DATA FROM HACKER ATTACKS WHILE YOU ARE BROWSING
THE INTERNET WITH YOUR SMART DEVICES, PC OR TELEVISION

© Copyright 2020 - All rights reserved.

PYTHON PROGRAMMING

Table of Contents

JAVA PROGRAMMING

Table of Contents

C++ PROGRAMMING

Table of Contents

CYBERSECURITY

Table of Contents

PYTHON

PROGRAMMING

THE EASIEST PYTHON CRASH COURSE TO GO DEEP
THROUGH THE MAIN APPLICATIONS AS WEB
DEVELOPMENT, DATA ANALYSIS AND DATA
SCIENCE
INCLUDING MACHINE LEARNING

ALAN GRID

Introduction

The introduction of technologies, especially computers, has influenced our behavior differently. Some people spend most of their time on computers that create programs and websites to make a living, while others mess around with computers to try to understand many different things about how machines work. Programming is one of the areas in networks that most people in the world focus on as a source of income. They can work in a company or computer repair to protect computers from attacks such as hackers or viruses.

One of the most advanced programming tools is Python because anyone, including beginners or experts, can easily use and read it. The secret to using Python is that you can read it because it contains syntax, which allows you as a programmer to express your concepts without necessarily creating a coding page. This is what makes Python easier to use and read than the other codes, including C ++ and Java. Overall, Python is the best language for you because of its usability and readability. We are therefore confident that it will be easy for you to read and understand all the codes you enter while creating your first program during and after this course.

Features of the Python

Python has the following characteristics:

- Large library: it works with other programming projects such as searching for texts, connecting to the web servers, and exchanging files.

- Interactive: Using the Python is very simple because you can easily test codes to determine if they work.

- It is free software; so, you can always download it from the internet with your computer.

- Python programming language can be extended to other modules such as C ++ and C.

- Has an elegant syntax that makes it easy for beginners to read and use.

- Has several basic data types to choose from.

History of the Python

Python programming was discovered by Guido Van Rossum in 1989 while he was carrying out a project at the Dutch research institute CWI, but it was later discontinued. Guido has successfully used a number of basic languages, the so-called ABC language, to work on the Python. According to Van Rossum, the strength of the python language is that you can either keep it simple or extend it to more platforms to support many platforms at once. The design allowed the system to easily communicate with the libraries and various file formats.

Since its introduction, many programmers now use Python in the world, and in fact, many tools are included to improve operation and efficiency. Many programmers have taken various initiatives to educate everyone about using python programming language and how it can help ease the fear of complex computer codes.

However, the Python was made open source by Van Rossum a few years ago to allow all programmers access and even make changes to it. This has changed a lot in the field of programming. For example, there was a release of the Python 2.0. Python 2.0 was community-oriented, making it transparent in the development process. While many people don't use Python, there are still some programmers and organizations that use part of the version.

The Python 3, a unique version, was released in 2008. Although the version has many different functions, it is completely different from the first two versions, and it is not easy to update the program. While this version is not backwards compatible, it has a small creator to show what needs to be changed when uploading the files.

Why you should use Python

There are many types of computer coding programs in the world, each with its advantages and disadvantages. However, Python has proven to be the best option for a variety of reasons, such as readability, and can be used on many platforms without changing things.

Using Python has the following advantages;

- **Readability**

Since it is designed in the English language, a beginner will find it easy to read and us. There are also a number of rules that help the programmer understand how to format everything, and this makes it easy for a programmer to create a simple code that other people can follow when using their projects with it.

- **Community**

Today, there are many workshops for Python worldwide. A beginner can visit online, offline, or both to learn more or even seek clarification on Python. Also, online and offline workshops can improve your understanding of Python, as well as your socialization skills. It is best for the personal computer as it works successfully on many different platforms. In fact, all beginners find it easy to code or learn from the expert.

- **Libraries**

For over 25 years, programmers have been using Python to teach the beginners how to use different codes written with it. The system is very open to programmers, and they can use the available codes indefinitely. In fact, a student can download and install the system and use it for their personal use, such as writing your codes and completing the product.

General terms in the Python

Understanding the standard terms used in Python is essential to you. It makes everything easy to know when you get started. Following are the most common terms in the Python programming language;

- Function: Refers to a code block that is called when a programmer uses a calling program. The goal is to also provide free services and accurate calculation.

- Class: A template used for developing user-defined objects. It is friendly and easy to use by everyone, including the beginners.

Ver Immutable: refers to an object with a fixed value and is contained within the code. These can be numbers, strings, or tuples. Such an object cannot be changed.

St Docstring: Refers to a string that is displayed in the function, class definition, and module. This object is always available in the documentation tools.

- List: Refers to the data type built into the Python and contains values sorted. Such values include strings and numbers.

LE IDLE: Stands for an integrated development environment that allows the users to type the code while interpreting and editing it in the same window. Best suited for beginners because it is an excellent example of code.

Interactive: Python has become the most suitable programming language for beginners due to its interactive nature. As a beginner, you can try out many things in the IDLE (interpreter to see their response and effects).

Qu Triple Quoted String: The string helps an individual to have single and double quotes in the string, making it easy to go through different lines of code.

- Object: It refers to all data in a state such as attitudes, methods, defined behaviors, or values.

- Type: Refers to a group of data categories in the programming language and differences in properties, functions, and methods.

- Tuple: Refers to the datatype built into the Python and is an unchanging set of values, although it contains some changeable values.

Advantages of Python Language

Using the Python program has many advantages over other programming languages such as C ++ and Java. You will be happy to see the availability and how easy it is to learn and use the Python program. Ideally, these are the best programming languages you can use right now, especially if you are a beginner. Following are some of the advantages of using Python language;

- **It is easy to use, write and read**

Many programmers face some challenges when using programming languages such as Java and C ++. They are difficult to view due to their design. One has to spend a lot of his/her time learning about the use of parentheses, and it is not easy to recognize some of the words used in these programming languages. Such words can scare you, especially if you are just getting acquainted with the programming languages. Unlike Java and C ++ languages, Python does not use crazy brackets. It only uses indents, making it easy to read the page. It uses English, which makes it easy to understand characters.

In addition to using indents, Python uses a lot of white spaces, making it easy to learn and read what's needed. It consists of many places with comments to allow you to understand or get clarification in case the program confuses you. So, check it out, and you will see how easy it is to use the Python programming language.

- **It uses English as the primary language**

Using Python is easy because the main language is English. As a beginner, you will spend less time reading and understanding the basic words used when programming in Python. So, whether you speak native or non-native English, Python is best for you because most words are simple and easy to understand.

- **Python is already available on some computers**

Some computers, such as macOS systems and Ubuntu, come with Python pre-installed. In this case, you just need to download the text interpreter to get started with Python programming. However, you must download the program on your computer if you are using a Windows computer. In fact, Python works fine even if you didn't install it from the beginning.

- **Python works perfectly with other programming languages**

For the first time, you will be using Python alone. However, you will realize that Python can work with other languages as you continue programming. Some of the programming languages that you can work with Python include C ++ and JavaScript. Try to learn more about Python and what it can do practically. You will be able to discover many things over time.

- **The Python can be used to test many things**

You need to download the test interpreter once you have downloaded the Python. The test interpreter plays an important role in enabling Python to read the information. It's good to use a simple product like Notepad that is available in your Windows or other interpreters.

Disadvantages of using Python programming

While there are many advantages to using Python, it is essential to recognize some of the adverse effects of using it. Some individuals prefer to use other programming languages such as C ++ and JavaScript for Python because of the following negative effects of Python.

- **Python has a slow speed**

While Python works well with other programming languages and is suitable for beginners, it is unfortunate that Python is not ideal for programmers looking for a high-speed program as it is a slower translated language than the other options. The level of speed depends on the content you are translating because some benchmarks with Python code work faster compared to other codes. Currently, many programmers around the world are trying to solve this problem by making the interpreting speed faster. It is hopeful that Python will run at the same rate or even faster than C and C ++ soon.

- **Python is not available in most mobile browsers**

While Python works well for those who have regular computers and is accessible on many server platforms and desktops to help individuals create the codes they are looking for, it is not yet ready for mobile computing. Programmers are trying to transition the program to mobile computing to cater to today's large numbers of people who use cell phones.

• Limited design

Python program is not a better option for programmers looking for a program with many design options. For example, the design language is not available in some other options; so, you will need more time to test, and sometimes, a lot of errors can occur when you run the program.

CHAPTER 1:

Python Basics

O nce you have the software installed on your system, it is time to begin your programming adventure with Python. I will start with the fundamentals such as variables, strings, and keywords. Now, you will learn and write your very first program in Python, the different data you can work with, how to use variables, and keywords. Let us begin with the basics to get your coding started right away.

Keywords

async	assert	as	and
def	from	nonlocal	while
continue	for	lambda	try
elif	if	or	yield
else	import	pass	

global	not	with	del
in	raise	false	await
return	none	break	except
true	class	finally	Is

Let us begin with the fundamental "Hello" program that is the first step for any programmer.

> Print ("Hello, Welcome to Python Programming!")

When this program code is run, your output will be:

> Hello, Welcome to Python Programming!

Python programs always end with the extension .py Let us save this program as Hello.py. Please always remember to save each example using its name in order to recall them when necessary. When you use your editor or IDE, the file is run via the interpreter, which then determines the words used in the program. For instance, in the program below, the interpreter will see the word encircled in parenthesis and prints what is inside the parentheses. In the course of writing Python codes, the editor may highlight certain parts of the program. For instance, it recognizes that print () is a function name and uses a particular color to differentiate it. However, when it gets to the word "Hello Welcome to Python Programming!" it recognizes that it is a Python program code. Therefore, it uses a different color to differentiate it from the other code. This unique feature is known as syntax highlighting and is useful for beginners.

Indentation and Lines

There is nothing like braces to indicate a block of code for function and class in Python. Normally, a block of code is represented by a line indentation that gets enforced in a strong manner. Importantly, the spaces in the indentation vary; however, every statement in the block must have the same amount of indentation. For instance,

```
if False:

    print "False"

else:

    print "True"
```

However, the block of the statement below will generate an error

```
if False:
```

```
print "Result"

print "False"

else:

print "Result"

print "True"
```

Consequently, all continuous lines you indent using the same number of spaces will for a block. Let us use another example to show various statement blocks. I will advise you not to try to understand the logic of the program. However, your aim is to understand the various blocks irrespective of their structure.

```
import sys

try:

    # open file stream

    file = open(fileName, "w")

except IOError:

    print "Error when writing to," fileName

    sys.exit()
```

```
print "Enter '," fileFinish,

print "' When finished"

while fileText != fileFinish:

  fileText = real_input("Enter text you want: ")

  if fileText == fileFinish:

    # close the file

    file.close

    break

  file.write(file_text)

  file.write("\n")

file.close()

fileText = real_input("Enter filename: ")

if len(fileName) == 0:

  print "Next time input something"

  sys.exit()

try:
```

```
file = open(fileName, "r")

except IOError:

    print "Error reading file requested"

    sys.exit()

fileText = file.read()

file.close()

print fileText
```

Multiple Line Statements

These statements normally terminate with a new line. Though, it allows you to use a special character (\) to continue a statement. Check the code below:

```
Total_Number = number1 + \

    number2 + \

    number3
```

Notwithstanding, there is an exception to this situation if such statements contain brackets such as (), {}, or []. For instance;

```
months = ['December', 'November,' 'October,' 'September,'
'August,'

                    'July,' 'June,' 'May,' 'April,' 'March,' 'February,'
'January']
```

Variables

A variable is a storage location, which has a name assigned to it. In Python, we can assign a value to a variable and recall these variables. I believe an example will make things clearer. Remember our first program (hello.py), let us add an additional two lines. Consider the program below:

```
outcome= "Hello, Welcome to Python Programming!"

print(outcome)
```

When you run the program, your output will be the same as the previous one, which was:

```
Hello, Welcome to Python Programming!
```

The only difference is that we added a variable called "outcome." Each variable always has a value assigned to it. In this situation, the value of "outcome" is "Hello Welcome to Python Programming!"

Let us add two additional lines to the previous code. However, ensure to insert a blank line in the first code before adding the new codes.

```
outcome= "Hello, Welcome to Python Programming!"

print(outcome)

outcome = "Hello, Welcome to Learning Python!"

print(outcome)
```

After adding the two lines, save the file and run the program again. Your output will be as follows:

```
Hello, Welcome to Python Programming!

Hello, Welcome to Learning Python!
```

Rules to Variable Naming

There are important rules to adhere to when naming variables in Python. If you break any of these rules, you will get an error message. Therefore, ensure to keep them in your mind when writing your programs.

- Variable names must have only numbers, underscores, and letters. You can begin your variable names with an underscore or a letter; however, it must not begin with a number. For example, your variable name can be outcome_1, but using 1_outcome is completely wrong.

- A variable name must not contain space between them. Notwithstanding, you can use underscores to separate two words. For instance, outcome_program will work; however, the outcome program will cause errors in your program.

- Avoid using function names and keywords as variable names

- Variable names must be short and descriptive when used. For instance, the score is preferable than using s, serial_name is better than sn.

Avoiding Variable Name Errors

As a beginner, you will make mistakes. Professionals aren't exempted from this situation, but they know how to tackle these errors efficiently. Let us look at a more likely mistake you will make as you beginning your Python-programming course. I will intentionally write an error code by misspelling the word "outcome."

```
outcome = "Hello, Welcome to Learning Python!"

#program will generate an error

print(outcom)
```

When such an error occurs, the Python interpreter figures the best way to solve the problem. It provides a traceback once the program cannot run successfully. Not many programming languages have this feature to traceback an error. Let us look at how the interpreter will respond to our program above

```
Trackback (most recent call last):

    1.  File "hello.py," line 3, in <module>

    2.  Print(outcom)

    3.  NameError: name 'outcome' is not defined
```

Line 1 reports the presence of an error in line 3 with filename "hello.py" however, the interpreter quickly identifies the error and informs us what particular type of error it is in line 3. In a situation like this, it will signify a name error. Additionally, it will reports that our variable hasn't been properly defined. Whenever you see a name error, it means there is a spelling error, or we didn't set a value to the variable. However, in this example, it was a wrong spelling where we didn't include the letter "e" from our variable name.

```
outcom= "Hello, Welcome to Python Programming!"

print(outcome)

outcom = "Hello, Welcome to Learning Python!"

print(outcome)
```

The program output will be:

```
Hello, Welcome to Python Programming!

Hello, Welcome to Learning Python!
```

You must understand that programming languages are strict; however, they disregard bad and good spellings. Because of this, you don't need to contemplate about grammatical and spelling procedures when creating a variable name.

Exercises to Try

Write a program that intends to perform the following things. Ensure to save the file and following the variable naming rules.

- Write a program that assigns a message to a variable name of your choice and print the message

- In this second program, change the value and use a new message. Then print the message.

- Tick the wrong variable names from the list below

  o 1_school

  o Fred Love

  o Fred_love

  o _exercises

  o Firsttwoletters

Data Types in Python

When writing codes, we need to store data into memory. These data cannot be stored in the same memory because a number will be different from a letter. For instance, a person's name is alphabetic; address can be alphanumeric characters, whereas age can be stored as a numerical value. Python has data types to define various operations and methods of storing these data types. There are five data types in Python; these are:

- String

- Numbers

- Tuple

- List

- Dictionary

String

This is a series of characters, which is enclosed in quotes. In Python, anything in quotes is regarded as a unique character. Both single and double quotes can be used to form a string in Python.

'Hello World'

"Hello World"

The two statements would produce the same output if we were to run it.

Using Quotes Inside Strings

In Python programming, when using strings, an opening string with a quote must match the ending quote. When you begin a string using a double quotation mark, Python takes the next double quotation mark as the ending of the string. This applies to a single quotation mark.

If you decide to use double quotes inside a string, you have to place them inside single quotes. The example below will show it better.

statement = 'Fred is "a boy that lives in New York"'

Let's assume you want to use both single and double quotes in a string. In this situation, you have to escape the single, and double quote misses up by using a backslash (\). The example below will demonstrate it.

```
statement_in_single = 'Fred "own\'s a wonderful car in his garage"'

statement_in_double = "Fred \ 'own's a wonderful car in his garage\""
```

Using Methods to Change Case in String

One simple task you can perform when using strings is to change the case of a particular word. What do you think the output will be for the code below?

```
full_name = "johnson boris"

print(full_name.title())
```

Once you write the code, save the file as name.py before running it. The output will be as follow:

```
Johnson Boris
```

If you observe, the variable full_name refers to the string in lowercase "johnson boris." After the variable name comes to the method title(). In Python, a method is an action upon which certain manipulation can be taken on a piece of data. Furthermore, the dot (.) that comes after the variable name informs the interpreter to allow the title() method to interact with our variable name. Parentheses always follow a method because they require additional information to perform their function. The function of the title() method is to change the first letter of each word to capital letter. Furthermore, Python allows us to change string to all lowercase or uppercase.

```
full_name = "Johnson Boris"

print(full_name.lower())

print (full_name.upper))
```

The output will be as follows:

> johnson boris
>
> JOHNSON BORIS

Using Variables in Strings

In certain scenarios, you may decide to use a variable, which contains a value in a string. For instance, you may want to use two variables to hold the first name and last name of a person, respectively. Additionally, these two variables must be combined to produce the individual's full name. Let us consider how that is possible in Python.

```
first_name = "johnson"

last_name = "boris"

        1. full_name = f "{first_name} {last_name}"

print(full_name)
```

If you want to insert a variable value to a string, you have to add the letter "f" directly before the opening quotation mark

Consider the code below

```
state = 'United Nation!'   #Assign the variable "state" to a string 'New York'
```

```
print state        # Prints the complete string

print state[0]     # Prints the first character of the string

print state[0:4]   # Prints characters starting from 1st to 4th

print state[3:]    # Prints string starting from 4th character

print state * 3    # Prints string three times

print state + " United State" # Prints concatenated string
```

The output will be –

```
United Nation!

U

United

Nations!

United Nation! United Nation!

United Nation! United State
```

CHAPTER 2:

Conditional Statements

N
ow, it is time to move on to the topic of conditional statements, which can also go by the name of decision control statements. These are going to be the statements that allow the computer to make some decisions based on the input that the user has, as well as what you would like to happen with the program. You will have many times in your program where you will want the computer to make some decisions and complete itself when you are not there. If you are working on a code where you would like the user to put in their answer, rather than giving them two options to work with, then these decision control statements are going to be good options to work with.

There are going to be a few different options that you can work with when you are making these conditional statements. The three most common ones are going to include the if statement, the if-else statement, and the elif statement. As a beginner, we are going to start with the basics of the if statement to get a good idea of how these can work, and then we will build up to understand some of the more complicated things that you can do with these conditional statements.

The first option that we are going to take a look at is the if statement. The if statement is going to work with the ideas, and the answer that your user gives to the computer is going to be either true or false. If the user does an input of information that is seen as true based on your code, then the interpreter can continue with the program, and it will show up the statements or the information that you would like. But, if the user is on the program and puts in something that doesn't match up with your code, and is seen as false, then the program is automatically going to end.

The good news is that we can go through a bit later, and look at the steps that you can take to ensure that you are going to get the program to respond no matter what answer your user gives, but that is not what the if statement is going to focus on. We need to take a look at this simplified form for now, and then build up from there. To help us look at how the if statement is meant to look when your user interacts with it, you will need to work with the following code:

age = int(input("Enter your age:"))

if (age <=18):

print("You are not eligible for voting, try next election!")

print("Program ends")

Once you have added this conditional statement to your compiler, we need to explore what is going to happen with the above code. If the user does come to this part of the program, and they say that they are under the age of 18, then there will be a message that comes up on the screen. In this case, we wrote in that the message that will come up is going to be, "You are not eligible for voting, try next election!" Then the program, because we don't have any other parts of the code here right now, is going to end. But, this brings up the question of what is going to happen with this particular code if the user does say that they are older than 18?

When a computer programmer is working with the if statement, if the user puts their age in at over 18, then nothing is going to happen. The if statement is going to be the option that you use when you only want the user to pick out the one answer that your code says is true. The user has to say that they are younger than 18 in this situation, or the program is going to be done.

As you can imagine here, this is going to cause us some problems. You most likely would want to allow your user to put in any age that works for them. Some of the users who will come to this program are going to be older than 18, and you don't want the program to end without anything there because they are older than that age range. This is going to end the program before you want it to, and it doesn't look that professional with the program that you are working with when the code ends. This is a big reason why you are not going to see the if statements all that often.

But this is where we are going to bring in the if-else statements and use those to fix this problem. These take the idea that we were going through, the issues that we brought up, and helping us to deal with them. Let's say that you are working with the code that we had before, and you want to make sure that your program brings up a result, no matter what answer the user decides to put into the program. You can write out an if-else statement so that you can get an answer for those who are under the age of 18, and then a different answer for those who are 18 and older. The code for this expands out the option that we talked about before, but here is an example that you can use.

```
age = int(input("Enter your age:"))

if (age <=18):

print("You are not eligible for voting, try next election!")

else

print("Congratulations! You are eligible to vote. Check out your local polling station to find out more information!)

print("Program ends")
```

This code is going to be a lot more useful to your endeavors and what you want to happen in your code, and it provides you with some more options than before. And the best part is that your code is not going to end because the user puts in their age. It is going to provide them with a statement on the screen based on the age that they put into it.

This code can also be expanded out to include some more possibilities if you would like. The example above just had two options, those under the age of 18 and those above. But you can have more options if it works for your program. For example, you can split up the age ranges a bit more if you would like. Maybe you want to know who is under the age of 18, who is in their 20's, who is in their 30's, and those who are older than 40. You can use this same idea and add in some more lines to it, to help meet the needs of your program using the if-else statement.

Another example that you may want to use when it comes to the if-else statement is when you ask the program to pick out their favorite color. You probably do not want to go through and write out enough code to handle each color that is out there in the world, but you will leave this open so that the user can put in the information that corresponds with their favorite color.

For this code, you may choose to have a list of six colors that you write out in the code (you can have more or less for what you need), and then you will have a message that corresponds to these six colors. You may pick out the colors of yellow, orange, green, blue, purple, and red. Then, you can add an else statement so that the user can pick out a different color. If the user decides to have white as their favorite color here, then the seventh, and the final message will come up. This final message is going to be the same for any of the colors that don't fit in with the original six.

Adding this else statement, or the catch-all, to the end of the code can be an important thing that you need to consider. You can't possibly list out all of the different colors that your user may choose to work with. You may take the time to put in a hundred different colors (but this takes a lot of time and code, and you won't want to do this), but then the user could go with the one color that you forget. If you don't add this else statement to the end, then the program is going to be lost at how you would like it to behave here.

The else statement is nice because it is going to be the one that you can use to catch more than one result from the user, and it can catch all of the answers that you don't account for, but that the user may choose to use. If you don't add a statement in the code, then your program isn't going to be sure how to behave when the user puts that answer in.

The Elif Statements

The other two options of conditional statements are going to be important for a lot of the codes that you would like to work with. The if statement is a good one to learn as a beginner getting into these statements, and they will help you to mostly get a good idea of how the conditional statements are supposed to work. These if statements are going to have a basis on the idea of the answer being either true or false.

In this case, if the answer received from the user is seen as true based on the conditions that you add to the code, then the program will see this and continue on its path. But if the condition is seen to be false, then the program is not going to have anything set up, and it is going to end.

This is a simple idea to work with and is a good way to learn more about the conditional statements, but for many of the codes that you want to write out in Python, it is not going to give you the results that you want.

Then we took a look at the if-else statements. These took this idea a bit further, and it understood that the ideas that come with the original if statements are going to be too simple.

These if-else statements can help us handle any answer that the user will give to the system, and ensure that the program doesn't just stop. We even took a look at an example code that shows us how these kinds of statements work.

From here, we need to spend some time working on the elif statements. This is going to handle things a bit different than what the other two did, but it is still going to be useful and can add an element of fun and something different to your code.

The elif statement is going to give the user a chance to pick from a few options that you present to them. And then, the answer that the user chooses is going to provide them with a predetermined statement that you added into the code.

There are different places where you can see these conditional statements.

The elif statement is a unique code for the Python language, and it is often going to be used for many games, or for a different program that you would like to have with the menu style of choices for the user.

These statements are going to be used most often if the computer programmer would like to provide their user with some options rather than just one or two.

CHAPTER 3:

Data Structures

Python is based on three reference structures: tuples, lists, and dictionaries. These structures are actually objecting that may contain other objects. They have quite different utilities and allow you to store information of all types.

These structures have a number of common features:

To extract one or more objects from a structure, we always use the []

For numerically indexed structures (tuples and lists), the structures are indexed to 0 (the first position is position 0)

The Tuples

This is a structure that groups multiple objects in indexed order. Its form is not modifiable (immutable) once created and is defined using parentheses. It has only one dimension. Any type of object can be stored in a tuple. For example, if you want to create a tuple with different objects, we use:

tup1 = (1, True, 7.5.9)

You can also create a tuple by using the tuple () function. Access to the values of a tuple is done by the classical indexing of structures. Thus, if we want to access the third element of our tuple, we use:

In []: tup1 [2]

Out []: 7.5

Tuples can be interesting because they require little memory. Else, on the other hand, they are used as outputs of functions returning several values. Tuples as structures are objects. They have methods that are clean. These are few for a tuple:

In []: tup1.count (9)

Out []: 1

We often prefer lists that are more flexible.

Lists

The list is the reference structure in Python. It is modifiable and can contain any object.

Creating a list

We create a list using square brackets:

list1 = [3,5,6, True]

You can also use the list () function. The structure of a list is editable. It has many methods:

.append (): add value at the end of the list

.insert (i, val): insert value to the index i

.pop (i): retrieves the value of the index i

.reverse (): reverse the list

.extend (): extends the list with a list of values

Note—All of these methods modify the list, the equivalent in terms of classic code would be the following:

liste1.extend (list2)

equivalent to

list1 = list1 + list2

Lists have other methods including:

.index (val): returns the index of the value val

.count (val): returns the number of occurrences of val

.remove (val): remove the first occurrence of the value val from the list

Extract an Item from a List

As we have seen above, it is possible to extract an element using the brackets:

list1 [0]

We are often interested in the extraction of several elements. It is done by using the two points:

list1 [0: 2] or list1 [: 2]

In this example, we see that this system extracts two elements: the indexed element in 0 and the one indexed in position 1. So we have as a rule that i: j goes from the element I included in element j not included. Here are some other examples:

Extract the last element

list1 [-1]

Extract the last 3 elements list1 [-3: -1] or list1 [-3:]

A concrete example

Suppose we wanted to create a list of countries. These countries are ordered in the list according to their population. We will try to extract the first three and the last three.

In []: country_list = ["China," "India," "United States," "France," "Spain," "Swiss"]

In []: print (country_list [: 3])

['China', 'India', 'United States']

In []: print (country_list [-3:])

['France', 'Spain', 'Switzerland']

In []: country_list.reverse ()

print (liste_pays)

['Switzerland', 'Spain', 'France', 'United States', 'India', 'China']

The Comprehension Lists

These are lists built iteratively. They are often very useful because they are more efficient than using loops to build lists. Here is a simple example:

In []: list_init = [4,6,7,8]

list_comp = [val ** 2 for val in list_init if val% 2 == 0]

The list comp_list allows you to store the even elements of list_init set to the square.

We will have:

In []: print (list_comp)

[16,36,64]

This notion of comprehension list is very effective. It avoids useless code (loops on a list) and performs better than creating a list iteratively. It also exists in dictionaries but not on tuples that are unchangeable. We will be able to use comprehension lists in the framework of the manipulation of data tables.

Strings—Character Lists

Strings in Python are encoded by default (since Python 3) in Unicode. You can declare a string of characters in three ways:

string1 = "Python for the data scientist"

string2 = 'Python for the data scientist'

string3 = "" "Python for the data scientist" ""

The last one allows having strings on several lines. We will most often use the first. A string is actually a list of characters, and we will be able to work on the elements of a string as on those of a list:

In []: print (string1 [: 6])

print (string1 [-14:])

print (string1 [3:20 p.m.])

Python for the Data Scientist

Data strings can be easily transformed into lists:

In []: # we separate the elements using space

list1 = chaine1.split ()

print (list1)

['Python', 'for', 'the', 'Data', 'Scientist']

In []: # we join the elements with space

string1bis = "" .join (list1)

print (chaine1bis)

Dictionaries

The dictionaries constitute a third central structure to develop in Python. They allow key-value storage. So far, we have used items based on numerical indexing. So in a list, you access an element using its position list1 [0]. In a dictionary, we will access an element using a key defined when creating the dictionary. We define a dictionary with braces:

dict1 = {"cle1": value1, "cle2": value2, "cle3": value3}

This structure does not require any homogeneity of type in the values. From this, we can have a list like value1, a boolean like value2, and an integer a value3.

To access an element of a dictionary, we use:

In []: dict1 ["cle2"]

Out []: value2

To display all the keys of a dictionary, we use:

In []: dict1.keys

Out []: ("cle1," "cle2," "cle3")

To display all the values of a dictionary, we use:

In []: dict1.items ()

Out []: (value1, value2, value3)

One can easily modify or add a key to a dictionary:

In []: dict1 ["key4"] = value4

You can also delete a key (and the associated value) in a dictionary:

In []: del dict1 ["cle4"]

As soon as you are more experienced in Python, you will use more dictionaries. At first, we tend to favor lists dictionaries because they are often more intuitive (with numerical indexing). However, more expert Pythonist will quickly realize the usefulness of dictionaries. In particular, we will be able to store the data as well as the parameters of a model in a very simple way. Plus, the flexibility of Python's for loop adapts very well to dictionaries and makes them very effective when they are well built.

Programming

The Conditions

A condition in Python is very simple to implement; it is a keyword. As mentioned before, the Python language is based on the indentation of your code. We will use an offset for this indentation with four spaces. Fortunately, tools like Spyder or Jupyter notebooks will automatically generate this indentation.

Here is our first condition, which means "if a is true, then display" it is "true":

if a is True:

print ("it's true")

There is no exit from the condition; it is the indentation that will allow to manage it. Generally, we are also interested in the complement of this condition; we will use else for that:

if a is True:

```
print ("it's true")

else:

print ("it's not true")
```

We can have another case if our variable a is not necessarily a boolean, we use elif:

```
if a is True:

print ("it's true")

elif a is False:

print ("it's wrong")

else:

print ("it's not a boolean")
```

The Loops

Loops are central elements of most programming languages. Python does not break this rule. However, you must be very careful with an interpreted language such as Python. Indeed, the treatment of loops is slow in Python, and we will use it in loops with few iterations. We avoid creating a loop repeating itself thousands of times on the lines of an array of data. However, we can use a loop on the columns of a data table to a few dozen columns.

The for loop

The Python loop has a somewhat specific format; it is a loop on the elements of a structure. We will write:

for elem in [1, 2]:

print (elem)

This piece of code will allow you to display 1 and 2. So the iterator of the loop (elem in our case) thus takes the values of the elements of the structure in the second position (after the in). These elements may be in different structures, but lists will generally be preferred.

Range, zip and enumerate functions

These three functions are very useful functions, they make it possible to create specific objects that may be useful in your code for your loops. The range () function is used to generate a sequence of numbers, starting from a given number or 0 by default and up to a number not included:

In []: print (list (range (5)))

[0, 1, 2, 3, 4]

In []: print (list (range (2,5)))

[2, 3, 4]

In []: print (list (range (2,15,2)))

[2, 4, 6, 8, 10, 12, 14]

We see here that the created range object can be easily transformed into a list with the list ().

In a loop, this gives:

for i in range (11):

print (i)

The zip and enumerate functions are also useful functions in loops and they use lists.

The enumerate () function returns the index and the element of a list. If we take our list of countries used earlier:

In []: for i, in enumerate (country_list):

print (i, a)

1. Swiss
2. Spain
3. France
4. United States
5. India
6. China

The zip function will allow linking many lists and simultaneously iterating elements of these lists.

If, for example, we want to simultaneously increment days and weather, we may use:

In []: for day, weather in zip (["Monday," "Tuesday"], ["beautiful," "bad"]):

print ("% s, it will make% s"% (day.capitalize (), weather))

Monday, it will be nice

Tuesday, it will be bad

In this code, we use zip () to take a pair of values at each iteration. The second part is a manipulation of the character strings. If one of the lists is longer than the other, the loop will stop as soon as it arrives at the end of one of them.

We can link enumerate and zip in one code, for example:

In []: for i, (day, weather) in enumerate (zip (["Monday," "Tuesday"], ["good," "bad"])):

print ("% i:% s, it will make% s"% (i, day.capitalize (), meteo))

0: Monday, it will be nice

1: Tuesday, it will be bad

We see here that i is the position of the element i.

Note—Replace in a string.

While loop

Python also allows you to use a while () loop that is less used and looks a lot like the while loop that we can cross in other languages. To exit this loop, we can use a station wagon with a condition. Warning, we must increment the index in the loop, at the risk of being in a case of an infinite loop.

We can have:

i = 1

while i <100:

i + = 1

if i> val_stop:

break

print (i)

This code adds one to i to each loop and stops when i reaches either val_stop, that is 100.

Note—The incrementation in Python can take several forms i = i + 1 or i + = 1.

Both approaches are equivalent in terms of performance; it's about choosing the one that suits you best.

CHAPTER 4:

Dealing with Local vs. Global in Python

Now we need to take a look at some of the different types of variables that you are able to work with when it is time to handle them in Python. The two main types of variables that we are going to work within this language will include the local variable and the global variable.

There are some big differences that are going to show up when we are talking about these variables. To start with is the global variable. This is mainly going to mean that we are looking at a variable that the rest of the program, or any part of the program, is able to declare. It doesn't matter where that part of the program is located; it will be able to use and rely on that global variable when it would like to.

Sometimes this is a good thing and will allow your modules to declare the variables that they want, even when they are not near one another. But other times, this is going to cause some issues. If the wrong part of the code tries to declare some of the variables that it shouldn't, it can cause the code to not behave the way that you want, and some of the variables are going to get declared at the wrong time. This is never a good thing, and it is going to require you to take some chances if you want to avoid this issue.

The solution to this issue is going to be the local variables. These are the ones that can't be accessed throughout the code. These are the variables that are only going to be declared in a specific method or function that you determine ahead of time. This will make sure that the variable is going to only be used in the manner that you would like, and nowhere else.

The Local Variable

The first option that we are going to take some time to look at is the local variable. This is going to be similar to what we will see with a local variable in other languages, and it is going to be the one that is declared at the beginning of the block that the variable is supposed to be local to at that time. It can also show up when we are working with a statement, a switch statement, and more depending on your needs.

The local variable is going to have a declaration with it that can explicitly define the type of the variable that has been declared along with some of the identifiers that will name out the variable at the same time. We will recognize the local variable as a type of variable that we are able to use where the scope and the extent of the variable are within the method or the statement block in which it is declared.

We are able to use these local variables more like an iteration variable in the foreach statement, the exception variable in the specific catch clause, and the resource variable when we are doing the using statement. It can also be used as a type of constant whose value can't be modified within the method or the statement block in which we declare it.

A local variable that is implicitly typed whose type is going to be inferred by the computer from the expression on its right is going to be useful when you would like to deal with the language-integrated queries. These are going to be the types of queries that will return to us some anonymous types in creating a custom type for each of the sets of results that you have.

The memory allocation that you are going to find with this kind of a variable is often going to be based on the type of variable that you are working with. If you are working with something like an integer or a structure, then the entirety of the contents will be stored in a stack. But if you are using a reference type of variable, it is going to be placed in the reference portion of the stack, and the contents will be in the heap that goes with it.

A local variable is one that needs to not be referred to in the code in any kind of textual position that will proceed with the declaration statement of your local variable. In addition, we have to remember that when we are in one single block, there can never be more than one variable that has the same name. Doing this is going to be a bad thing because it is going to cause an error to show up and will basically just confuse the code that you are working with. However, multiple local variables of the same type can be declared, and it can be initialized, in one single statement.

Within the method of a class that you find one of these local variables and it is named in a manner that is similar to its field, you will find that the local variable is going to hide the field while still being able to access it within the method. It is often more efficient for us to work with a local variable rather than a field.

Looking at a Global Variable

The other thing that we need to take a look at here is what a global variable is all about. This is going to be a type of variable that we will declare outside of any of our functions, which means that it is easy to access by all of the functions that are found in the program that you are writing. A group of these variables is called a global environment or a global state, because when they are combined, and they are going to define various aspects of a program or an environment when the program is going to run.

A global variable is going to be the one that is declared on top of all the other functions, and it is usually best if we can keep this to a minimum. This is because all of the functions will be able to manipulate these variables during the run time of the program. For most of the programs that you want to handle in this language, this can be dangerous because there is the possibility that they can be changed on accident, and that causes bugs in the system.

Global variables, as we can guess by the name, will be some variables that we can access globally, or everywhere throughout the program.

Once we go through the process of declaring them, these are going to stay in the memory throughout the runtime of the program. This means that we are able to get them changed with any function that we want, at any time when the program is running, and this can definitely cause some issues with the program as a whole.

During some of the earlier years when computers can be used, but they had a limited amount of memory, these global variables were seen as bad practice because they would take up a lot of valuable information and memory, and it was easier for the programmer to start losing track of the values they worked with, especially in longer programs. And basically, it brought in a lot of bugs to the program that was hard to locate and fix.

Source code is always going to be easier to use and to understand when the scope of its elements is limited. This is something that is hard to do when we are working with the global variables because they are not local, and it becomes really hard to figure out and see where these variables have been changed or even the reason why they were changed in the first place.

Even with this kind of stigma, these global variables are going to be pretty valuable when we are working in functions that do not chare a relation that is known as caller and called. This means that the function is not going to have signal handlers or any kind of concurrent threads. With the exception of those global variables that are declared as read-only values in the protected memory, the codes need to make sure they are able to deploy some of the proper encapsulation in order to be seen as thread-safe in the process.

As we can see here, there are some benefits, and even some negatives, that come with working on this kind of variable. There are still some uses of working with this, which is why we spent some time taking a look at them and figuring out why they are important, but for the most part, the local variables are better and will keep some more control in the codes that you are writing.

Putting It All Together

This may seem a bit confusing in the beginning, but the good news is that there are a number of things that we are able to do when it is time to work with these two variables. And to help us gain a better understanding of the differences between global and local variables with the program that we used below:

1. The variable "f" is going to be one that has a global scope, and it is going to be assigned value 101, which is printed in the output.
2. The variable f is also going to be declared in a function and assumes local scope. It is going to be assigned to a value, and in this case, it is going to be assigned to a value "I am learning Python." Which is going to then be printed out as an output. This variable is different from that global variable f that we tried to define in the previous step.

3. Once we have been able to call the function over, the local variable f is going to be destroyed. At line 12, when we again go through and print off the value off, it is going to show us the global variable that is f = 101.

We can then go through and use the keyword of global, and this will make sure that we are then able to reference the variable that is global inside of the function.

Some of the things that we are going to be able to follow with this one will include:

1. The variable "f" is going to be global with its scope, and then it is going to be given a value of 101, which is going to be printed as the output.

2. This same variable is going to be declared when we use the global keyword. This is not going to be the local variable here, but the same global variable that we were able to declare earlier. This means that when we go through and print out the value, the output that we get is going to be 101.

3. We then went and changed the value of 'f' inside of the function. Once we are done with the function call, the changed value of the variable "f" will persist. At line 12, when we again go through and print off the value of "f," the value that we are going to get here is "changing a global variable."

There are a lot of times when you will be able to use the idea of the global and local variables that you would like to handle. Knowing how each of these is going to work, and when each one is going to be the most important part of working with these when you would like them.

CHAPTER 5

Modules in Python

What are the Modules?

In Python, a module is a portion of a program (an extension file) that can be invoked through other programs without having to write them in every program used. Besides, they can define classes and variables. These modules contain related sentences between them and can be used at any time. The use of the modules is based on using a code (program body, functions, variables) already stored on it called import. With the use of the modules, it can be observed that Python allows simplifying the programs a lot because it allows us to simplify the problems into a smaller one to make the code shorter so that programmers do not get lost when looking for something in hundreds of coding lines when making codes.

How to Create a Module?

To create a module in Python, we don't need a lot; it's very simple.

For example: if you want to create a module that prints a city, we write our code in the editor and save it as "mycity.py."

Once this is done, we will know that this will be the name of our module (omitting the .py sentence), which will be assigned to the global variable __city_.

But, beyond that, we can see that the file "mycity.py" is pretty simple and not complicated at all, since the only thing inside is a function called "print_city" which will have a string as a parameter, and what it will do is to print "Hello, welcome to," and this will concatenate with the string that was entered as a parameter.

Locate a Module

When importing a module, the interpreter automatically searches the same module for its current address, if this is not available, Python (or its interpreter) will perform a search on the PYTHONPATH environment variable that is nothing more than a list containing directory names with the same syntax as the environment variable.

If in any particular case, these previous actions failed, Python would look for a default UNIX path (located in /user/local/lib/python on Windows).

The modules are searched in the directory list given by the variable sys.path.

This variable contains the current directory, the PYTHONPATH directory, and the entire directory that comes by default in the installation.

Import Statement

This statement is used to import a module. Through any Python code file, its process is as follows: The Python interpreter searches the file system for the current directory where it is executed. Then, the interpreter searches for its predefined paths in its configuration.

When it meets the first match (the name of the module), the interpreter automatically executes it from start to finish. When importing a module for the first time, Python will generate a compiled .pyc extension file. This extension file will be used in the following imports of this module. When the interpreter detects that the module has already been modified since the last time it was generated, it will generate a new module.

You must save the imported file in the same directory where Python is using the import statement so that Python can find it.

As we could see in our example, importing a module allows us to improve the functionalities of our program through external files.

Now, let's see some examples. The first one is a calculator where will create a module that performs all the mathematical functions and another program that runs the calculator itself.

The first thing we do is the module "calculator.py" that is responsible for doing all the necessary operations. Among them are the addition, subtraction, division, and multiplication, as you can see.

We included the use of conditional statements such as if, else, and elif. We also included the use of exceptions so that the program will not get stuck every time the user enters an erroneous value at the numbers of the calculator for the division.

After that, we will create a program that will have to import the module previously referred to so that it manages to do all the pertinent mathematical functions.

But at this time, you might be thinking that the only existing modules are the ones that the programmer creates. The answer is no since Python has modules that come integrated to it.

With them, we will make two more programs: the first one is an improvement of the one that we have just done, and the second one will be an alarm that will print on screen a string periodically.

Example:

Create a python module called dummymodule.py and write the following inside

def testF():

```
print("this is a module, goodbuy")
```

save the module in the python installation directory.

In the shell

Import dummymodule

Now call the function

dummymodule.testF()

You have used your first module.

Module example One

The first thing that was done was to create the module, but at first sight, we have a surprise, which is that math was imported.

What does that mean to us?

Well, that we are acquiring the properties of the math module that comes by default in Python.

We see that the calculator function is created that has several options.

If the op value is equal to 1, the addition operation is made.

If it is equal to 2, the subtraction operation is made, and so on.

But so new is from op is equal to 5 because, if this is affirmative, then it will return the value of the square root of the values num1 and num2 through the use of math.sqrt(num1), which returns the result of the root.

Then, if op is equal to 6, using functions "math.radians()," which means that num1 or num2 will become radians since that is the type of value accepted by the functions "math.sin()," meaning that the value of the sin of num1 and num2 will return to us, which will be numbers entered by users arbitrarily who will become radians and then the value of the corresponding sin.

The last thing will be to create the main program, as it can be seen next:

Here, we can see the simple program, since it only imports the module "calculator.py," then the variables num1 and num2 are assigned the value by using an input.

Finally, an operation to do is chosen, and to finish is called the calculator function of the calculator module to which we will pass three parameters.

Module example Two

We are going to create a module, which has within itself a function that acts as a chronometer in such a way that it returns true in case time ends.

In this module, as you can see, another module is imported, which is called as "time," and as its name refers, functions to operate with times, and has a wide range of functions, from returning dates and times to help to create chronometers, among others.

The first thing we do is to create the cron() function, which starts declaring that the start Alarm variables will be equal to time.time, which means that we are giving an initial value to this function o know the exact moment in which the function was initialized to then enter into an infinite cycle.

Since the restriction is always True, therefore, this cycle will never end, unless the break command is inside it.

Then, within the while cycle, there are several instructions.

The first is that the final variable is equal to time.time() to take into account the specific moment we are located and, therefore, to monitor time.

After that, another variable is created called times, and this acquires the value of the final minus start Alarm.

But you will be wondering what the round function does. It rounds up the values; we do that to work easier. But this is not enough; therefore, we use an if since, if the subtraction between the end and the beginning is greater or equal to 60, then one minute was completed, and what happens to this?

Why 60?

This is because the time module works with a second and for a minute to elapse, 60 seconds have to be elapsed; therefore, the subtraction between the end and the beginning has to be greater than or equal to 60, in the affirmative case, True will be returned, and finally, we will get out of the infinite cycle.

Once the alarm module is finished, we proceed to make the program, as we can see below:

We can see that the program imports two modules, the one we have created, the alarm and the time module.

The first thing we do is to create the variable s as an input, which tells the user if he wants to start.

If the answer is affirmative, then the variable h representing the time will be equal to "time.strftime ("%H:%M:%S"),'' which means that we are using a function of the time module that returns the hour to use in the specified format so that it can then be printed using the print function.

The next action is to use the alarm module using the command alarm.cron(), which means that the cron() function is being called.

When this function is finished, the time will be assigned to the variable h, again, to finish printing it and being able to observe its correct operation.

As a conclusion of this chapter, we can say that the modules are fundamental for the proper performance of the programmer since they allow to make the code more legible, in addition, that it allows subdividing the problems to attack them from one to one and thus to carry out the tasks easily.

CHAPTER 6:

Object-Oriented Programming and File Handling

Object-Oriented programming is an extensive concept used to create powerful applications. Data scientists are required to build applications to work on data, among other things. This chapter will explore the basics of object-oriented programming in Python.

Object-Oriented Programming abbreviated as OOP has several advantages over other design patterns. The development process is faster and cheaper, with great software maintainability. This, in turn, results in better software, which is also filled with new attributes and methods. The learning curve, is; however, complex. The idea might be complicated for newbies. In terms of computation, OOP is slower and consumes a lot of memory because more lines of code have been written.

Object-oriented programming relies on the important programming concept, which makes use of statements to change a program's state. It concentrates on illustrating how a program should operate. Examples of imperative programming languages are Java, C++, C, Ruby, and

Python. This is different from declarative programming, which deals with the type of computer program that should achieve, without detailing how. Examples consist of database query languages such as XQuery and SQL.

OOP relies on the property of classes and objects. A class can be considered as a 'blueprint' for objects. These can feature their own characteristics and methods they execute.

Example of OOP

Take an example of a class Dog. Don't consider it as a specific dog or your own dog. We're describing what a dog is and what it can do in general. Dogs have an age and a name. These are instance properties. Dogs can also bark; this is a method.

When you discuss a certain dog, you would have an object in programming: an object is a class instance. This is the basic state on which object-oriented programming depends.

Now let's look at OOP in Python language.

Python is a powerful programming language that allows OOP. You will use Python language to define a class with properties and methods, which you will later call. Python has extra benefits than other languages. First, the language is dynamic and a high-level data type. This implies that development takes place faster than Java. It doesn't need the programmer to declare variable types and arguments. This makes

Python easy to learn for beginners. Its code is more intuitive and readable.

It is important to remember that a class basically provides the structure. This is a blueprint that outlines how something needs to be defined. However, it doesn't offer any real content. For example, shape () class may specify the size and name of shapes, but it will not indicate the exact name of a shape.

You can view a class as a concept of how something should be executed.

Python Objects

Although the class is the blueprint, objects or instances are members of a given class. It's not a concept anymore. It's an actual shape, like a triangle with three sides.

Put differently; a class is like a questionnaire. It will define the required information. Once you complete the form, your actual copy is an instance of the class. It has original information relevant to you.

You can complete different copies to have multiple instances, but without the form, you'll be lost, not knowing the kind of information required. Therefore, before you can create individual objects, you need to define what is required by the class.

Defining a Class in Python

Below is a simple class definition in Python:

- Class Dog (object)

- Pass

When defining a class in Python, you begin with the class keyword to show that you're writing a class, then you follow it with the name of the class. In the above example, Dog is the name of the class. The above class definition has the Python keyword pass; this is normally used as a placeholder where code will finally go. Why this keyword has been used is to avoid the code from throwing an error.

The object section enclosed in parentheses demonstrates the parent class that you're inheriting from. But this is no longer required in Python 3 because it's the implicit default.

Objects Attributes

All classes define objects, and all objects have properties known as attributes. The _init_ () method is used to specify an object's original properties by outlining their default value.

This method requires at least one argument as the self-variable, which describes the object itself.

```
class Dog:

    # Initializer / Instance Attributes
    def __init__(self, name, age):
        self.name = name
        self.age = age
```

In the following example, each dog has a unique name and age, which is critical to know, especially when you begin to define different dogs. Don't forget that the class is only defining the Dog, and not creating objects of individual dogs with unique names and ages.

Similarly, the self-variable also belongs to an instance of the class. Because class instance has different values, you can write Dog.name = name instead of self.name = name.

Class Attributes

While instance attributes are unique to every object, the characteristics of a class are the same for all instances. In this case, all dogs.

Methods

When you have attributes that belong to a class, you can proceed to define functions that will access the class attribute. These functions are referred to as methods. When you declare methods, you will want to provide the first argument to the method using a self-keyword.

For instance, you can define a class Snake, which contains the attribute name and the method change_name. The method change name will accept an argument new_name plus the keyword self.

Now, you can instantiate this class with a variable snake and change the name using the method change_name.

```
>>> # instantiate the class
>>> snake = Snake()

>>> # print the current object name
>>> print(snake.name)
python

>>> # change the name using the change_name method
>>> snake.change_name("anaconda")
>>> print(snake.name)
anaconda
```

Instance Attributes and the init Method

You can still provide the values for the attributes at runtime. This occurs by defining the attributes within the init method. Check out the example below:

```
class Snake:

    def __init__(self, name):
        self.name = name

    def change_name(self, new_name):
        self.name = new_name
```

Now you can proceed to directly define different attribute values for different objects.

So far, you know how to define Python classes, methods, and instantiate objects, and call instance methods. These skills will be useful when you want to solve complex problems.

With object-oriented programming, your code will increase in complexity as your program expands. You'll have different classes, objects, instance methods, and subclasses. You'll want to maintain your code and ensure it remains readable. To accomplish this, you will need to adhere to design patterns. These are principles that help a person to avoid bad design. Each represents a particular program that always reoccurs in OOP, and describes the solution to that problem, which can then be repeatedly used.

File Handling

Python provides a critical feature for reading data from the file and writing data into a file.

In most programming languages, all the values or data are kept in some volatile variables.

Since data will be stored in those variables during run-time only and will disappear once the program execution ends, therefore, it's better to save these data permanently using files.

Once you store data on a file, the next important thing is its retrieval process because it's stored as bits of 1s and 0s, and in case the retrieval does not occur well, then it becomes completely useless, and that data is said to be corrupted.

How Python Handles Files?

If you're working in an extensive software application where they execute a massive amount of data, then we can't expect those data to be kept in a variable because variables are volatile.

Therefore, when you want to deal with these situations, the role of files will come into the picture.

Since files are non-volatile in nature, the data will remain permanently in a secondary device such as Hard Disk and using Python to deal with these files in your applications.

Do You Consider How Python Will Handle These Files?

Let's assume how normal people will deal with these files. If you want to read the data from a file or write the data into a file, then you need to open the file or create a new file if the file doesn't exist and then conduct the normal read/write operations, save the file and close it.

Similarly, the same operations are accomplished in Python with the help of in-built applications.

Types of Files in Python

There are two kinds of files:

1. Text files
2. Binary files

A file whose contents can be examined using a text editor is known as a text file. A text file refers to a sequence of ASCII characters. Python programs are examples of text files.

A binary file stores the data in the same manner as stored in the memory. The mp3 files, word documents are some of the examples of binary files. You cannot read a binary file using a text editor.

In Python language, file processing takes the following steps.

- Open a file that returns a filehandle.
- Use the handle to read or write action.
- Close the filehandle.

Before you perform a read or write operation to a file in Python, you must open it first. And as the read/write transaction finishes, you should close it to free the resources connected with the file.

Let's now look at each step in detail.

Access_mode: This is represented with an integer e.g read, write, and append. The default setting is the read-only <r>.

Buffering: The default value for buffering is 0. A zero value shows that buffering will not happen. If the value is 1, then the line buffering will happen while accessing the file. If it's more than 1, then the buffering action will proceed based on the size.

File_name: This is a string that represents the name of the file you want to access.

File open modes in Python language

<r>

<rb+>

<rb>

<w+>

<wb+>

<r+>

<w>

<wb>

Python File Object Properties

Once you call the Python open () function, it returns an object, which is the filehandle. Additionally, you need to understand that Python files have different features. And you can take advantage of the filehandle to list the features of a file it belongs.

Close a File in Python

It is good always to close a file when you finish your work. However, Python has a garbage collector to clean up the unused objects. However, you need to do it on your own instead of leaving it for the GC.

The Close Method

Python offers the <close ()> method to close a file.

When you close a file, the system creates resources allocated to it. And it's easy to accomplish.

Closing a file releases essential system resources. If you forgot to close the file, Python will do it automatically when the program ends, or the file object is no longer referenced inside the program. However, in case your program is large, and you're reading or writing multiple files that can consume a massive amount of resources on the system. If you continue opening new files carelessly, you might run out of resources.

CHAPTER 7

Development Tools

How to Run Python

Now before we start running our first python program, it is important that we understand how we can run python programs. Running or executing or deploying or firing a program simply means that we are making the computer process instructions/lines of codes.

For example, if the lines of codes (program) require the computer to display some message, then it should. The following are the ways or modes of running python programs. The interpreter is a special program that is installed when installing the Python package and helps convert text code into a language that the computer understands and can act on it (executing).

Immediate Mode

It is a way of running python programs that are not written in a file. We get into the immediate mode by typing the word python in the command line and which will trigger the interpreter to switch to immediate mode. The immediate mode allows typing of expressions directly, and pressing enter generates the output. The sign below is the Python prompt:

>>>

The python prompt instructs the interpreter to accept input from the user. For instance, typing 2+2 and pressing enter will display 4 as the output. In a way, this prompt can be used as a calculator. If you need to exit the immediate mode, type quit() or exit().

Now type 5 +3, and press enter, the output should be 8. The next mode is the Script Mode.

Script Mode

The script mode is used to run a python program written in a file; the file is called a script.

The scripts can be saved to external storage such as a disk for later use. All python scripts have the file extension .py, which implies that the filename ends with .py. An example is myFirstProg.py. We shall explain later how to write python scripts.

What is the IDE?

An IDE provides a convenient way of writing and running Python programs. One can also use text editors to create a python script file instead of an IDE by writing lines of codes and saving the file with a .py extension. However, using an IDE can simplify the process of writing and running Python programs. The IDEL present in the Python package is an example of an IDE with a graphical user interface and gets installed along with the Python language. The advantages of IDE include helping getting rid of repetitive tasks and simplify coding for beginners. IDE provides syntax highlighting, code hinting, and syntax checking, among other features. There also commercial IDE, such as the PyScripter IDE, that performs most of the mentioned functions.

The IDE is going to be important to what we are able to do inside of our language. You need to have some kind of IDE or environment in place in order to handle any of the coding. Without this, you will find that the programs will not work.

The good news is that the IDE is simple to install, and will not be too difficult to get to work with. And there are many Python IDE"s that you will be able to choose from. It often depends on the features and other add-ons that you would like to have with the environment that you choose.

Keep in mind that a few of these are going to cost a bit of money based on who designs them, and what kinds of features you find in them. You can choose whether those features are important to what you want to do or not.

If you are looking to keep costs down, while still ensuring that you get a good IDE that has all of the features and more that you need, you can go visit the www.python.org website. This will ensure, along with the Python download, that you get the IDE and all of the other files that you need to make coding in Python possible. And it will do all of this for free to help you keep costs down!

Your First Program in Python

The rest of the illustrations will assume you are running the python programs in a Windows environment.

- Start IDLE
- to the File menu and click New Window
- Type the following:

  print ("Hello World!")

- On the File, menu clicks Save. Type the name of myProgram1.py
- Navigate to Run and click Run Module to run the program.

The first program that we have written is known as the "Hello World!" and is used to not only provide an introduction to a new computer coding language but also test the basic configuration of the IDE. The output of the program is "Hello World!" Here is what has happened, the Print() is an inbuilt function; it is prewritten and preloaded for you, is used to display whatever is contained in the () as long as it is between the double-quotes. The computer will display anything written within the double-quotes.

Work to do: Now write and run the following python programs:

- Print("I am now a Python Language Coder!")

- Print("This is my second simple program!")

- Print("I love the simplicity of Python")

- Print("I will display whatever is here in quotes such as owyhen2589gdbnz082")

Now we need to write a program with numbers, but before writing such a program, we need to learn something about Variables and Types.

Remember, python is object-oriented and it is not statically typed, which means we do not need to declare variables before using them or specify their type. Let us explain this statement; an object-oriented language simply means that the language supports viewing and manipulating real-life scenarios as groups with subgroups that can be linked and shared mimicking the natural order and interaction of things. Not all programming languages are object-oriented; for instance, Visual C programming language is not object-oriented. In programming, declaring variables means that we explicitly state the nature of the variable. The variable can be declared as an integer, long integer, short integer, floating integer, a string, or as a character, including if it is accessible locally or globally. A variable is a storage location that changes values depending on conditions.

For instance, number1 can take any number from 0 to infinity. However, if we specify explicitly that int number1 it then means that the storage location will only accept integers and not fractions, fortunately, or unfortunately, python does not require us to explicitly state the nature of the storage location (declare variables) as that is left to the python language itself to figure out that.

Before tackling types of variables and rules of writing variables, let us run a simple program to help us understand how to make this happen.

    a.   Start IDLE

    b.   Navigate to the File menu and click New Window

    c.   Type the following:

```
num1=4

num2=5

sum=num1+num2

print(sum)
```

    d.   On the File, menu clicks Save. Type the name of myProgram2.py

    e.   Navigate to Run and click Run Module to run the program.

The expected output of this program should be "9" without the double-quotes.

At this point, you are eager to understand what has just happened and why the print(sum) does not have double quotes like the first programs we wrote. Here is the explanation.

The first line num1=4 means that variable num1(our shortened way of writing number1, first number) has been assigned 4 before the program runs.

The second line num2=5 means that variable num2(our shortened way of writing number2, second number) has been assigned 5 before the program runs.

The computer interprets these instructions and stores the numbers given

The third line sum=num1+num2 tells the computer that takes whatever num1 has been given and add to whatever num2 has been given. In other terms, sum the values of num1 and num2.

The fourth line print(sum) means that display whatever sum has. If we put double quotes to sum, the computer will simply display the word sum and not the sum of the two numbers! Remember that cliché that computers are garbage in and garbage out. They follow what you give them!

Now let us try out three exercises involving numbers before we explain types of variables. Remember variables values vary, for instance, num1 can take 3, 8, 1562, 1.

Follow the steps of opening the Python IDE and do the following:

    f.   The output should be 54

num1=43

num2=11

sum=num1+num2

print(sum)

    g.   The output should be 167

num1=101

num2=66

sum=num1+num2

print(sum)

iii.   The output should be 28

num1=9

num2=19

sum=num1+num2

print(sum)

CHAPTER 8:

Proper Installation

Installing Python (Windows)

Part of getting started with Python is installing the Python on your Windows. For the first step of the installation, you will need to download the installation package for your preferred version from this link below: https://www.python.org/downloads/

Visiting this link, you will be directed to a page. On that page, you will need to choose between the two latest versions for Python 2 and 3: Python 3.8.1 and Python 2.7.17.

In the other way round, if you are looking for a specific release, you can explore the page to find download links for earlier versions. Normally, you would opt to download the latest version, which is Python 3.8.1 — which was released on October 14, 2019 —or you download the latest version of Python 2, 2.7.17. However, the version you download must be because of the kind of project you want to do, compatibility, and support for updates.

Once you're finished with the download, you can proceed to installation by clicking on the downloaded .exe file. A standard installation has to incorporate pip, IDLE, and the essential documentation.

Installing Python (Mac)

If you're using a Mac, you can download the installation package from this   link:

https://www.python.org/downloads/mac-osx/

The progression of learning is getting further into Python Programming Language. In reality, Python is an adaptable yet powerful language that can be used from multiple points of view. This just implies Python can be used intelligently when code or a declaration is to be tried on a line-by-line premise or when you're investigating its highlights. Incredibly, Python can be used in content mode, most particularly when you want to decipher a whole document of declarations or application program.

Working with Python, be that as it may, requires most extreme caution – particularly when you are drawing in or connecting with it. This caution is valid for each programming language as well. So as to draw in with Python intelligently, the Command Line window or the IDLE Development Environment can be used.

Since you are an apprentice of either programming by and large or using Python, there will shift ventures on how you could connect with and cooperate with Python programming language. The following are basic highlights of activities for brisk cooperation with Python:

The Command-Line Interaction

Associating with the order line is the least difficult approach to work, as a novice, with Python. Python can simply be imagined by seeing how it functions through its reaction to each finished direction entered on the >>> brief. The Command-Line probably won't be the most favored commitment with Python; at the same time, throughout the years, it has demonstrated to be the easiest method to investigate how Python functions for learners.

Launching Python using the Command Line

If you're using macOS, GNU/Linux, and UNIX frameworks, you should run the Terminal tool to get to the command line. Then again, if you are using Windows, you can get to the Python order line by right-clicking on the Start menu and launching Windows PowerShell.

As directions on programming require a contribution of an order, when you need Python to do something for you, you will train it by entering directions that it knows about a similar yield. This is an adjustment in the order may give the ideal yield; be cautious.

With this, Python will make an interpretation of these directions to guidelines that your PC or gadget can comprehend and execute.

Let's take a look at certain guides to perceive how Python functions. Note that you can use the print order to print the all-inclusive program

"Heydays, Savants!"

1. Above all else, open Python's command line.

2. At that point, at the >>>prompt, type the accompanying (don't leave space among print and the section): print ("Heydays, Savants!")

3. Now, you should press enter so as to disclose to Python that you're finished with the direction. Promptly, the direction line window will show Heydays, Savants! In the interim, Python has reacted similarly as it has been told in the composed arrangement that it can relate with. Then again, to perceive how it will react wrongly when you request that it print a similar string using a wrong linguistic structure for the print order, type and enter the accompanying direction on the Python order brief: Print("Heydays, Savants!")

The outcome will be: Syntax error: invalid language structure

This is a case of what get when you use invalid or fragmented explanations. Note that Python is a case-touchy programming language, so at whatever point you misunderstand the message, it could be that you composed print with a capital letter. Obviously, there is a choice to print direction; you can simply type your announcement inside statements like this: "Primes, Savants!" Note that an announcement is the words you wish to show once the order is given; the words that can fit in are not confined to the model given here, however.

The most effective method to leave the Python order line

To exit from Python, you can type any of these commands: quit() or exit(). Subsequently, hold Control-Z and afterward press Enter; the Python should exit.

Your commonality with Python Programming ought to get fascinating now; there are still parts to learn, tolerance will satisfy.

The area of IDLE: Python's Integrated Development Environment (IDE)

A standout amongst the fascinating pieces of Python is the IDLE (Integrated Development and Learning Environment) apparatus. Despite the fact that this specific device is incorporated into Python's establishment bundle, you can download increasingly refined outsider IDEs as well. The IDLE instrument gives you access to an increasingly effective stage to compose your code and work engagingly with Python. To get to IDLE, you can experience a similar organizer where you found the direction line symbol or on the begin menu (as you've gained from order line collaboration). When you click on the IDLE symbol, you will be coordinated to the Python Shell window. This will take us to the segment on cooperation with the Python Shell Window.

Connecting with the Python Shell Window

When you're at the Python Shell Window, you will see a dropdown menu and a >>>prompt that resembles what you've found in the direction line window (the principal connection talked about). There is a specific IDLE's function of altering for the drawing in past order. Now, you will use a similar IDLE's altering menu to look back to your past directions, cut, copy, and glue past statements and, taking all things together, make any type of editing.

Clearly, the IDLE is increasingly similar to a jump from the direction line association. Incredibly, in the menu dropdown of the Python Shell window are the accompanying menu things: File, Windows, Help, Shell, Options, Edit, and Debug. Every one of these menus has various functions. The Shell and Debug menus are used while making bigger projects as they give get highlights to the procedure. In any case, while the Shell menu gives you a chance to restart the shell or look the shell's log for the latest reset, Debug Menu has loads of valuable things for following the source record of an exemption and featuring the blundering line.

With the Debugger option, you will most likely introduce an intelligent debugger window that will enable you to stop and look through the running projects on the Python. The Options menu of the window enables you to edit and set IDLE to suit your own Python working inclinations.

Moreover, at the Help menu, you are opened to choice Python Help and documentation.

Using the File Window menu, you will most likely make another document, open a module, open an old record, as well as spare your session through the essential things naturally made once you get to this menu. With the 'New File' alternative, you will almost certainly make codes you should simply to tap on it. When you have, you will be taken to another window with a straightforward and standard word processor where you can type or alter your code. You will see that the record is 'untitled' don't freeze; this is the underlying name of the document, which will change when you spare your code. One awesome thing about the File window menu is that refuse to have both the 'Shell' and 'Menu' choices together, so the bar changes just somewhat with the Shell Window. What happens is that in the Shell Window, two new Menus have been presented, to be specific: the Run and the Format menus. At whatever point you need to run the codes you have composed on the record window, the yield will be given on the Shell Window individually.

Toward the start of this area, you're informed that Python can be used in the Script Mode. How would you do this? The method of getting the outcome is very extraordinary at this point. When working in a content mode, the outcome you will get won't be programmed as in the manner you would in connecting with or associating mode. You should summon them out of your code. To get your yield on this mode, run the content or order it through the print() work inside your code.

To finish up this section, you've been taken through the essential two methods of the Python Programming Language; the drawing in or associating and the Script modes. Whatever the circumstance, realize that the fundamental change in that one outcome is getting dependent on order while the other is programmed.

CHAPTER 9:

Data Science

Data Science and Its Significance

Data Science has come a long way from the past few years, and thus, it becomes an important factor in understanding the workings of multiple companies. Below are several explanations that prove data science will still be an integral part of the global market.

1. The companies would be able to understand their client in a more efficient and high manner with the help of Data Science. Satisfied customers form the foundation of every company, and they play an important role in their successes or failures. Data Science allows companies to engage with customers in the advance way and thus proves the product's improved performance and strength.

2. Data Science enables brands to deliver powerful and engaging visuals. That's one of the reasons it's famous. When products and companies make inclusive use of this data, they can share their experiences with their audiences and thus create better relations with the item.

3. Perhaps one Data Science's significant characteristics are that its results can be generalized to almost all kinds of industries, such as travel, health care, and education. The companies can quickly determine their problems with the help of Data Science, and can also adequately address them

4. Currently, data science is accessible in almost all industries, and nowadays, there is a huge amount of data existing in the world, and if used adequately, it can lead to victory or failure of any project. If data is used properly, it will be important in the future to achieve the product 's goals.

5. Big data is always on the rise and growing. Big data allows the enterprise to address complicated Business, human capital, and capital management problems effectively and quickly using different resources that are built routinely.

6. Data science is gaining rapid popularity in every other sector and therefore plays an important role in every product's functioning and performance. Thus, the data scientist's role is also enhanced as they will conduct an essential function of managing data and providing solutions to particular issues.

7. Computer technology has also affected the supermarket sectors. To understand this, let's take an example the older people had a fantastic interaction with the local seller. Also, the seller was able to meet the customers' requirements in a personalized way. But now this attention was lost due to the emergence and increase of supermarket chains. But the sellers are able to communicate with their customers with the help of data analytics.

8. Data Science helps companies build that customer connection. Companies and their goods will be able to have a better and deeper understanding of how clients can utilize their services with the help of data science.

Data Technology Future: Like other areas are continually evolving, the importance of data technology is increasingly growing as well. Data science impacted different fields. Its influence can be seen in many industries, such as retail, healthcare, and education.

New treatments and technologies are being continually identified in the healthcare sector, and there is a need for quality patient care.

The healthcare industry can find a solution with the help of data science techniques that helps the patients to take care of. Education is another field where one can clearly see the advantage of data science. Now the new innovations like phones and tablets have become an essential characteristic of the educational system.

Also, with the help of data science, the students are creating greater chances, which leads to improving their knowledge.

Data Structures

A data structure may be selected in computer programming or designed to store data for the purpose of working with different algorithms on it. Every other data structure includes the data values, data relationships, and functions between the data that can be applied to the data and information.

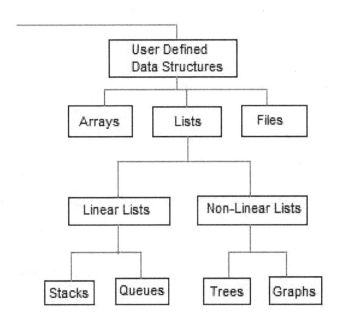

Features of data structures

Sometimes, data structures are categorized according to their characteristics. Possible functions are:

- Linear or non-linear: This feature defines how the data objects are organized in a sequential series, like a list or in an unordered sequence, like a table.

- Homogeneous or non-homogeneous: This function defines how all data objects in a collection are of the same type or of different kinds.

- Static or dynamic: This technique determines to show to assemble the data structures. Static data structures at compilation time have fixed sizes, structures, and destinations in the memory. Dynamic data types have dimensions, mechanisms, and destinations of memory that may shrink or expand depending on the application.

Data structure Types

Types of the data structure are determined by what sorts of operations will be needed or what kinds of algorithms will be implemented. This includes:

Arrays: An array stores a list of memory items at adjacent locations. Components of the same category are located together since each element's position can be easily calculated or accessed. Arrays can be fixed in size or flexible in length.

Stacks: A stack holds a set of objects in linear order added to operations. This order may be past due in first out (LIFO) or first-out (FIFO).

Queues: A queue stores a stack-like selection of elements; however, the sequence of activity can only be first in the first out.

Linked lists: In a linear order, a linked list stores a selection of items. In a linked list, every unit or node includes a data item as well as a reference or relation to the next element in the list.

Trees: A tree stocks an abstract, hierarchical collection of items. Each node is connected to other nodes and can have several sub-values, also known as a child.

Graphs: A graph stores a non-linear design group of items. Graphs consist of a limited set of nodes, also called vertices, and lines connecting them, also known as edges. They are useful for describing processes in real life, such as networked computers.

Tries: A tria or query tree is often a data structure that stores strings as data files, which can be arranged in a visual graph.

Hash tables: A hash table or hash chart is contained in a relational list that labels the keys to variables. A hash table uses a hashing algorithm to transform an index into an array of containers containing the desired item of data. These data systems are called complex because they can contain vast quantities of interconnected data. Examples of primal, or fundamental, data structures are integer, float, boolean, and character.

Utilization of data structures

Data structures are generally used to incorporate the data types in physical forms. This can be interpreted into a wide range of applications, including a binary tree showing a database table. Data structures are used in the programming languages to organize code and information in digital storage. Python databases and dictionaries, or JavaScript array and objects, are popular coding systems used to gather and analyze data. Also, data structures are a vital part of effective software design.

Significance of Databases Data systems is necessary to effectively handle vast volumes of data, such as data stored in libraries, or indexing services.

Accurate data configuration management requires memory allocation identifier, data interconnections, and data processes, all of which support the data structures. In addition, it is important to not only use data structures but also to select the correct data structure for each assignment.

Choosing an unsatisfactory data structure could lead to slow running times or disoriented code. Any considerations that need to be noticed when choosing a data system include what type of information should be processed, where new data will be put, how data will be organized, and how much space will be allocated for the data.

How significant is Python for Data Science?

- Efficient and simple to use—Python is considered a tool for beginners, and any student or researcher with only basic understanding could start working on it. Time and money spent debugging codes and constraints on different project management are also minimized. The time for code implementation is less compared to other programming languages such as C, Java, and C #, which makes developers and software engineers spend far more time working on their algorithms.

- Library Choice—Python offers a vast library and machine learning and artificial intelligence database. Scikit Learn, TensorFlow, Seaborn, Pytorch, Matplotlib, and many more are among the most popular libraries.

- Scalability—It gives flexibility in solving problems that can't be solved with other computer languages. Many companies use it to develop all sorts of rapid techniques and systems.

- Visual Statistics and Graphics—Python provides a number of visualization tools. The Matplotlib library provides a reliable framework on which those libraries such as gg plot, pandas plotting, PyTorch, and others are developed. These services help create graphs, plot lines ready for the Web, visual layouts, etc.

How Python is used for Data Science

First phase—First of all, we need to learn and understand what form a data takes. If we perceive data to be a huge Excel sheet with columns and crows lakhs, then perhaps you should know what to do about that? You need to gather information into each row as well as column by executing some operations and searching for a specific type of data. Completing this type of computational task can consume a lot of time and hard work. Thus, you can use Python's libraries, such as Pandas and Numpy, that can complete the tasks quickly by using parallel computation.

Second phase—The next hurdle is to get the data needed. Since data is not always readily accessible to us, we need to dump data from the network as needed. Here the Python Scrap and brilliant Soup libraries can enable us to retrieve data from the internet.

Third phase—We must get the simulation or visual presentation of the data at this step. Driving perspectives gets difficult when you have too many figures on the board. The correct way to do that is to represent the data in graph form, graphs, and other layouts. The Python Seaborn and Matplotlib libraries are used to execute this operation.

Fourth phase—The next stage is machine-learning, which is massively complicated computing. It includes mathematical tools such as the probability, calculus, and matrix operations of columns and rows over lakhs. With Python's machine learning library Scikit-Learn, all of this will become very simple and effective.

CHAPTER 10

Learning Machine

Computers have become an integral part of modern-day operations in almost every sphere of life. Teaching computers how to operate and progressively improve on functionality takes different approaches. The types of machine learning are categorized into taxonomies depending on the underlying problems or the anticipated outcomes. These types of machine learning allow the computer to learn patterns and regularities that are useful across a variety of business and health-related fields in the modern world. The following are some of the types of learning algorithms useful in the process of machine learning.

Supervised Learning

Supervised learning occurs where the algorithms create a function that maps raw data into desired outputs. Supervised learning is one of the most common paradigms for machine learning. It is easy to comprehend. The process of implementation of supervised learning may be achieved through systems from the training dataset. The training data or examples contain more than one input and the desired output. The output is also known as a regulatory signal, which is represented within the mathematical model. An array of vectors represents the training example. When provided with data in the form of illustrations, the algorithms may be useful in the prediction of each name. Forecasting takes place in the process of giving a response on whether the answers were right or wrong. The approach allows the algorithms a chance to learn to make approximations over time that allow for the distinction between the labels and the examples. The method makes supervised learning a common option in the process of finding solutions...

The most common supervised learning approaches include classification and regression. In the case of classification, the use of supervised learning occurs where the outputs may have restrictions on a fixed number of values. Classification typically deals with the identification in a given data set with a view to linking new observations into such categories. On the other hand, the use of regression occurs when the outputs have a wide range of numerical values within a given subset. The goal in both examples is to ensure that machine learning utilizes a fixed set of training examples to make the necessary comparisons on how similar or different a collection of data may be in a given subset. The optimal scenarios in such data sets ensure that the algorithms can determine the class labels for all the unseen occurrences within such a subgroup.

Unsupervised Learning

Machines learning may occur through unsupervised cluster analysis. The approach involves using a set of data that is made up of inputs, which is necessary for the development of a structure. The clustering of data points is an example of unsupervised learning. Unlike in the case of supervised learning, the test data in unsupervised learning does not have labels and is not within a specific classification. Unsupervised learning does not respond to feedback but instead focuses on the commonalities. The method seeks to identify the possibility of commonalities in a given set of data and use these commonalities to develop a pattern. Essentially, this means that the goal is to task a computer with learning how to do something without providing a logical approach to achieve this task. The unsupervised approach is, therefore, more complicated and more complex than the supervised process. This method means using a reward approach to affirm success in the achievement of the tasks without necessarily providing explicit instructions on how to achieve the set goals.

The purpose of the unsupervised approach is more aligned towards the decision-making process as opposed to the mere classification of these data. Unsupervised learning trains the agent to act or respond to tasks based on the reward system or punishment built over time. A computer gradually learns how to navigate past commands without having prior information on the anticipated outcomes. This approach may be time-consuming and tedious. But unsupervised learning can be powerful because it operates from the point of trial and error, which may produce discoveries. Unsupervised learning does not consider any pre-classified information and therefore works from an aspect of the invention.

The unsupervised learning approach is critical in a world where most of the data sets in the world are unlabeled. This indisputable reality means that having intelligent algorithms that can utilize terabytes of unlabeled data and make sense of such information is critical. In the future, there will be different instances where unsupervised learning will become a crucial area of focus. Recommender systems will be a vital area where unsupervised learning will be applicable in the future. The recommender system allows for a distinct link to relationships, which makes it easy to categorize and suggest content based on shared likes.

Reinforcement Learning

Reinforcement learning is useful when the exact models are unrealistic because they rarely assume knowledge of an accurate mathematical model. The approach focuses on how machines should operate to maximize some aspects of cumulative rewards. In modern research, the application of reinforcement learning is observed from a behavioural psychology point of view. The method thus functions through interacting with the immediate environment. As we noted earlier, supervised learning operates based on existing examples. The user of interaction with the situation in the case of reinforcement learning indicates a difference between the two approaches.

The application of reinforcement learning in the field of Artificial Intelligence is an indication of the ability of the machines to learn and adjust to new tasks through interactions with the immediate environment. The algorithms adapt to taking specific action based on the observation of the contextual setting. The pattern of behavioural reaction to environmental stimuli is an indication of the process of learning that has become synonymous with artificial intelligence. Every action in reinforcement learning has a direct implication of the operational context, and this reaction provides an opportunity for the machine to receive feedback, which is critical in the process of learning. Reinforcement learning tends to rely on time-dependent sequences or labels. The results in the case of reinforcement learning depend on the connection between the agent and the environmental context. The agent is then given a set of tasks that have a direct implication on the environment. The method then approves a specific reinforcement signal, which provides negative or positive feedback depending on the job and the anticipated result.

Semi-supervised Machine Learning

The use of semi-supervised learning algorithms is essential, where there is a small amount of labelled data and enormous amounts of unlabelled data. The method utilizes the combination of both labelled and unlabelled data. The programmer, therefore, uses both data types to identify patterns. The deduced models become the basis on which relationships target variables, and the data examples become easy to identify and analyse. The approach refers to semi-supervised learning because it utilizes data from labelled and unlabelled examples and still makes sense out of this information. Semi-supervised learning is, therefore, a hybridization of supervised and unsupervised learning approaches. Semi-structured data is used in this case because it does not obey the formal structuring of data models. The tags and other indicators used in the semi-supervised approach aids in the separation of semantic elements. This is essential when there lack enough examples to develop an accurate model. Semi-structured models often make critical sense when there is a lack of adequate resources and limited capacity to increase the available data examples.

The approach allows for the labelling process of the defined data; then, it uses the trained model to classify the other data based on the specific model. In some instances, you may find situations where you have a wide range of data with a known outcome, yet also have another set of data that is unidentified. The use of semi-supervised machine learning allows the process to utilize the known data models to build a sequence that can be effective in the course of making labels for the rest of the data sets. As a result, when compared to other models, this approach provides the best option because it is time-saving and also reduces drastically the overall resources used towards achieving the intended outcome. The creation of an appropriate function when using semi-supervised approaches may be a critical solution in a modern setting where unlabelled data is likely to supersede labelled data in the process of classification. The use of semi-supervised methods in spam identification and detection from standard messages is the most realistic example in the modern world. The use of human knowledge to sieve through such messages would otherwise be impossible to achieve. Using semi-supervised techniques helps in resolving the high dimensionality concern that often affects the process of classification.

Conclusion

You're on your way to work listening to your favorite Spotify playlist and scrolling through your Instagram feed. Once you arrive at the office, you head over to the coffee machine, and while waiting for your daily boost, you check your Facebook notifications. Finally, you head to your desk, take a sip of coffee, and you think, "Hey, I should Google to learn what Python is used for." At this point, you realize that every technology you just used has a little bit of Python in it.

Python is used in nearly everything, whether we are talking about a simple app created by a startup company or a giant corporation like Google. Let's go through a brief list of all the ways you can use Python.

In conclusion, Python and big data provide one of the strongest capabilities in computational terms on the platform of big data analysis. If this is your first time at data programming, Python will be a much easier language to learn than any other and is far more user-friendly.

And so, we've come to the end of this book, which was meant to give you a taste of data analysis techniques and visualization beyond the basics using Python. Python is a wonderful tool to use for data purposes, and I hope this guide stands you in good stead as you go about using it for your purposes.

I have tried to go more in-depth in this book, give you more information on the fundamentals of data science, along with lots of useful, practical examples for you to try out.

Please read this guide as often as you need to and don't move on from a chapter until you fully understand it. And do try out the examples included – you will learn far more if you actually do it rather than just reading the theory.

This was just an overview to recap on what you learned in the first book, covering the datatypes in pandas and how they are used. We also looked at cleaning the data and manipulating it to handle missing values and do some string operations.

There are a lot of other coding languages out there that you are able to work with, but Python is one of the best that works for most beginner programmers, providing the power and the ease of use that you are looking for when you first get started in this kind of coding language. This guidebook took the time to explore how Python works, along with some of the different types of coding that you can do with it.

In addition to seeing a lot of examples of how you can code in Python and how you can create some of your programs in this language, we also spent some time looking at how to work with Python when it comes to the world of machine learning, artificial intelligence, and data analysis. These are topics and parts of technology that are taking off, and many programmers are trying to learn more about it. And with the help of this guidebook, you will be able to handle all of these, even as a beginner in Python.

When you are ready to learn more about how to work with the Python coding language and how you can make sure that you can even use Python along with data analysis, artificial intelligence, and machine learning, make sure to check out again this guidebook to help you get started.

JAVA

PROGRAMMING

LEARN HOW TO CODE WITH AN OBJECT-ORIENTED
PROGRAM TO IMPROVE YOUR SOFTWARE
ENGINEERING SKILLS. GET FAMILIAR WITH
VIRTUAL MACHINE, JAVASCRIPT AND
MACHINE CODE

ALAN GRID

Introduction

J ava is a widely-used programming language on the Web and in computing applications. It is a free download solution that allows users to access the latest versions and implement updates. This particular programming language is present in the majority of today's web applications and computing technologies. Java's scalable characteristics make it suitable for deployment in a wide range of applications, including apps for small electronic devices like cell phones and software solutions for large scale operations such as data centers. The growing preference for deploying Java is attributable to its robust functional features and sound security credentials.

Java is a programming language that is built by Sun Microsystems, which was later taken over by the Oracle Corporation. It is designed to run on any operating system that supports Java. This is what made the language so popular, because the developer just had to write the program once, and the program could then run on any operating system without the need for the programmer to change the code.

Most of the modern applications built around the world are made from the Java programming language. Most of the server-side and business logic components of major applications are built on the Java programming language.

During the entire course of this book, you will learn how to write programs such as the one above, and also learn advanced concepts that will enable you to start writing complete application programs.

Some of the design goals for Java are mentioned below:

— The language is intended to be written once and have the ability to be run on any operating system.

— The language should provide support for numerous software engineering principles.

Portability is an important factor. This is why Java has the ability to run on Windows, Linux, and the MacOS operating system.

Support for internationalization is very important.

Java is intended to be suitable for writing applications for both hosted and embedded systems.

Other design goals are discussed next:

Strong Type Checking

Java is a strong type language. Every variable that is defined needs to be attached to a data type.

You don't need to understand the complete program for now, but let's just have a quick look at 2 lines of the code.

1) int i=5;

Here we are defining something known as a variable, which is used to hold a value. The value that can be stored depends on the data type. In this example, we are saying that 'i' is of the type 'int' or Integer, which is a numeric data value.

Array Bounds Checking

At runtime, Java will check whether the array has the required number of values defined. If one tries to access a value which is outside the bounds of the array, an exception will be thrown.

You don't need to understand the complete program for now, but let's just have a quick look at the following lines of the code.

1) int[] array1 = new int[2];

Here we are declaring an array, which is a set of integer values. The value of '2' means that we can only store two values in the array.

2) array1[0] = 1;
   array1[1] = 2;
   array1[2] = 3;

With this code, we can see that we are assigning 3 values to the array. When you run this program, you will get an error because the program will see that the array has gone out of its maximum allowable bounds of two. You will get the below error at runtime.

Exception   in   thread   "main"
java.lang.ArrayIndexOutOfBoundsException: 2

at HelloWorld.main(HelloWorld.java:8)

Why Java is important?

Next, Java has syntax and features that resemble other programming languages like C and C++. If you have any prior programming experience, you will find learning Java a breeze. Even if you are totally new to programming, you can rest assured that Java is designed to be a relatively easy language to learn. Most programmers find it easier to learn Java than say, C or C++.

Java is also designed to be platform-independent. As mentioned earlier, Java code is compiled into bytecode first, which can be run on any machine that has the Java Virtual Machine.

Hence with Java, you can write the code once and run it anywhere you want.

Why Java?

Of course, one of the key reasons to use Java is its focus on Object-oriented programming.

Object-oriented programming, or "OOP" is a type of programming language model which allows the program's code to be organized around data, rather than functions and logic, which is known as procedural programming.

These "data clusters" are organized into things called "objects," hence the moniker of "object-oriented programming."

These objects are created by something called "classes," understood here in the traditional sense of how classes are: types of objects, allowing the programmer to "classify" them according to two major criteria: attributes and methods.

The attributes of a class are the raw data that will create the object: these are its descriptors, such as the values that it possesses, and other relevant data that will make up the object. The second criterion is the "method" of the object.

This "method" is the behavior, or the logical sequences contained within the class, describing how it interacts or can be interacted with natively.

CHAPTER 1:

Java Basics

O f course, one of the key reasons to use Java is its focus on Object-oriented programming. Object-oriented programming, or "OOP" is a type of programming language model which allows the program's code to be organized around data, rather than functions and logic, which is known as procedural programming.

These objects are created by something called "classes," understood here in the traditional sense of how classes are types of objects, allowing the programmer to "classify" them according to two major criteria: attributes and methods.

The attributes of a class are the raw data that will create the object: these are its descriptors, such as the values that it possesses, and other relevant data that will make up the object.

The second criterion is the "method" of the object.

In order to make this clearer, say that there is a class "Human." This "class" will have attributes such as height, weight, gender, and race. The "human" class can also have methods such as "run," "walk," "talk."

These theoretical components make up the "human" class, a blueprint for an object.

Now that the class has been defined, the programmer, if they so wish, can create an object using the "human" class as a blueprint.

They can invoke the class "Human" and "populate" its attributes, giving it a specific height, weight, gender, and race. In addition, the object already has built-in functions such as "run," "walk," and "talk," so upon the creation of an object, let's say named "Mike" from the "Human" class, it already contains the functions to run, walk, and talk, without need for the programmer to code those specific functions again, as they are already "inherent" in the created object.

In a nutshell, that is what Object-oriented programming is meant to be: a way of programming that allows the programmer to draw on pre-defined classes so that it will be easier to describe them and use their internal, or built-in functions in order to operate them.

Assuming that the reader is not a total newbie to programming, and has been introduced to the world of programming using C or another procedural—heavy language, the next logical question would be: why even use object-oriented programming?

Well, one of its main advantages is that in the long run, it saves time.

Procedural programming is usually much quicker and more straightforward in simpler algorithms and programs; rather than having to construct and define a class, and create an object based on that class, all the programmer really has to do is to simply declare the necessary variables and write the functions, and create the algorithm in order to solve the problem that they need the code to address.

However, when it comes to more complex programs, needing more complex solutions, this is where object-oriented programming begins to shine, and this is where it starts to show its strength.

In a lot of programs, there will be times that there will be a number of "objects" or data clusters that have to be grouped together, and that the programmer will be treated in a certain way.

This is what "classes" are meant to address.

Instead of declaring a new set of variables per data cluster, they can simply draw on a pre-made "class" and create a new "object."

Let's see how this would work in practice.

If a programmer were to code a chess game in procedural fashion, then they would have to manually describe each and every piece, all sixteen pawns, four bishops and four knights, four rooks, two queens, and two kings. In addition, they will have to write the functions that allow each piece to move in its own separate way.

However, if the programmer makes use of object-oriented programming, instead of having to code sixteen pawns, four bishops, four knights, four rooks, two queens, two kings, they simply have to code six classes: one class to describe each piece on the board.

The programmer can now simply include the movement functions within each class, and have the attributes describe their position: whether they're white king's pawn, or black queen's pawn, these are all things that can be inserted through the "attributes" portion of the "pawn" class. Instead of thirty—two clusters of code, the programmer only has to do six.

Now it's much easier, much shorter, and also much more elegant.

Java tokens

Java tokens are the values that are smaller than other integers.

These numbers are going to fall between the value of -32768 and 32767.

The code that I have been using is not going to work for shorts, instead, I am going to need to use the short function so that I can make sure that the values are going to fall between the set limitations.

Large values are going to be stored inside of a double value along with floating-point values.

A double does not have to be used if I can use a floating-point. As I am storing a floating variable.

I am going to need to put a letter at the end of my value amount.

This value should be f because it is a floating-point number.

Keywords

In Java, the Boolean type refers to false or true values. J

Ava finds out if it is true or false using the reserved keywords. Therefore, a Boolean expression type will assume one of these values.

An example to demonstrate include:

There are a few things to note about this program.

First, the println(), displays a boolean value. Secondly, the boolean values control the flow of an if statement.

You don't need to go a long way in writing the boolean type this way: if (b == true)

The result shown by the operator, such as < is boolean. It is one of the reasons why we have the expression 11 > 8 showing the value true.

In addition, the other pair of parentheses near the 11 > 8 is important since plus comes before the >.

Identifiers

The top layer of the diagram above is for the identifier or name. This top layer is the name you give to a class. The name should specifically identify and also describe the type of object as seen or experienced by the user. In simple terms, the name or identifier should identify the class.

Operators

Java has an extensive list of operator environment. If you are wondering what an operator is, you can look at it as a symbol that conveys a specific message to the compiler to carry out a logical or mathematical operation. In Java, you will interact with four classes of operators.

The four classes include:

- Logical operator
- Bitwise operator
- Relational operator
- Arithmetic operator

Like other computer languages, Java has a defined list of additional operators to take care of certain specific scenarios. When it comes to learning JAVA programming language, or any programming language for that matter, there are five basic concepts you must understand before you get started. These five basic concepts include:

- Variables
- Data Structures
- Control Structures
- Syntax
- Tools

Each of these concepts will be thoroughly explained on a beginner's level to ensure that they are understood.

Separators

They are not suitable for high-level abstraction: note that a lot of these programs make use of low-level constructs which are primarily used for low-level abstraction. The usual approach with these programming languages is that they focus on the machine—how to make a computer do something rather than how these functions can help solve the issues of a user.

These languages deal with the minute details, which is already beyond the scope of high-level abstraction, which is the more common approach that we see today.

In low-level abstraction, data structures and algorithms are taken separately, whereas these are taken as a whole in high-level abstraction.

Literals

When it comes to literals in Java, we mean the fixed values which appear in the form in which human beings can read. We can say the number 200 is literal. Most of the time, literals can be constants. Literals are important in a program. In fact, most Java programs use literals. Some of the programs we have already discussed in this book use literals.

Literals in Java can fall on various primitive data types.

The manner in which every literal is shown is determined by its type. Like it was mentioned some time back, we enclose character constants in single quotes such as 'c' and '%.'

We define literals in integers without involving the fractional part. For instance, 12 and -30 are integer literals. A floating-point literal should contain the decimal point plus the fractional part. 12.389 is a floating literal.

Java further permits for one to apply the scientific notation for the floating-point literals.

Integer literals contain int value, and anyone can initialize them with a variable of short, byte, and char.

Comments

When this occurs, we call the grey's comments. In the running stages of the program, the grey's (comments) are moot.

This is to means that you can use the comment feature to state or explain what the code you are creating wants to achieve.

You can achieve this by typing two slashes and then the comment. Here is a sample.

//Place your single line comment here

You can have more than one comment line by doing either of the following:

//We are going to

//spread the comments into two

Or

/*

This comment spreads over two lines

*/

If you look at the comment above, you will notice that it starts with /* but ends with */

Additionally, if you look at the previous image (figure 8, you will notice that there are comments that begin with a single forward slash and two asterisks (/**), but end with one asterisk and one forwards slash; this is called a Javadoc comment.

CHAPTER 2:

Variables

What are variables?

A variable, on the other hand, is an "object" that contains a specific data type and it's assigned or received value. It is called a variable because the value contained can change according to how it is used in the code, how the coder can declare its value, or even how the user of the program chooses to interact with it. A variable, in short, is a storage unit for a data type. Having access to variables allow programmers to conveniently label and call stored values at hand.

Types of variables in Java

Java requires the programmer to use declaration statements, lines of code used to declare variables and define them by specifying the particular data type and name. Java has a specific way of treating variables, by defining variables as containers that contain a certain type and value of information, unlike some languages such as python, which only requires a declaration of a variable, and the variable can dynamically change its type; Java variables are static, which retain their type once declared.

Int number = 20;

Boolean completed = true;

String hello = "Hello World!"

The syntax in declaring is seen in the previous examples, with the type of the variable coming first, then the name of the variable, then the value. Note as well that the declaration statement can be composed of multiple declarations in one line, as in the following example:

Int number = 20, Boolean completed = true, string hello = "Hello World!";

Java variables can be declared without any value at the start; in cases such as these, Java chooses to declare these variables with a particular default value, for example:

Byte   a;

Short num;

Boolean answer;

Will result in the values 0, 0, and false, respectively. A more complete list of default values is as follows: the byte, short, int, and long data types will all result in a default value of 0, while the float and double data types will have a default 0.0 value, the char data type will result in 'u\0000' value, a string or any other object will have a null default value, and all Booleans will begin with a false default value.

In Java, variables are static when declared, meaning that the programmer must define the data type that the variable will be containing. To illustrate, if we wish to use a variable num to store a number, we would first have to declare the variable: "int num," before we can assign a value, such as "num = 10."

The process above is usually known as and referred to as an "assignment statement," where a value is assigned to the variable as declared by the programmer. However, one prominent thing about how Java, and in fact how most programming languages, works is that in the assignment statement, such as in our example of num = 10, the actual value stored is the one on the right side of the equals sign, the value of 10, and num is just the "marker" to call that stored value. This is why there are many Java programmers that tend to prefer the jargon of "getting" a value rather than "assigning," though for the most part, they may be employed interchangeably, and outside of some rare scenario, function mostly the same way.

Note, however, that once values have been assigned to variables, functions need to be carried out in order for the data inside that variable to change its data type.

Naming a variable

Creating variables is an easy task, especially given how Java programmers tend to create and name them after the data type or the purpose of what the variable will store. However, there are a few rules when it comes to naming these variables, else Java will not recognize it, and an error message will result. The main restrictions around variable names are that it should not begin with a special character, such as an underscore or a number. However, variable names can consist of characters such as letters and numbers, and even an underscore, provided that the underscore is not placed at the start. No other characters may be used, such as the # or even $, as these special characters have different uses in Java, and thus will not be recognized in a variable name.

While those are the major rules, here are some tips when it comes to naming variables. The variable name should be descriptive, as in longer codes it may be difficult to recall just what "x" is for. Having a variable name such as "count" or "output" is much easier to recall as compared to having a generic "x" or "y" and will help in avoiding confusion. In addition to being descriptive, variables will also be easier to use if their names are kept fairly short. While having a variable name such as banking information account records is very descriptive, typing it repeatedly as needed in the program will get exhausting, and having longer variable names increase the chances of typographical errors, which will lead to bugs in the code, resulting in a run - time error or the code not working as intended, or working, but introducing bugs along the way. Note as well that it has always been a practice for Java variables to be written in all lower—case letters, and while there is no restriction on capitalization, keeping things in lowercase simplifies things, as a missed capitalization may result in the variable not being recognized, as Java reads an upper—case letter as an entirely different character versus a lower—case letter.

Java primitive types

Method Naming Conventions

We shall revisit the naming conventions in Java since you will be using member methods. Methods in Java programming perform operations, they also receive any argument provided by a caller, and it can also return a result of an operation to a caller. Here's the syntax for declaring a method:

[Access Control Modifier] Return Type methodName ([set of parameters]) {

// body of the method

......

}

Here are a few rules to remember when you make the names for the methods that you will write. Method names are always verbs or more specifically verb phrases (which means you can use multiple words to name them). The first word of the method name should all be in lower case letters, while the rest of the words should follow a camel case format. Here is an example:

writeMethodNamesThisWay( )

Now, you should remember that verbs are used for method names, and they indicate an action while nouns are used for variable names, and they denote a certain attribute.

Following the syntax for declaring a method and following the name conventions for this Java construct, here's a sample code that can be used to compute the area of a circle.

```java
public double computeCircleArea() {

return radius * radius * Math.PI;

}
```

Using Constructors in Your Code

We'll just go over some additional details as they relate to object-oriented programming. As stated earlier, a constructor will look like a method, and you can certainly think of it and treat it like a special kind of method in Java programming.

However, a constructor will still be different from a method in several ways. The name of a constructor will be the same as the class name. Use the keyword or operator "new" to create a new instance of the constructor and also to initialize it. Here's an example using the class "Employee" and a variety of ways to initialize it in your code:

Employee payrate1 = new Employee( );

Employee payrate2 = new Employee(2.0);

Employee payrate3 = new Employee(3.0, "regular");

A constructor will also implicitly return void—that simply means it doesn't have a return type. You can't put a return statement inside the body of a constructor since it will be flagged by compilers as an error. The only way you can invoke a constructor is via the use of the "new" statement. We have already given you several ways how you can invoke constructors in the samples above.

One final difference is that constructors can't be inherited. Let's go back to the examples provided above—the first line includes "Employee( );"– –that is called a default constructor. As you can see, it has no parameters whatsoever. The job of a default constructor is to simply initialize the member variables to a specific default value. In the example above, the member variable payrate1 was initialized to its default pay rate and employee status.

Can constructors be overloaded too? Yes, they can. Constructors behave like methods too, so that means you can overload a constructor just the same way you overload a method. Here are a few examples of how you can overload a constructor. We use the Employee class and overload it using different parameters.

Employee( )

Employee(int r)

Employee(int r, String b)

How to initialize a variable

Now that we know how to declare variables, and we know the various types of variables that are available to us, the next thing to do is to learn how to make use of these variables, in something called "expressions." Expressions are the most used building blocks of a Java program, generally meant to produce a new value as a result, though in some cases, expressions are used to assign a new value to a variable. Generally, expressions are made up of things such as values, variables, operators, and method calls. There are also some expressions that produce no result, but rather affect another variable. One example would be an expression that changes the value of a variable based on an operation: there is no new value output, and there is no true "assignment" of a new value, but rather there is what is called a side effect that results in a changed variable value.

The "Hello World" printing program, we introduced raw values into the print function, also known as "hard coding" the output. However, at this point, we should try to incorporate what we have learned about variables. Variables operate much the same way as raw values, as they simply reference a previously stored value by the computer, and as such, the programmer can just use the variable name instead of the value. In

COMPUTER PROGRAMMING FOR BEGINNERS AND CYBERSECURITY

order to demonstrate this, let us remember the previous "Hello World" program:

print ("Hello World") ;

input ("\n\nPlease press the return key to close this window.") ;

Now, instead of hard—coding the "Hello World" string, we can simply declare it into a variable and have the program output that variable. This should end up looking as:

String = "Hello World" ;

print(string) ;

input ("\n\nPlease press the return key to close this window.") ;

This should come out with the same result as the previous program, looking something similar to:

Hello World

Please press the return key to close this window.

154 | P a g .

CHAPTER 3:

Java Basics

Java Development Kit

The JDK provides the tools needed to build, test, and monitor robust Java-anchored applications. It allows developers to access software components and compile applications during Java programming operations. For example, a developer needs a JDK-powered environment to be able to write applets or implement methods.

Since the JDK more or less performs the operations of a Software Development Kit (SDK), one could easily confuse the scope and operations of the two items. Whereas the JDK is specific to the Java programming language, an SDK has broader applicability. But a JDK still operates as a component of an SDK in a program development environment. This means that a developer would still need an SDK to provide certain tools with broader operational characteristics and that are not available within the JDK domain. Developer documentation and debugging utilities, as well as application servers, are some of the crucial tools that SDK supplies to a Java programming environment.

The scope of JDK deployment depends on the nature of the tasks at hand, the supported versions, and the Java edition that is in use. For example, the Java Platform, Standard Edition (Java SE) Development Kit is designed for use with the Java Standard Edition. The Java Platform, Enterprise Edition (Java EE), and the Java Platform, Macro Edition (Java ME), are the other major subsets of the JDK. Details of each of these Java editions are described in detail in the subtopics below. The JDK has been a free platform since 2007, when it was uploaded to the OpenJDK portal. Its open-source status facilitates collaborations and allows communities of software developers to clone, hack, or contribute ideas for advancements and upgrades.

Java SE

The Java SE powers a wide variety of desktop and server applications. It supports the testing and deployment of the Java programming language within the development environment of these applications. Some of the documentations associated with the recent releases of Java SE include an advanced management console feature and a revamped set of Java deployment rules. Java SE 13.0.1 is the latest JDK version for the Java SE platform at the time of writing this book.

The Java SE SDK is equipped with the core JRE capabilities alongside a portfolio of tools, class libraries, and implementation technologies that are designed for use in the development of desktop applications. These tools range from simple objects and types for Java program implementations to advanced class parameters that are suited for building applications with networking capabilities and impenetrable security characteristics. Java programmers can also apply this particular JDK on the development of Java applications used to simplify access to databases or to enhance GUI properties.

Java EE

The Java EE platform is an open-source product that is developed through the collaborative efforts of members of the Java community worldwide. Java EE is closely related to the Java SE because the former is built on top of the latter. This particular software is integrated with transformative innovations that are designed for use in enterprise solutions. The features and advancements that are introduced in new releases often reflect the inputs, requirements, and requests of members of the Java community. The Java EE actually offers more than twenty implementations that are compliant with Java programming.

The Java EE SDK is meant for use in the construction of applications for large-scale operations. Just as its name suggests, this particular Java SDK was created to provide support for enterprise software solutions. The JDK features a powerful API and runtime properties that Java programmers require to build applications with scalable and networkable functionalities. Developers in need of developing multi-tiered applications could find this JDK useful as well.

The Java EE 8 is the latest release at the time of writing this book. Java EE's revised design provides enhanced technologies for enterprise solutions as well as modernized applications for security and management purposes. The release features several advancements that included greater REST API capabilities provided through the Client, JSON Binding, Servlet, and Security APIs. This version also features the Date and Time API as well as the Streams API, according to information published in the Oracle Corporate website as of December 2019.

Java ME

The Java ME platform deploys simplicity, portability, and dynamism to provide a versatile environment for building applications for small gadgets and devices. Java ME is known for having an outstanding application development environment, thanks to its interactive and user-friendly navigation interfaces, as well as built-in capabilities for implementing networking concepts. It is largely associated with the Internet of Things (IoT) and is useful when building applications designed for built-in technologies or connected devices that could be used to invent or implement futuristic concepts. Java ME's portability and runtime attributes make it suitable for use in software applications for wearable gadgets, cell phones, cameras, sensors, and printers, among other items and equipment.

The Java ME SDK is equipped with the requisite tools meant for use within an independent environment when developing software applications, testing functionalities, and implementing device simulations. According to information published in the Oracle

Corporate website as of 2019, this JDK is well suited for accommodating "the Connected Limited Device Configuration (CLDC)" technology alongside "the Connected Device Configuration (CDC)" functionality. This results in a single and versatile environment for developing applications.

There are several other Java ME solutions that support the deployment of the Java programming language in applications. Java ME Embedded provides a runtime environment integrating IoT capabilities in devices, while the Java ME embedded client facilitates the construction of software solutions that run and optimize the functionality of built-in programs. Java for Mobile makes use of the CLDC and the stack of Java ME developer tools to create innovative features for mobile devices.

Java Runtime Environment

Remember that there are certain conditions that must prevail for Java applications to run efficiently. The JRE contains the ingredients responsible for creating these requisite conditions. This includes the JVM and its corresponding files and class attributes. Although JRE operates as a component of the JDK, it is capable of operating independently, especially if the tasks are limited to run rather than build application instructions.

The JRE lends important operational properties to different programs in the Java programming ecosystem. For example, a program is considered self-contained if it runs an independent JRE within it. This means that a program does not depend on other programs to access the JRE. This independence makes it possible for a program to achieve compatibility with different OS platforms.

Java Virtual Machine

The JVM operates as a specification for implementing Java in computer programs. It is the driving force behind the platform-independence characteristics of the Java language. This status is accentuated by JVM's status as a program that is executed by other programs. The programs written to interact with and execute the JVM see it as a machine. It is for this reason that similar sets, libraries, and interfaces are used to write Java programs to be able to match every single JVM implementation to a particular OS. This facilitates the translation or interpretation of Java programs into runtime instructions in the local OS, and thereby eliminating the need for platform dependence in Java programming.

As a developer, you must be wary of the vulnerability your development environment and applications have to cyber attacks and other threats. The JVM provides enhanced security features that protect you from such threats. The solid security foundation is attributable to its built-in syntax and structure limitations that reside in the operational codes of class files. But this does not translate to limitations on the scope of class files that the JVM can accommodate. The JVM actually accepts a variety of class files so long as they can be validated to be safe and secure. Therefore, the JVM is a viable complementary alternative for developing software in other programming languages.

The JVM is often included as a ported feature in a wide variety of software applications and hardware installations. It is implemented through algorithms that are determined by Oracle or any other provider. As such, the JVM provides an open implementation platform. The JVM actually contains the runtime instance as the core property that anchors its command operations. For example, the creation of a JVM instance simply involves writing an instruction in the command prompt that, in turn, runs the class properties of Java.

A Java programmer needs to be familiar with the key areas of JVM, such as the classloader and the data section for runtime operations as well as the engine that is responsible for executing programs. There are also performance-related components, such as the garbage collector and the heap dimension tool, that are equally important to the deployment of the JVM. There is a close affiliation between the JVM and bytecodes.

Bytecodes

Bytecodes are essentially JVM commands that are contained in a class file alongside other information that include the symbol table. They operate as background language programs responsible for facilitating the interpretation and execution of JVM operations. Bytecodes are actually the substitutes for native codes because Java does not provide the latter. The structure of the JVM register is such that it contains methods which, in turn, accommodate bytecode streams—that is, sets of instructions for the JVM. In other words, each Java class has methods within it, and the class file loading process executes a single bytecode stream for any given method. The activation of a method automatically triggers a bytecode the moment a program begins to run.

The other important feature of bytecodes is the Just-in-time (JIT) compiler that operates during the runtime operations for compiling codes that can be executed. The feature actually exists as a HotSpot JIT compiler within the JVM ecosystem. It executes codes concurrently with the Java runtime operations because it has the ability to perform at optimized levels and the flexibility to scale and accommodate growing traffic of instructions. Previously, the JIT compiler required frequent tuning to rid it of redundant programs and refresh its memory. Tuning was a necessary procedure that ensured the JIT compiler delivered optimum performance. However, the frequent upgrades in the newer versions of Java gradually introduced automated memory refreshing mechanisms that eliminated the need for regular tuning.

Bytecodes can be either primitive types, flexible types, or stack-based. According to Venners (1996), there are seven parameters of primitive data, including byte, char, double, float, int, long, and short. The boolean parameter is also a widely used primitive type, taking the tally to eight. Each of the eight parameters is meant to help developers deploy variables that can be acted upon by the bytecodes. Bytecode streams actually express these parameters of the primitive types in the form of operands. This ends up designating the larger and more powerful parameters to the higher levels of the bytes' hierarchy, with the smaller ones occupying the lower levels of the hierarchy in a descending order.

Java opcodes are similarly crucial components of the primitive types, thanks to their role of classifying operands. This role ensures that operands retain their state, thereby eliminating the need for an operand identification interface in the JVM. The JVM is able to speed up processes because it is capable of multitasking while accommodating multiple opcodes that deliver domicile variables into stacks. Opcodes are also useful for processing and defining the value parameters for stack-based bytecodes. According to Venners (1996), this could be an implicit constant value, an operand value, or a value derived from a constant pool.

CHAPTER 4:

Java Environment

Writing Programs in Editors

To write programs, you use a simple editor such as Notepad, or you can use a full-fledged Integrated Development Environment (IDE). Below is a list of some of the most popular IDE's that are available for Java and some of their relevant features.

Eclipse

This IDE has been around for quite a long time and is very popular and widely used amongst the Java development community. Some of the core features of the IDE are:

- It's free and open source. Hence there are many developers who keep contributing to the IDE.

- It can be used to develop applications in other languages such as C++, Ruby, HTML5, and PHP.

- It has a rich client platform.

- It provides the ability of refactoring code.

- It helps in code completion.

- It has a wide variety of extensions and plugins.

- It also has support for most source code version control systems.

IntelliJ IDEA

This is another popular IDE used by the Java development community. Some of the core features of this IDE are:

- The community edition is free and open source.

- The paid edition provides many more features and allows developers to build enterprise applications with the Java Enterprise Edition.

- It provides the ability of refactoring code.

- It helps in code completion.

- It has a wide variety of extensions and plugins.

- It also has support for most source code version control systems.

Netbeans

NetBeans is a highly recommended IDE for beginners in Java language. It is a powerful and fast IDE that supports all Java platforms as well as mobile applications. It runs on a variety of platforms such as Windows, Linux, Mac OS X, and Solaris. It also provides support for languages such as HTML5, C/C++, and PHP.

The Upsides of Java

- Java epitomizes simplicity in programming, thanks to its user-friendly interface for learning, writing, deployment, and implementation.

- Java's core architecture is designed to facilitate ease of integration and convenience of use within the development environment.

- Java is platform-independent and readily portable, making it suitable for multitasking and use across software applications.

- The object-oriented characteristics of Java support the creation of programs with standard features and codes that can be redeployed.

- Java's networking capabilities make it easier for programmers to create software solutions for shared computing environments.

- The close relationship between Java, the C++, and the C languages makes it easier for anyone with knowledge of the other two languages to learn Java.

- Java's automated garbage collection provides continuous memory protection, making it convenient for programmers to eliminate security vulnerabilities while writing codes.

- Java's architecture is flexible for the implementation of multithreading programs.

- Java is readily reusable, thanks to the ability to redeploy classes using the interface or inheritance features.

The Downsides of Java

- Since Java is not a native application, it runs at lower speeds compared to other programming languages.

- Java may also lack consistency in the processing and displaying of graphics. For example, the ordinary appearance of the graphical user interface (GUI) in Java-based applications is quite different and of lower standards compared the GUI output of native software applications.

- Java's garbage collection, a feature that manages memory efficiency, may interfere with speed and performance whenever it runs as a background application.

CHAPTER 5:

Objects and Classes

Finally, we are going to look at classes and objects;

An object in Java has got to have a state, which will be stored in a field and a behavior, indicated by a method. A class is a sort of map, a blueprint if you like, from which an object is created. This is what a class looks like:

public class Dog {

String breed;

int ageC;

String color;

void barking() {

}

void whining() {

}

void sleeping() {

}

}

A class may have any of these variable types:

- Local—defined within a constructor, block, or method. The variable is declared and then initialized inside a method and destroyed once the method has ended.
- Instance—defined in a class but are outside a method. Initialized when instantiation of the class happens and can be accessed from inside any constructor, block, or method of the class.
- Class—declared inside the class, uses the static keyword, and are outside any method.

Classes can have multiple methods, as many as required to access all the different kinds of values in the method. In our example above, we had three methods—barking(), whining(), and sleeping().

Constructors

Every class will have a constructor; if you omit it, a default one will be built by the compiler. When you create a new object, at least one constructor must be invoked. As a rule, the name of a constructor must be the same as that of the class, and there can be as many constructors as a class requires.

This is what a constructor looks like:

public class Puppy {

public Puppy() {

  }

public Puppy(String name) {

  // This constructor has a single parameter, name.

  }

}

Creating Objects

We already know that a class is a kind of blueprint to create objects from, so it goes without saying that the object is created from the class. For a new object to be created, we need the new keyword.

These are the three steps needed to create an object from a class:

Declaration—A variable must be declared with a name and the object type

Instantiation—The new keyword is used for creating the object

Initialization—The constructor is called, and this initializes the object.

The next example shows how objects are created:

```java
public class Puppy {

public Puppy(String name) {

// This constructor contains a single parameter called name.

System.out.println("Passed Name is :" + name );

}

public static void main(String []args) {

// The next statement will create an object called myPuppy

Puppy myPuppy = new Puppy( "fluffy" );

}

}
```

Run this and see what happens.

Accessing Instance Variables and Methods

Objects can be used when we want to access instance variables and methods; this example shows how we access an instance variable:

```java
/* First we create the object */

ObjectReference = new Constructor();
```

/* Now we call our variable, like this */

ObjectReference.variableName;

/* Now a class method is called, like this */

ObjectReference.MethodName();

Next, we can see the instance variables and methods in a class are accessed:

public class Puppy {

int PuppyAge;

public Puppy(String name) {

// This constructor contains a single parameter called name.

System.out.println("Name chosen is :" + name);

}

public void setAge(int age) {

PuppyAge = age;

}

public int getAge() {

System.out.println("Puppy's age is :" + PuppyAge);

return PuppyAge;

}

public static void main(String[] args) {

/* Object creation */

Puppy myPuppy = new Puppy("fluffy");

/* Now we call the class method to set the Puppy's age */

myPuppy.setAge(2);

/* Next, we call another class method to get the Puppy's age */

myPuppy.getAge();

/* We access instance variable in this way */

System.out.println("Variable Value :" + myPuppy.PuppyAge);

}

}

Run this and see what happens.

Import Statements

One important thing to remember is that paths must be fully qualified, and that includes the names of the class and the package. If not, the compiler will struggle to load the source code and the classes. To qualify a path, we need to use import statements and, in this example, we see how a compiler loads the requested classes into the directory we specify:

import java.io.*;

Next, we need two classes created, one called Employee and one called EmployeeTest. We use the following code to do this—keep in mind that Employee is the name of the class, and it is a public class. Do this and then save the file, calling it Employee.java.

Also note that we have four instance variables here—age, name, designation, and salary, along with one constructor that has been explicitly defined and that takes a parameter:

public class Employee {

String name;

int age;

String designation;

double salary;

// This is the constructor of the class called Employee

public Employee(String name) {

this.name = name;

```
}

// We assign the age of the Employee to the variable called age.

public void empAge(int empAge) {

age = empAge;

}

/* We assign the designation to the variable called designation.*/

public void empDesignation(String empDesig) {

designation = empDesig;

}

/* We assign the salary to the variable called salary.*/

public void empSalary(double empSalary) {

salary = empSalary;

}

/* Print the Employee details */

public void printEmployee() {

System.out.println("Name:"+ name );

System.out.println("Age:" + age );
```

System.out.println("Designation:" + designation);

System.out.println("Salary:" + salary);

}

}

Code processing begins with a main method, so you need to ensure that your code has a main method, and we need to create some objects. We will start by creating a class called EmployeeTest, and this will create a couple of instances of the class called Employee. The methods for each object must be invoked so that the values may be assigned to the variables. Save this code in EmployeeTest:

public class EmployeeTest {

public static void main(String args[]) {

/* Create two objects by using constructor */

Employee empOne = new Employee("Bobby Bucket");

Employee empTwo = new Employee("Shelley Mary");

// Invoke the methods for each of the objects we created

empOne.empAge(28);

empOne.empDesignation("Senior Software Developer");

empOne.empSalary(1500);

```
empOne.printEmployee();

empTwo.empAge(22);

empTwo.empDesignation("Software Developer");

empTwo.empSalary(850);

empTwo.printEmployee();

}

}
```

Now the classes need to be compiled, and EmployeeTest run; do this and see what you get.

You should see this:

Output

C:\> javac Employee.java

C:\> javac EmployeeTest.java

C:\> java EmployeeTest

Name: Bobby Bucket

Age:28

Designation: Senior Software Developer

Salary:1850.000

Name: Shelley Mary

Age:22

Designation: Software Developer

Salary:850.00

CHAPTER 6:

Proper Working Code Examples

T raditionally, everyone's first program prints, "Hello World." This first program demonstrates how to create, save, and run a program. It also shows the basic structure used in all Java programs.

Here's a screenshot of the window created by the Hello World program:

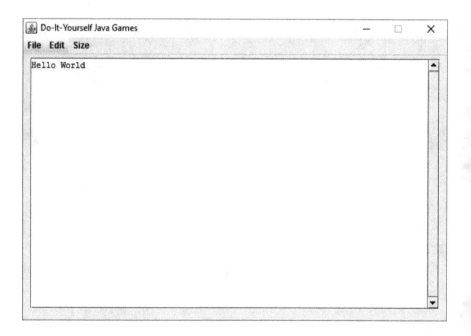

Lesson 1—Java Projects and Packages

Programs are first organized by Java projects, then by packages within the Java projects. You'll create a Java project for each program in this book.

Packages hold program files that are usually used together. Because the programs in this book will be small, most of the Java projects you create will have only one package.

In this lesson, you'll create one Java project and one package for your first program.

Try It

Create your first Java project, called Hello World:

1. If Eclipse is no longer open:

   a. Double-click the Eclipse shortcut you created on your desktop.

   b. Click OK to use your Java work folder as your workspace.

2. Right-click in the Package Explorer pane and choose New/Java Project.

3. Name the Java project Hello World, and select Use Default JRE if it is 1.7 or higher, then click next, as shown in the image below. If the default JRE is less than 1.7, select the

option to Use an execution environment JRE of 1.7 or higher.

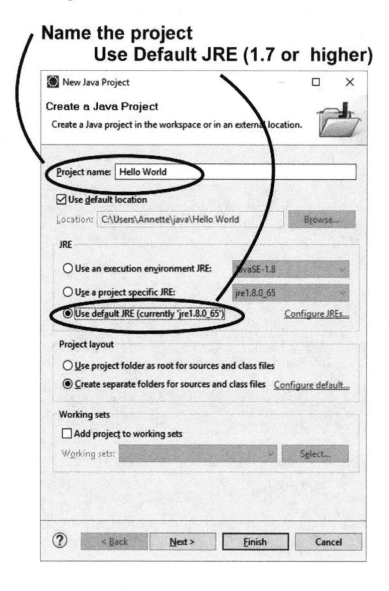

4. Click Libraries, then click Add External JARs..., as shown in the image below.

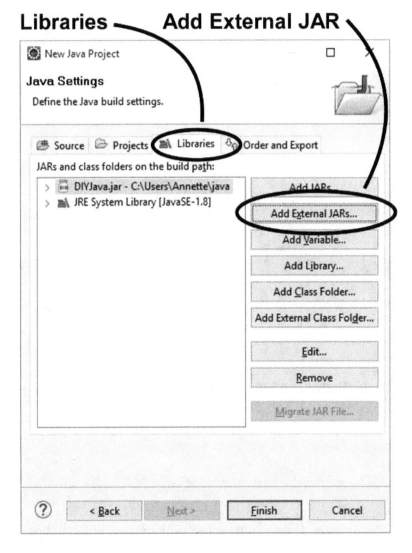

5. Browse to and select DIYJava.jar, which you installed in your Java work folder, and click Open.

6. Click Finish.

The Package Explorer pane now lists one project (Hello World) with the added JAR file (DIYJava.jar), as shown in this image:

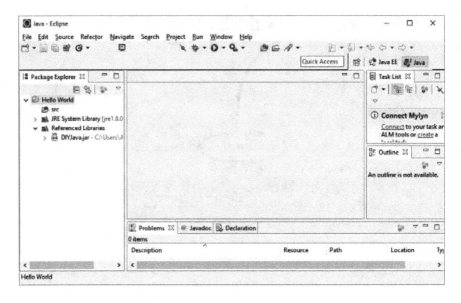

Create a package for your Hello World program in the Hello World project:

1. Right-click on the Hello World project and choose New/Package.

2. Name the package _____._____.helloworld, as shown in the image below. Use your own name as part of the package name. I used annette.godtland.helloworld for my package name.

Name the package

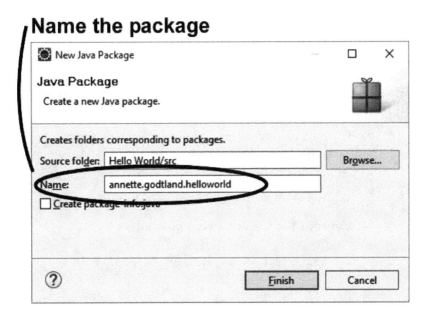

3. Click Finish.

The Package Explorer pane now shows the package you created in your Hello World project, as shown in this image:

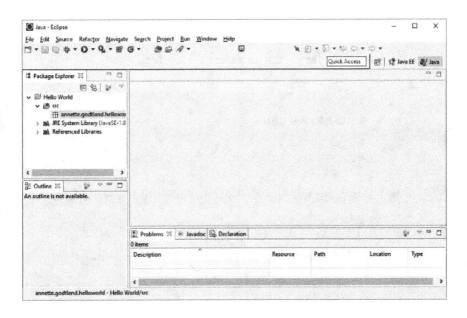

Key Points and More

- Right-click in the Package Explorer pane to create Java projects and packages.

- Create a different Java project for each program.

- Eclipse will create a folder on your computer named the same as the Java project. Give your Java project a name you want for the folder on your computer.

  o You now have a folder called Hello World in your Java work folder.

  o For example, capitalize the first letter of each word and put a space between each word like the Hello World project.

- Add DIYJava.jar to the Java projects you create with the help of this book.

  o DIYJava.jar is an external JAR file.

  o DIYJava.jar makes it easy to write programs that print text to a window.

- Organize your program files into packages in Java projects.

- Put program files that are usually used together into one package.

  o Because your programs will be small, most of your programs will have only one package.

- Package name rules:

  o Make your package name different from anyone else's package names. Java programmers traditionally use their name or business name as the first part of their package name.

  o Use all lowercase letters with no spaces.

  o Use periods between different categories in the package name. For example, if the package name identifies who created the package and what the package will be used for, put a period between the creator and its purpose.

- Make sure when you create the Java Projects in this book that you select the option to Use an execution environment JRE of JavaSE-1.7 or higher. Once you select this option for creating a project, Eclipse will default to that option for all future Java Projects.

- Java projects are for Eclipse; packages are for Java. Because you're using Eclipse, you'll use both Java projects and packages. If you were to create Java programs without Eclipse, you would probably use only packages.

Lesson 2—Classes, Superclasses, and Programs

Java programs are made from one or more classes. Classes contain the actual program code: the instructions that, when run in sequence, perform the desired task.

Every class must name some other class as its superclass. For example, programs intended to run in a window must name some type of window class as its superclass.

In this lesson, you'll create your first class: a program that runs in a DIYWindow.

Try It

Create your first class using the DIYWindow class as its superclass:

1. Right-click on your package in the Package Explorer pane and choose New / Class.

2. Enter HelloWorld for the class name, as shown in the image below. (Hint: there's no space between "Hello" and "World.")

3. Click Browse for Superclass.

   a. Enter "diy" for the type, select DIYWindow, as shown in the image below, and click OK.

4. Which method stubs would you like to create? Select these options, as shown in the image below:

a. Public static void main (String[] args).

b. Constructors from superclass.

c. It doesn't matter if the third option, Inherit abstract methods, is selected or not.

Name the class

Browse to and select Superclass DIYWindow

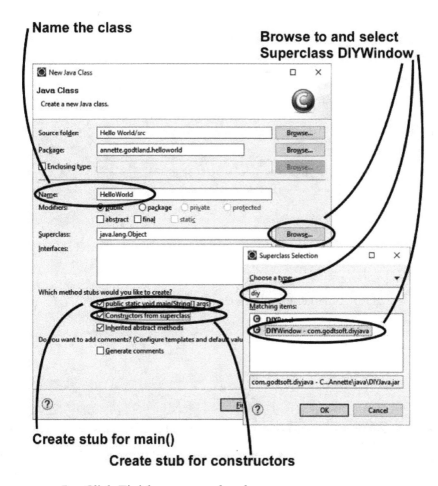

Create stub for main()

Create stub for constructors

5. Click Finish to create the class.

Eclipse will create code for a HelloWorld class that looks like the following listing.

You may find it easier to read the code listings in this book if you set your e-reader to a smaller font to minimize word wrapping.

Listing 1-1, from HelloWorld.java

```
package annette.godtland.helloworld;

import com.godtsoft.diyjava.DIYWindow;

public class HelloWorld extends DIYWindow {

public HelloWorld() {

   // TODO Auto-generated constructor stub

}

public static void main(String[] args) {

   // TODO Auto-generated method stub

}

}
```

Eclipse adds comment code you don't need. Comments are lines that begin with // or groups of lines that begin with /* and end with */.

1. Remove the automatically-generated comment lines from this class, where it says (Code was removed from here.) in the following listing.

Listing 1-2, from HelloWorld.java

package annette.godtland.helloworld;

import com.godtsoft.diyjava.DIYWindow;

public class HelloWorld extends DIYWindow {

public HelloWorld() {

(Code was removed from here.)

  }

  public static void main(String[] args) {

(Code was removed from here.)

  }

}

Remove the automatically-generated comments from the program code for every class you create for this book. You'll add your own comments in later lessons.

Click any Completed listing link to see how to complete the code. However, you'll learn more if you try to complete the code yourself before you look up the answer.

The block of code that starts as a public static void main is called the main() method. The block of code that starts as public HelloWorld() is called the constructor.

Now, add your first lines of code:

1. Add code to the constructor and main() method exactly as shown here. Changes to make to code are always shown bold in the listings.

Listing 1-3, from HelloWorld.java

```
package annette.godtland.helloworld;

import com.godtsoft.diyjava.DIYWindow;

public class HelloWorld extends DIYWindow {

public HelloWorld() {

print("Hello World");

}

 public static void main(String[] args) {

new HelloWorld();
```

}

}

1. Press Ctrl-S to save the program.

2. Click the Run button, as shown in this image, to run the program:

What happened?

A window should open that displays "Hello World," as shown in this image:

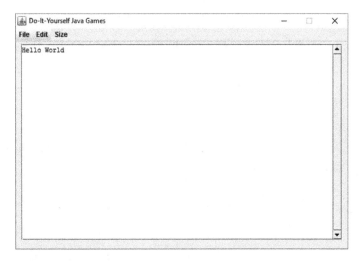

1. What would you have to change in your class to make it say hello to you?

Listing 1-4, from HelloWorld.java

...

```
public HelloWorld() {

print("Hello

_____

");

}
```

...

1. Save the program and run it.

What happens if you make a mistake?

1. Type the word "print" incorrectly and save the program.

Listing 1-5, from HelloWorld.java

...

```
public HelloWorld() {

print

ttt

("Hello Annette");
```

```
}

...
```

What happened?

Many error indicators appear, as shown in this image:

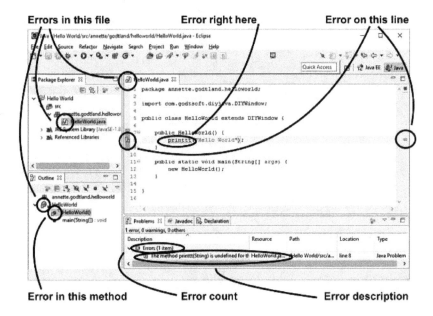

1. Double-click the Error count in the Problems pane of Eclipse to see the list of errors found.

2. Double-click on the Error description in the Problems pane to move your cursor to the line with the error.

3. Rest your cursor on the actual error (where it says Error right here in the above image). Eclipse will list ways to fix the problem, as shown in the image below. This feature of Eclipse is called Quick Fix.

Quick Fixes

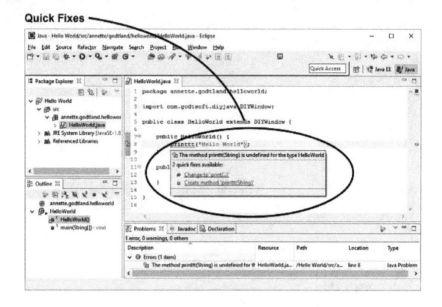

4. Click the quick fix called Change to "print(...)."

That action will fix the error for you.

1. Save changes.

All error indicators should disappear.

Now, print more:

1. Change the code to make your program say this:

Hello, earthling.

Take me to your leader.

Listing 1-6, from HelloWorld.java

...

```
public HelloWorld() {

    print

("_____");

    print("_____");

}

...
```

Throughout the lessons, unless there are syntax errors, save changes, and run the program after every code change.

Did it print the correct lines? If not, fix the code and try again.

1. What do you think you would have to print to put a blank line between the two sentences, as shown below. (Hint: you want nothing printed on that line.)

Hello, earthling.

Take me to your leader.

Listing 1-7, from HelloWorld.java

```
...

public HelloWorld() {

    print("Hello, earthling.");
```

```
print(____);

    print("Take me to your leader.");

}

    ...
```

Key Points and More

- Java programs are made up of classes. Every program requires a main() method in one of its classes.

  o The main() method must be written as public static void main(String[] args). Later lessons will explain what all those words mean.

- Multiple classes are often used together to create one program. However, most of the programs in this book will be made of only one class.

- Every class must have a superclass. Any class can be used as a superclass. You'll create your own superclass in a later lesson.

- Classes with the same superclass are considered to be of the same type. For example, the main class you create for every program in this book will use the DIYWindow class as its superclass. So every program in this book will be a type of DIYWindow.

- To create classes, right-click in the Package Explorer pane.

  o Class names can contain numbers, letters, dollar signs, and underscores. Dollar signs and underscores are usually not used.

  o Blanks or periods aren't allowed in class names.

  o Class names cannot start with a number.

  o Class names typically start with an uppercase letter.

  o If the class name includes more than one word, the first letter of each word is usually uppercase, and the rest of the letters are lowercase.

- Classes can have one or more constructors.

  o The class constructor is named the same as the class and must be declared as public. Constructors will be explained more in later lessons.

  o A constructor is called by using new, followed by the name of the constructor and parentheses. For example, new HelloWord() in the main() method calls the HelloWorld constructor.

- Blocks of code are enclosed in curly brackets, { }, and each line of code ends with a semicolon;

  o Every Java program runs the main() method first.

o The main() method calls the class constructor in all the programs in this book. Therefore, the main() method will run first, followed by the class constructor.

o Each statement within the curly brackets is run, one at a time, in the order it appears in the code.

o Blank lines between lines of code have no effect on how the code runs. Blank lines are added to make the code easier for you to read.

- Print () statements print the text in the parentheses to a window.

o Each print() statement prints on a new line.

o To print a blank line, use print() with empty parentheses.

o The print() method is part of DIYWindow, which is in DIYJava.jar. That's why you added the external JAR file, DIYJava.jar, to the project, and why you chose DIYWindow as the superclass for the HelloWorld class.

- Comments are lines that begin with // or a group of lines that begin with /* and end with */.

CHAPTER 7

Object-Oriented Programming

Y ou have learned earlier that Java is an object-oriented programming language. As such, it supports the fundamental principles of this programming paradigm.

An object refers to real entities such as bag, car, chair, or pen. Object-oriented programming languages allow programmers to design programs that use objects and classes. They provide and support features that can simplify software development and maintenance. The most important concepts of this programming paradigm are the following:

- Objects
- Classes
- Method
- Instance
- Inheritance
- Abstraction
- Polymorphism
- Message Parsing
- Encapsulation

Objects

In the real world, you will encounter objects such as humans, dogs, cars, and cats. These objects possess state and behavior. For instance, when you think of a cat, its state can consist of its breed, color, or name. Its behavior may consist of running, jumping, or wagging its tail. A software object resembles a real-world object in terms of these characteristics. Its state is saved in fields, and its behavior is exhibited through methods. In development, the methods are performed on an object's internal state, and the methods facilitate communication between objects.

Classes

Classes are used to set the definitions for objects. These specifications serve as blueprints for creating objects. While they are not immediately applied when classes are created, the definitions are available in case an object of the class is instantiated. An object or class can have multiple copies or instances within a program.

Following is an example of a class definition for a class named Cat:

```
public class Cat {
    String breed;
    int ageC
    String color;

    void running() {
    }

    void sleeping() {
    }

    void jim ping() {
    }
}
```

A class can have the following types of variable:

Class variables

Class variables are those that are declared inside a class using the static modifier and outside any method.

Local variables

Local variables are those that are defined within the methods, blocks, or constructors. These variables are declared and instantiated inside the method and are destroyed once the method had been carried out.

Instance variables

Instance variables are those that are inside a class but outside of the methods. They are initialized at the same time as the class. They can be accessed from a method, block, or constructor of that specific class.

A class can contain as many methods as necessary to obtain the values it needs. For example, the Cat class has three methods: running(), sleeping(), and jumping().

Constructors

A constructor is a method which is used to initialize an object. A class must contain at least one constructor.

The following are the important rules for constructors:

The name of the constructor should match the name of the class

It should have no explicit return type.

Types of Constructors

- Default or no-arg constructor
- Parameterized constructor
- Default Constructor

A constructor without a parameter is called default constructor.

Here's the syntax:

<class_nam e>(){}

Parameterized Constructor

A parameterized constructor is a constructor with parameters. It is used to supply values to specific objects.

The following example shows both types of constructors. The first one is a default constructor, and it doesn't have any parameter. The second constructor has one parameter, the name.

```
public class Kitten {
  public Kitten() {
  }

  public Kitten(String nam e) {
    // This constructor has one param eter, nam e.
  }
}
```

Creating Objects

Classes provide the template for objects. Objects are basically created from a class. To create new objects, you will use the 'new' keyword.

The following steps are taken to create a new object from a class:

Declaration—This refers to a variable declaration where you will write the name of the variable and its object type.

Instantiation—To create a new object; you will use the 'new' keyword.

Initialization—A call to a constructor follows the 'new' keyword and initializes a new object.

The following examples show the different steps taken to create a new object from class:

```java
public class Kitten {
  public Kitten(String name) {
    // This constructor contains a parameter, the name name.
    System.out.println("Passed Name is:" + name);
  }

  public static void main(String[]args) {
    // Following statement would create an object myPuppy
    Puppy myKitten = new Kitten("spotty");
  }
}
```

Here's the output:

Passed Name is: spotty

How to Access Methods and Instance Variables

The created objects are used to access methods and instance variables. To access instance variables, you will use these steps:

First, you must create an object:

ObjectName = New Constructor();

Next, call a variable like:

ObjectName.variableName;

To call a class method:

ObjectName.MethodName();

Java Package

A package is simply a way of grouping interfaces and classes. A Java package serves as container for classes. The usual basis for grouping is functionality. The use of packages facilitates code reusability. When interfaces and classes are categorized into packages, you can easily access them for use in other programs. The use of packages also helps prevent name conflicts among classes and interfaces.

To create a package, use the package statement before the package name as the first statement.

Here's an example:

```
package m ypack;
public class students
{
    ...statement
}
```

Import Statement

You may use the import keyword to import packages to your source file. An import statement makes it easy for the compiler to find the location of a class or source code.

You may want to import just one class from a package. You can use the dot operator to indicate the package and the class. For example:

```
import java.util.Date;
class MyDate extends Date
{
    //statement.
}
```

To import all classes from one package, you can use the wild character * after the dot operator.

For example:

```
import java.io.*;
```

Modifiers

Modifiers are keywords that alter the meaning of the definitions in your code. Java provides several modifiers.

Access Modifiers

The access modifiers are used to define access levels for methods, variables, classes, and constructors.

Private—only accessible within the class

When a method, variable, class, or constructor is declared private, it means that it is only available within the class. If the class, however, has public getter methods, you may be able to access a private variable outside the class. The private keyword indicates the highest access restriction. Take note that you cannot declare interfaces and class as private.

Public—accessible to the world

A method, interface, constructor, class, etc. that has been defined as public may be accessed from other classes. Similarly, blocks, methods, or fields that have been defined inside a public class may be accessed from Java class.

This is true as long as they are in the same package.

If you want to access a public class from another package, you will have to import the public class. Under the class inheritance concept, subclasses inherit all public variables and methods of a class.

Take note that an application's main() method will have to be declared public before the Java interpreter can call it to run the class.

Protected—accessible to all subclasses and package

Declaring a method, variable, or constructor as protected in a superclass makes it accessible only to classes within its package or to its subclasses in another package.

This access type is used if you want to allow the subclass to use variable or helper methods and prevent non-related classes from using them. Interfaces, as well as the fields and methods under them, should not be declared protected, but fields and methods outside of the interface can be declared protected.

Classes should not be declared as protected.

Default: Applicable when no modifier is provided—accessible to the package

A method or variable that has been declared without a modifier is accessible to other classes within the package.

The following table summarizes the different access modifiers and their effect:

Modifier	Inside class	Inside package	Outside package by subclass	Outside package
Private	Y	N	N	N
Public	Y	Y	Y	Y
Protected	Y	Y	Y	N
Default	Y	Y	N	N

Non-access Modifiers

The non-access modifiers can be used to access various functionalities in Java.

Final—used to finalize implementations of variables, methods, and classes

Final variables

You can only explicitly initialize a final variable once. When you declare a variable as final, you will never be able to reassign it to another object. Take note, however, that you can still change the data stored inside the object. This means that while you may change the object's state, you will not be able to change the reference. The final modifier is commonly paired with static to create a class variable out of the constant value.

Final methods

The final keyword is used to prevent a method from being changed by subclasses.

Final classes

The final modifier is used to prevent other classes from inheriting any feature from the class declared as a final class.

Static—used to create class methods or variables.

You can use this keyword to create a unique variable (called a static variable or class variable) that will exist independently from other instances of the class. You cannot declare a local variable as static.

You can also use the static keyword to create a method (called a static method or class method) that will exist independently from other instances of the class. Static methods recognize and work only on data from the arguments given without considering variables.

You may access class methods and class variables by writing the variable or method name after the class name and a dot (.).

Abstract—used to create abstract methods or classes

Abstract class

When a class is declared as abstract, it means that you will never be able to instantiate the class. The only reason for declaring a class as abstract is to extend the class. You cannot declare a class to be both final and abstract, as you can't possibly extend a final class. A class that uses abstract methods will have to be declared as abstract. Failure to do so will result in compile errors.

Abstract method

As it is declared with no implementation, an abstract method derives its methods body from the subclass. Abstract methods cannot be declared as strict or final. Unless it is also an abstract class, a class extending an abstract class must adopt the abstract methods of the superclass. A class that contains at least one abstract method should be declared as an abstract class. On the other hand, an abstract class need not have abstract methods.

Example:

```
abstract class Car {
    private double price;
    private String type;
    private String year;
    public abstract void goFast();   // abstract method
    public abstract void changeColor();
```

Synchronized

The synchronized modifier is used to indicate that only one thread can access a method at any given time. You can use this keyword with any access level modifier.

Example:

```
public synchronized void show Info() {
    ........
}
```

Volatile

This keyword is used to indicate that a thread accessing a volatile variable should merge its private copy with the master copy stored in memory. In effect, it synchronizes all cached copies of the variable with the main memory. You may only use this modifier to define instance variables of the private or object type.

Example:

```
public class M yRunnable im plem ents Runnable {
    private volatile boolean active;

    public void run() {
        active = true;
        w hile (active) {  // line 1
            // code here
        }
    }

    public void stop() {
        active = false;  // line 2
    }
}
```

Transient

The keyword transient is used to tell the compiler to skip an instance variable when it is serializing the object that contains the marked variable.

Example:

```
public transient int lim it = 50;  // w ill not persist
```

CHAPTER 8:

Decision Making and Loop Control

The decision making structures are used in situations where a set of instructions have to be executed if the condition is true and another set of instructions have to be executed when the condition is determined to be false. There are several constructs available in Java for programming such scenarios. These structures include—

If statement

This statement is used in situations where a condition needs to be tested, and if the condition is found true, the block of code that follows this statement needs to be executed. The syntax for this construct is—

if(condition){

/*Body*/

}

Sample implementation for this construct is given below—

public class ifDemo {

```java
public static void main(String args[]) {

int i = 10;

int j = 1;

if(i>j) {

System.out.print(i);

}

}

}
```

If else statement

This statement is used in situations where a condition needs to be tested, and if the condition is found true, the block of code that follows this statement needs to be executed else the block of code that follows the else statement is executed. The syntax for this construct is—

if(condition){

/*Body*/

}

else(

/*Body*/

}

Sample implementation for this construct is given below—

public class ifElseDemo {

public static void main(String args[]) {

int i = 1;

int j = 0;

if(i>j){

System.out.print(i);

```
}

else {

System.out.print(j);

}

}

}
```

Nested if statement

This statement is used in situations where a condition needs to be tested, and if the condition is found true, the block of code that follows this statement needs to be executed else the next condition is tested. If this condition is found true, the block of code corresponding to the if statement for this condition is executed. If none of the conditions are found true, the block of code that follows the else statement is executed. Multiple conditions can be tested using the nested if statements. The syntax for this construct is—

if(condition1) {

/*Body*/

}

else if (condition2) (

/*Body*/

}

else {

/*Body*/

}

Sample implementation for this construct is given below—

```java
public class nestedIfDemo {

public static void main(String args[]) {

int i = 0;

int j = 0;

if(i>j){

System.out.print(i);

}

else if(j>i) {

System.out.print(j);

}

else {

System.out.print("Equal");

}

}

}
```

Switch

If you have a variable and different blocks of code need to be executed for different values of that variable, the ideal construct that can be used is the switch statement. The syntax for this construct is—

switch(variable){

case <value1>:

/*body*/

break;

case <value2>:

/*body*/

break;

case <value3>:

/*body*/

break;

default:

/*body*/

break;

```
}
```

Sample implementation for this construct is given below—

```
public class switchDemo {

public static void main(String args[]) {

int i = 5;

switch (i) {

case 0:

System.out.print(0);

break;

case 2:

System.out.print(2);

break;

case 5:

System.out.print(5);

break;

default:

System.out.print(999);
```

```
break;

}

}

}
```

Conditional Operator

Java also supports the conditional operator, which is also known as the?: operator. This operator is used to replace the 'if else' construct. Its syntax is as follows—

Expression1? Expression2: Expression3

Here, Expression1 is the condition that is to be tested. If the condition is true, Expression2 is executed else Expression3 is executed.

Loop Control

There are several situations that require you to iterate the same set of instructions a number of times. For instance, if you need to sort a set of numbers, you will need to scan and rearrange the set several times to get the desired arrangement. This flow of execution is known as loop control.

Simply, a loop is a construct that allows the execution of a block of code many times. Java supports several constructs that can be used for implementing loops. These include a while loop, for loop, and do while loop.

A while loop executes a block of code iteratively until the condition specified for the while loop is true. The moment this condition fails, while loop stops.

For loop allows the programmer to manipulate the condition and loop variable in the same construct. Therefore, you can initialize a loop variable, increment/decrement it, and run the loop until a condition on this variable is true.

Do while loop is similar to while loop. However, in the while loop, the condition is checked before executing the block code. On the other hand, in a do while loop, the block of code is executed, and then the condition is checked. If the condition is satisfied, the loop execution is again initiated else the loop is terminated. It would not be wrong to state that the do while loop, once implemented, will execute at least once.

Loop statements

There are two keywords that are specifically used in connection with loops and are also termed as control statements as they allow transfer of control from one section of the code to a different section. These keywords are—

Break

This keyword is used inside the loop at a point where you want the execution flow to terminate the loop and directly start execution from the first instruction that appears after the loop.

Continue

This keyword is used inside the loop at a point where the programmer wants the computer to overlook the rest of the loop and move the control to the first statement of the loop.

In order to help you understand how loops are executed, let us take an example and implement it using all the three types of loop control.

For Loop Implementation

```
public class forDemo {

public static void main(String args[]) {

int [] numberArray = {100, 300, 500, 700, 900};

for(int i=0; i<5; i++) {

System.out.print(numberArray[i]);

System.out.print(,"");

}

System.out.print("\n");

}

}
```

While Loop Implementation

```java
public class whileDemo {

public static void main(String args[]) {

int [] numberArray = {100, 300, 500, 700, 900};

int i = 0;

while(i<5) {

System.out.print(numberArray[i]);

System.out.print(",");

i++;

}

System.out.print("\n");

}

}
```

Do While Loop Implementation

```
public class doWhileDemo {

public static void main(String args[]) {

int [] numberArray = {100, 300, 500, 700, 900};

int i = 0;

do {

System.out.print(numberArray[i]);

System.out.print(",");

i++;

} while (i<5);

System.out.print("\n");

}

}
```

Enhanced For Loop

Java also supports an enhanced loop structure, which can be used for array elements. The syntax for this loop construct is—

for(declaration : expression) {

/*Body*/

}

The declaration part of the Enhanced for loop is used to declare a variable. This variable shall be local to the 'for loop' and must have the same type as the type of the array elements. The current value of the variable is always equal to the array element that is being traversed in the loop. The expression is an array or a method call that returns an array.

Sample implementation of the enhanced for loop has been given below -

public class forArrayDemo {

public static void main(String args[]) {

int [] numberArray = {100, 300, 500, 700, 900};

for(int i : numberArray) {

System.out.print(i);

```java
System.out.print(",");

}

System.out.print("\n");

}

}
```

COMPUTER PROGRAMMING FOR BEGINNERS AND CYBERSECURITY

Exception Hierarchy

Java has an inbuilt class named java.lang.Exception and all the exceptions fall under this class. All the exception classes are subclasses of this class. Moreover, the Throwable class is the superclass of the exception class. Another subclass of the Throwable class is the Error class. All the errors like stack overflow described above fall under this Error class.

The Exception class has two subclasses, namely RuntimeException class and IOException class. A list of the methods, for which definitions are available in Java, as part of the Throwable class, is given below.

public String getMessage()

When called, this message returns a detailed description of the exception that has been encountered.

public Throwable getCause()

This method, when called returns a message that contains the cause of the exception.

public String toString()

This method returns the detailed description of the exception concatenated with the name of the class.

public void printStackTrace()

The result of toString(), along with a trace of the stack, can be printed to the standard error stream, System.err, can be done by calling this method.

public StackTraceElement [] getStackTrace()

There may be some scenarios where you may need to access different elements of the stack trace. This method returns an array, with each element of the stack trace saved to different elements of the array. The first element of the array contains the top element of the stack trace, while the bottom of the stack trace is saved to the last element of the array.

public Throwable fillInStackTrace()

Appends the previous information in the stack trace with the current contents of the stack trace and returns the same as an array.

Catching Exceptions

The standard method to catch an exception is using the 'try and catch' keywords along with their code implementations. This try and catch block needs to be implemented in such a manner that it encloses the code that is expected to raise an exception. It is also important to mention here that the code that is expected to raise an exception is termed as protected code. The syntax for try and catch block implementation is as follows—

try {

/*Protected code*/

}catch(ExceptionName exc1) {

/*Catch code*/

}

The code that is expected to raise an exception is placed inside the try block. If the exception is raised, then the corresponding action to be performed for exception handling is implemented in the catch block. It is imperative for every try block to either have a catch block or a final block.

As part of the catch statement, the exception, which is expected to be raised needs to be declared. In the event that an exception occurs, the execution is transferred to the catch block. If the raised exception matches the exception defined in the catch block, the catch block is executed.

A sample implementation of the try and catch block is given below. The code implements an array with 2 elements. However, the code tries to access the third element, which does not exist. As a result, an exception is raised.

```java
import java.io.*;

public class demoException {

public static void main(String args[]) {

try {

int arr[] = new int[2];

System.out.println("Accesing the 3rd element of the array:" + arr[3]);

}catch(ArrayIndexOutOfBoundsException exp) {

System.out.println("Catching Exception:" + exp);

}

System.out.println("Reached outside catch block");

}

}
```

Implementing Multiple Catch Blocks

A block of code may lead to multiple exceptions. In order to cater for this requirement, implementation of multiple catch blocks is also allowed. The syntax for such implementation is given below.

try {

/*Protected Code*/

}catch(ExpType1 exp1) {

/*Catch block 1*/

}catch(ExpType2 exp2) {

/*Catch block 2*/

}catch(ExpType3 exp3) {

/*Catch block 3*/

}

The syntax shown above has illustrated the implementation of three catch blocks. However, you can implement as many catch blocks as you want. When this code is executed, the protected is executed.

If an exception occurs, the type of exception is matched with the exception of the first catch block.

However, if the exception type does not match, the catch block 1 is ignored, and the exception type for the second catch block is tried for matching.

Whichever catch block has the same exception type as that of the raised exception; the corresponding catch block is executed.

CHAPTER 9:

ADT, Data Structure, and Java Collections

Abstract data type (ADT)

An abstract data type (ADT) is a logical description of the data and the operations that are allowed on it. ADT is defined as a user point of view of a data. ADT concerns about the possible values of the data and the interface exposed by it. ADT does not concern about the actual implementation of the data structure.

For example, a user wants to store some integers and find their mean value. ADT for this data structure will support two functions, one for adding integers and other to get mean value. ADT for this data structure does not talk about how exactly it will be implemented.

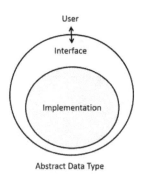

Abstract Data Type

Data-Structure

Data structures are concrete representations of data and are defined as a programmer point of view of data. Data-structure represents how data will be stored in memory. All data-structures have their own pros and cons. Depending upon the type of problem, we choose a data-structure that is best suited for it.

For example, we can store data in an array, a linked-list, stack, queue, tree, etc.

Note: In this chapter, we will be studying various data structures and their API. So that the user can use them without knowing their internal implementation.

JAVA Collection Framework

JAVA programming language provides a JAVA Collection Framework, which is a set of high quality, high performance & reusable data-structures and algorithms.

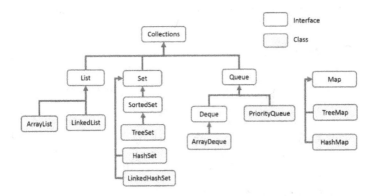

The following advantages of using a JAVA collection framework:

1. Programmers do not have to implement basic data structures and algorithms repeatedly. Thereby it prevents the reinvention of the wheel. Thus, the programmer can devote more effort in business logic

2. The JAVA Collection Framework code is well-tested, high quality, high-performance code. Using them increase the quality of the programs.

3. Development cost is reduced as basic data structures and algorithms are implemented in the Collections framework are reused.

4. Easy to review and understand programs written by other developers as most of Java developers uses the Collection framework. In addition, the collection framework is well documented.

Array

Array represents a collection of multiple elements of the same datatypes.

Array ADT Operations

Below is the API of the array:

1. Adds an element at the kth position. Value can be stored in an array at Kth position in O(1) constant time. We just need to store value at arr[k].

2. Reading the value stored at the kth position. Accessing the value stored at some index in the array is also O(1) constant time. We just need to read the value stored at arr[k].

3. Substitution of value stored in the kth position with a new value. Time complexity: O(1) constant time.

Example:

public class ArrayDemo {

    public static void main(String[] args) {

        int[] arr = new int[10];

        for (int i = 0; i < 10; i++)

        {

            arr[i] = i;

        }

    }

}

JAVA standard arrays are of fixed length. Sometimes we do not know how much memory we need, so we create a bigger size array. Thereby wasting space. If an array is already full and we want to add more values to it than we need to create a new array, which has sufficient space and then copy the old array to the new array. To avoid this manual reallocation and copy, we can use ArrayList of JAVA Collection framework or Linked Lists to store data.

ArrayList implementation in JAVA Collections

ArrayList<E> in JAVA Collections is a data structure which implements List<E> interface, which means that it can have duplicate elements in it. ArrayList is an implementation as a dynamic array that can grow or shrink as needed. (Internally array is used when it is full a bigger array is allocated, and the old array values are copied to it).

Example:

import java.util.ArrayList;

public class ArrayListDemo {

    public static void main(String[] args) {

        ArrayList<Integer> al = new ArrayList<Integer>();

al.add(1); // add 1 to the end of the list

        al.add(2); // add 2 to the end of the list

        System.out.println("Contents of Array: " + al);

        System.out.println("Array Size: " + al.size());

        System.out.println("Array IsEmpty: " + al.isEmpty());

        al.remove(al.size() -1); // last element of array is removed.

al.removeAll(al); // all the elements of array are removed.

System.out.println("Array IsEmpty: " + al.isEmpty());

    }

}

Output:

Contents of Array: [1, 2]

Array Size: 2

Array IsEmpty: false

Array IsEmpty: true

Linked List

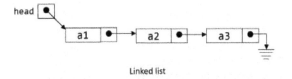

Linked list

Linked lists are a dynamic data structure, and memory is allocated at run time.

The concept of the linked list is not to store data contiguously. Nodes of the linked list contain a link that points to the next elements in the list.

Performance-wise linked lists are slower than arrays because there is no direct access to linked list elements. Linked list is a useful data structure when we do not know the number of elements to be stored ahead of time.

There are many types of linked lists: linear, circular, doubly, doubly circulare, etc.

Linked list ADT Operations

Below is the API of Linked list.

Insert(k): adds k to the start of the list

Insert an element at the start of the list. Just create a new element and move pointers.

So that this new element becomes the first element of the list. This operation will take O(1) constant time.

Delete(): Delete the element at the start of the list

Delete an element at the start of the list. We just need to move one pointer. This operation will also take O(1) constant time.

PrintList(): Display all the elements of the list.

Start with the first element and then follow the pointers. This operation will take O(N) time.

Find(k): Find the position of the element with value k

Start with the first element and follow the pointer until we get the value we are looking for or reach the end of the list. This operation will take O(N) time.

Note: Binary search does not work on linked lists.

FindKth(k): Find element at position k

Start from the first element and follow the links until you reach the kth element. This operation will take O(N) time.

IsEmpty(): Check if the number of elements in the list are zero.

Just check the head pointer of the list, if it is Null, then the list is empty otherwise not empty. This operation will take O(1) time.

LinkedList implementation in JAVA Collections

LinkedList<E> in by JAVA Collections is a data structure that also implements List<E> interface.

Example:

import java.util.LinkedList;

public class LinkedListDemo {

    public static void main(String[] args) {

        LinkedList<Integer> ll = new LinkedList<Integer>();

        ll.addFirst(2); // 8 is added to the list

```java
ll.addLast(10); // 9 is added to last of the list.

ll.addFirst(1); // 7 is added to first of the list.

ll.addLast(11); // 20 is added to last of the list

System.out.println("Contents of Linked List: " + ll);

ll.removeFirst();

ll.removeLast();

System.out.println("Contents of Linked List: " + ll);

    }

}
```

Output:

Contents of Linked List: [1, 2, 10, 11]

Contents of Linked List: [2, 10]

Stack

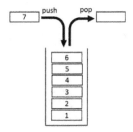

Stack is a special kind of data structure that follows the Last-In-First-Out (LIFO) strategy. This means that the element that is added last will be the first to be removed.

The various applications of the stack are:

Recursion: recursive calls are implemented using system stack.

1. Postfix evaluation of the expression.
2. Backtracking implemented using stack.
3. Depth-first search of trees and graphs.
4. Converting a decimal number into a binary number etc.

Stack ADT Operations

Push(k): Adds value k to the top of the stack

Pop(): Remove element from the top of the stack and return its value.

Top(): Returns the value of the element at the top of the stack

Size(): Returns the number of elements in the stack

IsEmpty(): determines whether the stack is empty. It returns true if the stack is empty otherwise return false.

Note: All the above stack operations are implemented in O(1) Time Complexity.

Stack implementation in JAVA Collection

The stack is implemented by calling push and pop methods of Stack <T> class.

Example:

```
public class StackDemo {

    public static void main(String[] args) {

        Stack<Integer> stack = new Stack<Integer>();

        int temp;

        stack.push(1);

        stack.push(2);

        stack.push(3);

        System.out.println("Stack : "+stack);

        System.out.println("Stack size : "+stack.size());

        System.out.println("Stack pop : "+stack.pop());
```

```
System.out.println("Stack top : "+stack.peek());

System.out.println("Stack isEmpty : "+stack.isEmpty());

    }

}
```

Output:

Stack : [1, 2, 3]

Stack size : 3

Stack pop : 3

Stack top : 2

Stack isEmpty : false

Stack is also implemented by calling push and pop methods of ArrayDeque<T> class.

JDK provides both ArrayDeque<T> and Stack<T>. We can use both of these classes. But there are some advantages of ArrayDeque<T>.

1. First reason is that Stack<T> does not drive from Collection interface.
2. Second Stack<T> drives from Vector<T> so random access is possible, so it brakes abstraction of a stack.
3. Third ArrayDeque is more efficient as compared to Stack<T>.

Queue

A queue is a First-In-First-Out (FIFO) kind of data structure. The element that is added to the queue first will be the first to be removed, and so on.

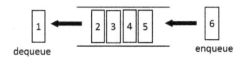

Queue has the following application uses:

1. Access to shared resources (e.g., printer)
2. Multiprogramming
3. Message queue
4. BFS, breadth-first traversal of graph or tree are implemented using queue.

Queue ADT Operations:

Add(K): Adds a new element k to the back of the queue.

Remove(): Removes an element from the front of the queue and return its value.

Front(): Returns the value of the element at the front of the queue.

Size(): Returns the number of elements inside the queue.

IsEmpty(): Returns 1 if the queue is empty otherwise returns 0

Note: All the above queue operations are implemented in O(1) Time Complexity.

Queue implementation in JAVA Collection

ArrayDeque<T> is the class implementation of a doubly ended queue. If we use add(), remove() and peek () it will behave like a queue. (Moreover, if we use push(), pop(), and peekLast() it behave like a stack.)

Example:

```java
import java.util.ArrayDeque;

public class QueueDemo {

    public static void main(String[] args) {

        ArrayDeque<Integer> que = new ArrayDeque<Integer>();

        que.add(1);

        que.add(2);

        que.add(3);

        System.out.println("Queue : "+que);

        System.out.println("Queue size : "+que.size());

        System.out.println("Queue peek : "+que.peek());

        System.out.println("Queue remove : "+que.remove());
```

```
        System.out.println("Queue isEmpty : "+que.isEmpty());

    }

}
```

Output:

Queue : [1, 2, 3]

Queue size : 3

Queue peek : 1

Queue remove : 1

Queue isEmpty : false

CHAPTER 10

File Handling

This chapter discusses the details of reading, writing, creating, and opening files. There are a wide array of file I/O classes and methods to choose from.

Reading a text File

Reading a text file is a crucial ability in Java and has many practical applications. FileReader, BufferedReader, and Scanner are useful classes for reading a plain text file in Java. Each of them possess specific qualities that make them uniquely qualified to handle certain situations.

BufferedReader

This technique reads text from a stream of character input. It buffers characters, arrays, and rows to be read efficiently. You can specify the buffer type or use the standard type. For most reasons, the default is big enough. In particular, each read application produced from a Reader leads the fundamental personality or byte stream to make a respective read application. Therefore, it is advisable to wrap a BufferedReader around any Reader whose read) (transactions, like FileReaders and InputStreamReaders, can be expensive.

For example:

BufferedReader in = New BufferedReader(Reader in, int size)

FileReader

Class of convenience to read character documents. This class ' constructors suppose the default character format and the default byte-buffer size is suitable.

Scanner

A simple text scanner that uses regular expressions to parse primitive types and strings. A Scanner uses a delimiter model to break its entry into tokens that suits white space by definition. Using distinct next techniques, the resulting tokens can then be transformed into values of distinct kinds.

```java
import        java.io.File;

import java.util.Scanner;

public class ReadFromFileUsingScanner

{

public static void main(String[] args) throws Exception

{

// filepath is set as a parameter now so that it can be scanned
```

```java
File example =

new File("C:\\Users\\userName\\Desktop\\example.txt");

Scanner example1 = new Scanner(file);

while (example1.hasNextLine())

System.out.println(example1.nextLine());

}

}
```

Using Scanner class but without using loops:

```java
import java.io.File;

import java.io.FileNotFoundException;

import java.util.Scanner;

public class example{

public static void main(String[] args)

throws FileNotFoundException {

File             example             =             new
File("C:\\Users\\userName\\Desktop\\example.txt");

Scanner example1 = new Scanner(file);
```

```java
// we will use \\Z as a delimiter

sc.useDelimiter("\\Z");

System.out.println(example1.next());

}

}
```

Read a text file as String in Java

```java
package io;

import java.nio.file.*;;

public class example{

public static example(String fileName)throws Exception {

String example1 = "";

example1 = new String(Files.readAllBytes(Paths.get(fileName)));

return example1;

}

public static void main(String[] args) throws Exception

{
```

String example1 =
example("C:\\Users\\userName\\Desktop\\example.java");

System.out.println(example1);

}

}

Writing to a text file

You can use one of the write methods to write bytes or lines to a file. Write methods include:

- Write(Path, byte[], OpenOption...)
- Write(Path, Iterable< extends CharSequence>, Charset, OpenOption...)

Renaming and Deleting Files

Renaming

In Java, there's a method called renameTo(fileName) within the File class that we can use to rename a file.

Deleting Files

Files that are saved using the java program will be permanently removed without moving to the trash/recycle bin. Using java.io.File.delete deletes this abstract pathname from the file or folder. Using java.nio.file.files.deleteifexists will delete a folder, if it occurs. If the folder is not open, it also deletes a folder listed in the route.

Advanced Topics In Java

Generics

In any non-trivial software project, bugs are simply a fact of life. Careful planning, programming, and testing may help diminish their omnipresence, but somehow they will always find a way to enter your system somewhere. This becomes especially apparent as new features are introduced, and your code base's magnitude and complexity increases.

Fortunately, it is easier to detect some bugs than others. Compile-time bugs, for instance, can be identified soon; you can use the compiler's error codes to determine what the issue is and solve it, right then and there. Runtime bugs, however, can be much harder; they do not always occur instantly, and when they do, they may be at a point in the program far apart from the true cause of the problem. Generics help stabilize your software by creating it feasible at compile time to identify more of your bugs.

Generics, in a nutshell, allow parameters for kinds (classes and objects) when defining courses, interfaces, and techniques. Like the more familiar formal parameters used in declarations of methods, type parameters provide you with distinct outputs to re-use the same code. The distinction is that values are the inputs to formal parameters, while kinds are the answers to type parameters. Code using generics has many advantages over the non-generic code. Through the use of generics, programmers can introduce generic algorithms that operate on distinct kinds of collections, can be tailored, and are secure and simpler to read form.

Generic Types

A generic form is a types-parameterized generic category or interface. It is possible to modify an easy box class to show the idea. Consider a non-generic box category that works on any sort of object. It only requires to provide two techniques: set), (adding an item to the cabinet, and get), (retrieving it. Because their methods accept or return an object, you are free to pass in whatever you want, as long as it is not one of the primitive types. There is no way to check how the class is used at compile time. One portion of the software may put an integer in the cabinet and expect to get integers out of it, while another portion of the software may erroneously move through a string, leading in a mistake in runtime.

The segment of the type parameter, delegated by angle brackets (< >), displays the title of the category. It indicates the parameters of the form (also known as factors of the sort) T1, T2, till T. You generate a generic type statement by altering the file "government class box" to "government class box <T >" to update the box category to use generics. This presents the type variable, T, which can be used inside the class anywhere. This replaces all Object events with T. Any non-primitive type you specify can be a type variable: any type of class, any type of interface, any type of array, or even some other type variable. It is possible to apply this same method to generic interfaces. Type designations are single, upper case letters by convention. This contrasts sharply with the variable naming conventions you already understand about and with an excellent reason: it would be hard to say the distinction between a type variable and a normal class or object name without this convention.

The most commonly used type parameter names are:

- E - Element (used extensively by the Java Collections Framework)
- K - Key
- N - Number
- T - Type
- V - Value
- S,U,V, etc.—2nd, 3rd, 4th types

You'll see these names used throughout the JDK and the API.

Invoking and Instantiating a Generic Type

To mention the generic box category within your system, a generic type invocation must be performed that brings T with a certain concrete value, such as Integer:

Box<Integer> integerBox;

You may believe that an invocation of a generic sort is comparable to a normal process invocation, but instead of adding an assertion to a procedure, you transfer a type argument—Integer, in this case—to the box category itself.

Many designers interchangeably use the words "type parameter" and "type statement," but not the same definitions. When coding, to generate a parameterized type, one offers sort arguments. The T in Foo < T > is, therefore, a type parameter, and the Foo < String > f string is a type contention. In using these words, this class follows this concept.

Like any other statement of variable, this software does not generate a fresh item of the box. It merely states that integerBox will have a reference to an "Integer Box," which is how it reads Box < Integer>. A generic type invocation is usually referred to as a parameterized type.

To instantiate this class, use the new keyword, as usual, but place <Integer> between the class name and the parenthesis:

Box<Integer> integerBox = new Box<Integer>();

The Diamond

In the latest versions of Java, you can replace the type arguments needed to invoke a generic class constructor with an empty set of type arguments (< >) as long as the compiler can determine, or infer from the context, the type arguments. This angle bracket couple, < >, is called "The Diamond loosely." For example, you can use the previous declaration to generate an instance of Box < Integer>:

Box<Integer> integerBox = new Box<>();

Generic Methods

Generic techniques are techniques which implement parameters of their own sort. This is similar to a generic type declaration, but the scope of the type parameter is limited to the method in which it is declared. In addition to generic class constructors, static and non-static generic techniques are permitted. The syntax for a generic technique involves a list of parameters of type inside angle brackets that appear before the return type of the procedure. The type parameter segment must occur before the return type of the method for static generic techniques. The Util class involves, compare, a generic technique comparing two Pair items.

Pair<Integer, String> ex1 = new Pair<>(49, "string1");

Pair<Integer, String> ex2 = new Pair<>(64, "string2");

boolean comparison = Util.<Integer, String>compare(ex1, ex2);

Bounded Type Parameters

Sometimes you want to limit the kinds that can be used in a parameterized type as form statements. For instance, a technique that works on figures could only recognize Number cases or its subclasses. That's what limit parameters of the sort are for.

List the name of the type parameter to indicate a defined type parameter, accompanied by the extension's keyword, followed by the upper bound, which is Number in this instance. Note that expands is generally used in this context to mean either "extends" (as in courses) or "implements" (as in interfaces).

Multiple Bounds

Type parameters can have more than one bound. A type variable with multiple bounds is a subtype of all the types listed in the bound. If one of the bounds is a class, it must be specified first. For example:

Class X { /* ... */ }

interface Y { /* ... */ }

interface Z { /* ... */ }

class R <T extends X & Y & Z> { /* ... */ }

If bound X is not specified first, you get a compile-time error:

class R <T extends Y & X & Z> { /* ... */ } // compile-time error

CHAPTER 11:

Collections

Functionalizing Collections

Whe hen we externalize code, we expose every step. This is the hallmark of imperative programming. However, one of the re-occurring themes of functional programming is the idea of doing the exact opposite: internalizing code. The act of internalizing code is to hide the details inside a function. But functional programming pushes this idea further by turning micro-patterns of everyday programming into functions. For example, iterating over data, be it with iterators, for-loops, or while-loops, is one of those micro-patterns. Functional programming changes the way we think about them.

Java's functionalization effort would not be complete without a revamp of its Collections library, namely the Collection, Map, List, and Set interfaces. This is because iteration is often done over collections, and they are the very fabric of Java programs. It is a natural place for the functionalization effort to occur. But making any kind of significant changes, like adding new methods to the Collection interface, would break backward compatibility to all programs written pre-Java 8. This includes not only the JDK's own hierarchy extending the Collection interface but any open or closed source 3rd party library and in-house classes. Java's designers never have and will never adopt such a strategy. Yet changes were necessary; the library was introduced in 1998, eons in software industry years, and was showing its age.

The motivation for the introduction of default methods was ushered by the need to modernize and functionalize the Collections library. Default methods are just the right tonic because they permit behavior to be added at the root of the hierarchy without disturbing dependent classes. Subclasses can either inherit or override the behavior. Unlike adding new interface methods, subclasses can automatically accept new default methods without recompilation. Instant compatibility is achieved. Default methods have proven useful in their own right but owe their existence to the need to functionalize the Collections library.

A second re-occurring theme in functional programming is parallelization. Quite simply, functional programming offers a better mousetrap for parallel processing. As a consequence, the Collections library has been enriched to benefit from multi-core CPUs when processing collections. Together with Streams, the Collections library is at center stage in bringing functional-style parallel processing to Java.

Now that we've studied Java's standard functional interfaces, we can begin to apply that knowledge to Collections. Let's look at what has become of the Collections library in Java 8.

Collection interface

We start by looking at a brand new default method in the Collection interface available to lists and sets. This is the forEach() method:

```
// Defined in the Iterable interface and extended in Collection
default void forEach (Consumer<? super T> action)
```

This method iterates through the entire collection letting the Consumer decide what to do for each element. This is the concept of internal iteration and a manifestation of declarative programming. The details of how to iterate are not specified. This is in opposition to external iteration, where the details of how to iterate as well as what to do with each element are specified in code.

We will show examples of these functionalized collection methods with the slapstick comedy trio from the golden age of Hollywood films: Larry, Moe, and Curly of The Three Stooges fame. To start, let's print the contents of a collection:

```
Collection<String> stooges = Arrays.asList("Larry", "Moe", "Curly");
// Print the contents of the stooges collection
stooges.forEach(System.out::println);
```

The forEach() method has a very wide range of applicability. It is a much more convenient way to iterate through collections and should be your de-facto standard. However, being a declarative construct, there are some things you will not be able to do. Most notably, you cannot change the state of local variables like you could in a while-loop. Algorithms must be re-thought functionally. For now, just know that forEach() is ideal for iterations that do not mutate state.

We now look at another new method available in Collection:

```
default boolean removeIf(Predicate<? super E> filter)
```

The method removeIf() internalizes the entire process of iterating, testing, and removing. It requires only to be told what the condition for removal is.

Using the now-familiar predicate functional interface, we can easily figure out what kind of lambda to use.

```java
// Remove all people not part of The Three Stooges comedy trio
List<String> theThreeStooges = new ArrayList<>
    (Arrays.asList("Larry", "Moe", "Curly", "Tom", "Dick", "Harry"));

// Create the predicate that determines who is a stooge
Predicate<String> isAStooge =
    s -> "Larry".equals(s) || "Moe".equals(s) || "Curly".equals(s);

// Negate the condition to remove non-stooges
theThreeStooges. removeIf (isAStooge.negate());
```

To replace all contents of a List, we can use replaceAll():

```java
List<String> theThreeStooges = new ArrayList<>
    (Arrays.asList("Larry", "Moe", "Curly"));

// Create the lambda to feminize the names
UnaryOperator<String> feminize =
    s -> "Larry".equals(s) ? "Lara" : "Moe".equals(s) ? "Maude" : "Shirley";

// Replace all male names with their female counterparts
theThreeStooges. replaceAll (feminize);
```

ReplaceAll() uses a UnaryOperator as its functional interface, which is a Function sub interface.

Both replaceIf() and replaceAll() are available to all subclasses with one caveat: the underlying class must support removal, or an exception will be thrown.

These examples show the compactness of functional programming. Most of the work was done by the function with the lambda providing the details.

Map interface

One of the biggest irritants of using lists as values in maps is the constant need to check for the presence of the map before adding, updating, or removing an element. First, you must try to extract the list and create it if it is not found. For example, say we have a method that updates a movie database implemented as a Map. The map's key is the year of the movie, and its value is a list of movies for that year. Pre-Java 8, the code would look like this:

```java
private Map<Integer, List<String>> movieDatabase = new HashMap<>();

private void addMovie(Integer year, String title) {
    List<String> movies = movieDatabase.get(year);

    if (movies == null) {
        // Need to create the array list if it doesn't yet exist
        movies = new LinkedList<String>();
        movieDatabase.put(year, movies);
    }

    movies.add(title);
}
```

Java 8 offers a better alternative with these default methods:

```
default V compute
    (K key,
     BiFunction<? super K, ? super V, ? extends V> remappingFunction)

default V computeIfPresent
    (K key,
     BiFunction<? super K, ? super V, ? extends V> remappingFunction)

default V computeIfAbsent
    (K key,
     Function<? super K, ? extends V> mappingFunction)

default V getOrDefault (Object key, V defaultValue);

default V putIfAbsent (K key, V value);

default V merge
    (K key, V value,
     BiFunction<? super V, ? super V, ? extends V> remappingFunction)
```

Let's start with the compute methods. Each variant allows the map's value to be generated by the mapping function. For computeIfPresent() and computeIfAbsent(), mapping occurs conditionally. So with these methods, we can refactor the previous code example:

```
private Map<Integer, List<String>> movieDatabase = new HashMap<>();

private void addMovie(Integer year, String title) {
    movieDatabase. computeIfAbsent (year, k -> new LinkedList<>());
    movieDatabase. compute (year,
        (k, v) -> {
            // K is the key of the map (the year)
            // V is the value containing the list strings (titles)
            v.add(title);
            return v;
        });
}
```

Notice that the creation of the list is handled by the computeIfAbsent() lambda. When it is time to add the movie to the list, via the compute() method, the add() will never throw a NullPointerException because the list is guaranteed to have been created.

In this case, using the computeIfAbsent() method is overkill, and we would be better off with putIfAbsent():

```
movieDatabase. putIfAbsent (year, new LinkedList<>());
```

This method is lambda-less and expects a value to be given—not calculated. This is still a functional style method even though no lambda was used. It proves the point that you can express code functionally without necessarily using lambdas.

If you still need to extract the data, you can use a more functional approach with the getOrDefault() method:

```
movieDatabase. getOrDefault (year, new LinkedList<>());
```

You can also use the merge() method as an alternative. It facilitates the checking of the existence of a list. In the example below, if the key (year) doesn't exist in the map, it puts the value (titles) on the map. If it does exist, it allows a BiFunction to decide what to do with the two lists:

```
private Map<Integer, List<String>> movieDatabase = new HashMap<>();

private void addMovies(Integer year, List<String> titles) {
    // Merge the contents of the current list at key=year with titles
    movieDatabaseb. merge (year, titles,
        (t1, t2) -> {
            // Append titles to current list - only gets called if
            // a value is stored at this key. Otherwise, titles is
            // stored.
            t1.addAll(t2);
            return t1;
        });
}
```

And it can be used this way:

```
List<String> titles = new ArrayList<>(
    Arrays.asList("Meet the Baron", "Nertsery Rhymes"));

movieDatabaseb. merge (1933, titles,
    // BiFunction to append t2 to t1
    (t1, t2) -> {t1.addAll(t2); return t1;});
```

The BiFunction can also return null, which tells the merge to delete the key.

The takeaway is that we have removed the overhead code of checking for the existence of an element and can now focus on what really matters: defining how to create the list and how to add an element to the list.

The map interface has been enriched with other functional methods such as forEach(), replace(), and replaceAll() and uses the same principle of code internalization. Consult the appendix for the complete listing.

Spliterator

The Collections library is still subject to the same constraints regarding concurrent access.

As always, you must choose the Collections library class that corresponds to your thread safety requirements.

This is because the new methods shown above are just functional abstractions riding above the same underlying data structures.

These methods are not particularly amenable to functional programming's take on parallel processing because they are still based on the notion of multiple threads mutating the collection and synchronizing access to the underlying data. However, there exists a new Java 8 abstraction that is compatible. It is designed to iterate over data in parallel.

The idea is embodied by the Spliterator interface.

The premise of this interface is to partition the data and handoff chunks to different threads. Spliterators can be obtained from the Collection interface, including subinterfaces List and Set.

Central to the Spliterator interface are these three methods:

```
Spliterator<T> trySplit ();

default void forEachRemaining (Consumer<? super T> action) {…}

boolean tryAdvance (Consumer<? super T> action);
```

The method trySplit() partitions the underlying data in two. It creates a new Spliterator with half the data and keeps the other half in the original instance. Each can be given to a thread which, in turn, iterates over the partitioned data using forEachRemaining().

The method tryAdvance() is a one-at-a-time variant that returns the next element or null if the list has been exhausted.

Spliterators do not handle parallel processing themselves but provide the abstraction to do so.

Here's the concept in action:

```java
public static boolean isMovieInList(String title, List<String> movieList)
    throws InterruptedException {
    // Obtain a spliterator from the movie list
    Spliterator<String> s1 = movieList. spliterator ();

    // Split the original list in half.
    // Now s1 and s2 each contains half the list.
    Spliterator<String> s2 = s1. trySplit ();

    BooleanHolder booleanHolder = new BooleanHolder();
    if (s2 != null) {
        Consumer<String> finder =
            movie -> {if (movie.equals(title)) booleanHolder.isFound = true;};

        // Each thread searches the movie list in parallel
        Thread t1 = new Thread(() -> s1. forEachRemaining (finder));
        Thread t2 = new Thread(() -> s2. forEachRemaining (finder));

        t1.start();
        t2.start();
        t1.join();
        t2.join();
    }

    return booleanHolder.isFound;
}

private static class BooleanHolder {
    public boolean isFound = false;
}
```

Given a title and a list of movies, the method isMovieInList() parallelizes the search to determine if it is contained in the list. It sets the flag in booleanHolder to true if found. It obtains a Spliterator instance from the list, splits it in half, and handsoff one half to each thread. The splitting process can be repeated if further threads are available.

Spliterators can be obtained from other Collection types as well as other libraries in the JDK. There are many implementations designed that deal with different characteristics, including finite/infinite, ordered/non-ordered, sorted/non-sorted, and mutable/immutable. They inherit the qualities of their underlying data structure.

Spliterators are a lower-level abstraction designed to give you more fine-grained control over parallelized iteration. However, the API lacks some of the refinements needed to implement functionally-friendly algorithms. In the above example, we needed to store the state in the BooleanHolder for the search.

Wrap up

This completes our overview of the new and improved Java 8 Collections library as well as the standard functional interfaces. Just as there have been many changes in the standard JDK libraries to support functional concepts, expect major changes from 3rd party APIs. But the biggest change is yet to come.

Key points

The new package java.util.function contains a set of functional interfaces. These are grouped into four families, each represented by their archetypes: Consumer, Function, Predicate, and Supplier.

Each family of functional interfaces defines variants that specialize in types and arity. Functional interfaces also define methods that enable functional composition. Multiple disparate lambdas can be fused to form super functions that appear as one.

The Collections library has been revamped and functionalized. This has been achieved using default methods at top levels of the hierarchy, thereby ensuring backward compatibility.

The new functional methods in Collections, Lists, Sets, and Maps have been designed with internal iteration in mind. Behavioral parameters in the form of lambdas and method references are given to methods that iterate over collections and act upon each element.

An internal iteration is a form of declarative programming that is fundamental to functional programming. It relieves the developer from having to describe the "how" to do it and focuses instead on the "what" to do.

Spliterators are designed for parallel iteration over collections. Data is partitioned, and each chunk is handed to different threads for parallel processing.

A number is greater than one that is not prime.

Conclusion

The JDK is the Java Development Kit, and it is a necessary tool required for compiling, documenting, and packaging Java programs. Together with JRE, an interpreter or loader is built-into the JDK, a compiler called javac, an archiver (JAR), the Javadoc document generator, and many other tools required for successful Java development.

The JRE is the Java Runtime Environment. It is the environment in which the Java bytecode may be executed, and it is used for implementing the Java Virtual Machine. The JRE also provides us with all the class libraries and many other support files required at runtime by the JVM. It is, in basic terms, a software package that provides us with everything we need for running Java programs, a physical implementation of the Java Virtual machine.

JVM stands for Java Virtual Machine. The JVM is an abstract machine, a specification that provides us with the JRE in which our bytecode is executed. The JVM must follow these notations— Specification, which is a document describing how the JVM is implemented, Implementation, which is a program meeting the JVM specification requirements, and Runtime Instance, which is the JVM instance that gets created whenever the command prompt is used to write a Java command and run a class.

All three are inextricably linked, and each relies on the others to work.

With this, I would like to thank you for choosing my guide on Java programming. As you can see, it is a simple yet complex language, with so many different aspects to learn. By now, you should have a good understanding of the core concepts of Java programming and how to use it.

Your next step is, quite simply, practice. And keep on practicing. You cannot possibly read this guide once and think that you know it all. I urge you to take your time going through this; follow the tutorials carefully and don't move on from any section until you fully understand it and what it all means.

To help you out, there are several useful Java forums to be found online, full of people ready, and willing to help you out and point you in the right direction. There are also loads of online courses, some free and some that you need to pay for, but all of them are useful and can help you take your learning to the next level.

Did you enjoy this guide? I hope that it was all you wanted and more, and it has put you on the right path to getting your dream job!

I hope that you found my introduction to computer programming helpful. It's a very basic start, but it should have given you some idea as to how to begin. It should also have shown you that computer programming really isn't all that difficult and can be quite exciting, especially as you start to see your results appear on the screen and see your computer, in short, doing what it's told to do!

If you found that this has given you a good idea of what to expect, then you may want to move on to more advanced programming in your chosen language. A word of warning here: don't try to learn more than one language at a time; otherwise, you'll find yourself in a muddle. The only other piece of advice I will give you at this stage is to practice…and keep on practicing. The more you do, the more you'll learn, and the more you'll want to learn.

Thank you for downloading my book; if you found it helpful, please consider leaving me a review at Amazon.com.

C++

PROGRAMMING

A STEP-BY-STEP BEGINNER'S GUIDE TO LEARN THE
FUNDAMENTALS OF A MULTI-PARADIGM
PROGRAMMING LANGUAGE AND BEGIN TO
MANAGE DATA

INCLUDING HOW TO WORK ON YOUR FIRST
PROGRAM

ALAN GRID

Introduction

There may be a lot of different coding languages, and C++ is not usually on the list when it comes to easy coding languages that we are able to work with along the way. We may find that there are a ton of benefits of working with this kind of language, but it is often seen to be a bit harder to work with compared to some of the others out there.

As we are going to explore throughout this guidebook, you will find that this is actually a really great language to work with. It is going to provide us with some of the best tips and tricks that we need and will show us how to actually write out some of the different codes that we need inside of this language. If you are looking for a coding language that is powerful, that can help with web applications, games, and so much more, and you want to learn how to use it today, then this is the guidebook for you.

Inside, we are going to learn everything that we need to know about coding in the C++ language. We will start out with some of the basics that come with working in this language, such as what this language is all about, some of the benefits of working with this language over some of the others that are out there, and a look at some of the history that is going to come with this language.

Once we have some of the basics down of the C++ language, you can then move on to some more of the things that we need to explore as well. We will take some in-depth looks at the syntax and the basics that come with this language. It is a bit different than some of the other coding languages out there, so it is important to learn how to make this happen, and then work on our codes from there. We will also explore some of the different libraries that are popular and work well with the C++ language that can extend out some of the functionality that we are able to see with this kind of language.

At this point, we have some of the basics of coding in C++ down, and we know a bit more about this language as a whole. It is now time to actually get into the information about how to do some of the coding that we want. There are so many different types of codes that we are able to focus on, and many different things that we are able to work within this language, and we are going to look at what these are, the codes that work with them, and so much more.

We will end this guidebook with a look at how we are able to do some of the basic debugging that is needed in this kind of language. There are times, especially as a beginner in this language, when the codes are not going to necessarily work the way that you would like, or there are going to be errors that you need to fix. This can be difficult for a beginner because they want to be able to handle these codes and get the programs to work, but they may be uncertain as to how to fix some of the mistakes that are made.

What is C++?

A lot of beginners categorize C++ as a complicated programming language. Whatever the reason it may be, C++ is not a complicated language but a computer language that is with a lack of good resources for beginners. This is the way it is because it is a programming language that has evolved from another major programming language (C programming language) for the past four decades.

"C++ is a programming language that is a spinoff to C programming language with the addition of Object-oriented principles such as inheritance and polymorphism. C++ is a subset language of C that evolved into a much bigger instance that it is intended to be."

History of C++

In the initial days, C++ is just used as a fork language for C and is used to be converted back to C before compiling as there is no direct compiler. A compiler called Cfront is famous for doing this job. However, after a few years, people working with C++ have found it too difficult to create code in a language that doesn't have an actual compiler. So, certain developers started developing a compiler, and the task is finally achieved by Bjarne Stroustrup with a working C++ compiler.

With the implementation of strict syntactical structures within few years, C++ has been recognized by ISO (International standard organization) in 1998. The first updated version was released in the same year, and people were surprised by the new additional features that C++ started to offer. It has started using advanced turing techniques to decrease the compile-time and has also introduced templates in the first version. All these robust new features have helped C++ to develop complex software that supports system programming. Within a few years, C++ has improved tremendously and has included a lot of advanced features that can be used to create generic applications.

It is important to appreciate Microsoft for the sudden up rise of C++ as a programming language. Microsoft started to use C++ for its development software Visual C++. A lot of programmers developing applications for Microsoft systems started to find how reliable and comfortable C++ is to work with. By 2009, C++ standard library has been updated with various complex systems, mathematical and time functions.

Why has C++ become successful?

The success of C++ is mainly due to its object-oriented nature. In the early 1980s, the object-oriented programming paradigm took the technological world by storm. People were impressed with the adaptability and simplicity it offers. A lot of built C libraries at that time can be easily transformed into C++ functional libraries.

All of these factors combinedly helped C++ to become one of the popular high-level programming languages of this decade. It is estimated that by 2025, 15% of the Robotic applications will use C++ as a primary language to develop their resources.

Setting up a C++ environment for different operating systems

All of the software that is used to create C++ software consists of a code editor and an inbuilt debugger to show possible errors. If you are an old cliched guy, you can simply use a text editor and run the program using the command-line environments. It still works perfectly. However, for this section, we will discuss advanced integrated development environment software that can be used to create C++ programs.

How does the IDE work?

IDE's use the combination of the editing program, Compiler chain mechanism, and debugging to create efficient programs.

Note:

Remember that C++ doesn't provide an interpreter if you are trying to work on the command line execution program.

C++ is famous among programmers for its advanced capabilities and easy syntax. Even with the impact of high-level programming languages such as Java and Python, C++ does not lose its charm. This chapter, a comprehensive introduction to C++ programming language and its history, will help you understand the importance and origins of one of the popular programming languages in detail. In this book, we have explained various complex programming topics in Layman's terms. To understand and appreciate much of the information, it is important to understand the importance of C++ as a programming language. Let us learn in detail about C++ now.

What is special about the New C++ version?

The newer versions of C++ are developed to support developers who are trying to implement complex real-world projects. Here are some of the notable advanced features that C++ provides.

a) Advanced data structure implementation

Simple data structures such as Tress and Linked lists can be easily implemented through basic C++ versions. However, it is impossible to implement advanced data structures such as graphs and binary trees using the older versions. Newer C++ versions, on the other hand, provide standard libraries that help us to implement map and hash values which can be further used to implement advanced data structures.

b) Cryptography features

The newer versions of C++ provide dedicated libraries that can be used to implement complex cryptography features in both web and mobile applications.

These libraries can also be used to create software that deals with ciphers and stenography.

c) Lambda implementation

Lambda implementation is essential to run data science and machine learning applications. For example, contemporary deep fake software use C++ rendering libraries that are built using lambda expressions.

d) Advanced Object-oriented features

We all know that C++ is an object-oriented language. The basic versions only support single inheritance, whereas the newer versions can provide multiple inheritances to your projects. With the newer versions, we will also be able to use multiple operating overloading and complex polymorphism features.

CHAPTER 1:

How to Work on Your First Program

Once you have downloaded the C++ environment that you would like to use, we are going to start right in with your first code. The code that you would have to use to make this work includes the following:

#include <iostream>

using namespace std;

int main ()

{

court << "Use This One!";

return 0;

}

You have a few options available when it comes to writing this out. You can choose to write this out in your compiler, which will be available in your environment, or you can choose to write it out and save it to your computer. The second option is sometimes nice because then you have the code saved and could copy and paste it any time that you would need it in your code.

Either way, you should carefully consider the type of text editor that you want to work with. Most of them are going to be device-specific, so you need to look for the one that goes well with your particular computer. Some of the options that you can go with are Windows Notepad, vlm, vl, Brief, and EMACS. If you would like to have an editor that is compatible with more than one platform, then the vlm and vl options are the best ones to choose.

When you write out your own codes, you should write them out in the text editor first to get a rough draft on the program, and then you can move them over to your compiler later on. This makes it easier for you to check your work and avoid mistakes with the code that you are currently working with.

C++ compilers

Just like with the text editors, there are many compilers out there that you can work with. The problem is that while you do get a lot of choices to pick from, many of these compilers are pretty expensive. That is because most of the compilers that you will come across are meant for elite hackers who have mastered what was in the other lower-level compilers, and now they want to make sure they can take it to the next level.

The good news is that there are some compilers that you can get for free. You just need to be careful and watch out, just make sure that you are getting ones that are good and will have all the features that you are looking for. One compiler that works out well with C++ and can be good for a beginner to use is GNU. It is best when used with the Linux systems, and you may already have this one on your system. To check whether the GNU compiler is available on your system, use the following code:

$ g++ -v

Basic syntax

The C++ language can be defined as a program that will use objects to help keep everything organized and will allow the code to communicate and complete other functions using various methods. There are four important parts that come with the C++ language and these include:

- Classes

These are the organizational tools for your language. They can be seen as boxes that can hold onto or store objects and will sort out similar ones. You can label your class anything that you would like, but it is good coding practice to place objects that, in one way or another, have similar characteristics into the same class.

- Object

Objects are things in your code that have states and behaviors. These could be things such as colors, texture, shapes, and so on. You will usually classify these objects into classes that have similar objects. So, if you had a class that was about dogs, you may put the different types of dogs in that same class.

- Method

This is a term used in coding for behavior. There can be as many or as few methods as you would like to work with. This is how you can manipulate the data, and actions will be played out based on the method that you are working with or using. Without using the right method, your program won't know exactly what it's supposed to do.

- Instant variable

These refer to the individual objects that you are working with. Each one is classified using a unique set of variables that act like the fingerprints to identify your object. You can use some values to assign the right variable to the object when you create it.

And that is the basics of writing a code in C++. You should take some time to write out the code above in your compiler to gain a little bit of practice to understand what it is that you should be doing here. We will have a look at some of the things that you can do with these codes later on, but this is a great place to start.

The C++ Data Types

Just like with some of the other coding languages that you may want to work with along the way, there are going to be quite a few data points that show up in your code as well with C++. You will often be working with variables, for example, which are just going to be spots that you reserve in the memory of your computer so that the different parts of the code will stay safe. There are a lot of data points that we are able to focus on when it comes to working in the C++ language, and these will include:

1. Boolean
2. Double floating point
3. Floating point
4. Integer
5. Character
6. Valueless
7. Wide character

The C++ Functions

We also need to take a look at some of the functions that are going to come up when we are working with the C++ language. A function is pretty simple and is just going to be a group of statements in order to perform a task. Each program that you want to write out in C++ is going to have a minimum of a function, which can be known as the main() function, but it is possible that you will need to add in some more functions to get their code to work the way that we would like.

You will be able to do this in a number of different ways. First, we have the option of choosing to divide up our code so that it is in several functions based on what we would like o see it work. How you decide to dive up the code and how many functions you use will depend on you, and what you are trying to write out on your code. But most programmers are going to dive it up in a manner so that each function is going to work on his own task.

A function declaration is going to tell the compiler about a function name, the parameters that come with the function, and the return type that we are going to see. Keep in mind though that the definition that we are going to see with the function though is going to be found in the actual body of this function.

The standard library that we are going to see with the C++ library will be able to provide us with numerous functions that are already built into the program that we are also able to call up any time that we want. For example, if we are working with the function for strcat(), it can be used in order to help us to concatenate two strings. Then we are able to work with the memcpy() to help us to copy one location of our memory over to another one. These are just a few of the different types of functions that you are able to work with, and you will find that each of them is going to work out in a similar manner.

With this in mind, we need to take this a bit further and actually see how we can apply the function in C++. The code that you will be able to use in order to define the function will include:

Return type function name (parameter list) {

Body of the function

}

These function definitions will consist of a function header and a function body. The parts of the function will include the following:

- Return type: The function that you are working on may return a value, and you will use the value of return type in order to get something to return here. Some functions will be able to do the operations that you want without returning value to you. With the syntax that we used above, you would end up with an answer to the void.

- Function name: This is the name that you will give to the function. When you add in the name of the function with the parameter, you will get what is called the function signature.

- Parameters: The parameter is a placeholder. When you invoke the function, you are passing a value over to the parameter. This value will be referred to as the actual parameter or as the argument. The parameter list will then be able to refer to the number, order, and type of the parameters of the function. It is possible to work on a function that does not have any parameters at all.

- Function body: And finally, the function body is going to contain a collection of statements that are able to define what the function does.

There are a lot of times when we are going to be able to use the functions to help us get some parts of our code done and to ensure that we get it all set up and ready to handle. Make sure to practice these functions to see how they are going to work for our needs.

The Types of Modifiers

Any time that you are working with some of the codes that you want to do in C++, you will find that you will be able to use char, double, and int in order to allow the modifier that shows up before it to be there. The modifier that we are talking about here is going to be used to help us alter up the meaning of that base type so that it is going to fit into any program or situation that we are trying to create. There are going to be different types of modifiers of the data that we are able to work with. These include signed, unsigned, long, and short.

These four modifiers are going to be applicable to any of the base types of integers that we have. You are able to take the signed and unsigned, for example, in order to work with a char, and then long can be used on a double for example. C++ is also going to make it easier for us to work with shorthand notation to help with these integers. This means that they are able to use those words without needing to add in the "int" part since this is always implied in the coding.

There are also different types of qualifiers in order to get things to work on your C++ code. The following types of qualifiers that you will be able to use in order to provide some additional information about the variables the precede include:

- Const: Objects that have the "const" will not have the ability to be changed by the program while you are executing it.
- Volatile: The modifier of volatility will tell the compiler that you are able to change the value but these changes may not be explicitly specified by the program.

Restrict: a pointer that has been qualified by restricting is initially the only means by which an object it points to can be accessed

CHAPTER 2:

Basic Facilities

Array

The Array is a data structure that holds a sequential collection of elements of the same data type.

For example, in the code below I declared two arrays of different data type: an array of characters and an array of integers.

#include "stdafx.h"

#include <iostream>

int main(int argc, char* argv[])

{

    int i;

    int length;

    int sum = 0;

    char char_array[10] = { 'p', 's', 'y', 'c', 'h', 'o', 'l', 'o', 'g', 'y' };

```cpp
// total number of bytes allocated for that array

//one char is one byte: the number of elements = number of bytes

length = sizeof(char_array);

std::cout << "Size of array of characters is " << length << std::endl;

for (i = 0; i<length; i++)

std::cout << char_array[i];

std::cout << '\n';

std::cout << '\n';

std::cout << '\n';

int numbers[10] = { 1, 5, 9, 4, 2, 7, 6, 3, 8, 0 };

//the total number of bytes allocated for that array.

length = sizeof(numbers);

std::cout << "Size of numbers array=" << length << std::endl;

//the total number of bytes allocated for array/number of bytes
allocated for one element

length = sizeof(numbers) / sizeof(numbers[0]);

std::cout << "Numbers of elements=" << length << std::endl;
```

```cpp
for (i = 0; i<length; i++)

{

    sum = sum + numbers[i];

    std::cout << "Sum of numbers=" << sum << std::endl;

}

int *p = numbers;

    std::cout << "Address of the first element is " << p << std::endl;

    std::cout << "The value in the address is " << *p << std::endl;

    p++; //move pointer to the next element

    std::cout << "Address of the second element is " << p << std::endl;

    std::cout << "The value in the address is " << *p << std::endl;

    int hold = 1;

    std::cin >> hold;

    return 0;

}
```

The function sizeof returns the number of bytes allocated for the array. Since char data type occupies one byte, the number of bytes returned by the sizeof function equals to the number of elements of the char array.

The integer data type occupies 4 bytes in the memory, and an array of 10 integers is stored in 40 bytes. As a result, the sizeof the array function returns 40 bytes for the integer array of 10 elements.

To calculate how many elements are stored in an array we can divide the number of bytes allocated for the whole array by the number of bytes allocated to one element of the array;

length=sizeof(numbers) / sizeof(numbers[0]);

40 / 4 = 10

To access the value of a single element, we have to use the array index. The index of array in C++ starts from 0.

The index of the first element is 0, the index of the second element is 1, and so on.

To access all elements of an array, we have to use for loop.

for(i=0; i<length; i++)

cout<<char_array[i];

If we declare a pointer and assign the array to the pointer, the pointer will hold the address of the first element of the array:

int *p =numbers;

cout<<"Address of the first element is "<<p<<endl;

The output of that line of code is:

Address of the first element is 0059F710

To access the value stored in the address of the first element of the array using the pointer, run the following line of code:

cout<<"The value in the address is "<<*p<<endl;

The output of the code is:

The value in the address is 1.

To move to the next element of the array, you have to increase p-value.

p++;

Now it will point to the second element of the array:

cout<<"Address of the second element is " <<p<<endl;

cout<<"The value in the address is"<<*p<<endl;

The output is:

The address of the second element of the numbers array on my PC is 0059F714

The value in the address of the second element is 5.

```
C:\amazon\book2017\cplus\cpluscode\cplus_new\simplearray\simplearray\Debu

Size of array of characters is 10
psychology


Size of numbers array=40
Numbers of elements=10
Sum of numbers=1
Sum of numbers=6
Sum of numbers=15
Sum of numbers=19
Sum of numbers=21
Sum of numbers=28
Sum of numbers=34
Sum of numbers=37
Sum of numbers=45
Sum of numbers=45
Address of the first element is 0059F710
The value in the address is 1
Address of the second element is 0059F714
The value in the address is 5
```

Figure The array program output.

String

String functions

I will show you how to use some of the string functions.

strcpy_s () - copies the content of a string to another.

strcat_s() - appends a copy of the source string to the destination string.

strlen() - returns the length of a string.

Our application will read the string from user input, copy it to another string, then copy the original string characters in the reverse sequence to the temporary string and concatenate the copy and the reversed copy in one string.

For example, if user enters string 'Concatenation' then the application will output

'ConcatenationnoitanetacnoC'

The following header files must be included in the main.cpp file:

#include "stdafx.h"

#include <stdio.h>

#include <cctype>

#include <iostream>

#include <cstring>

The <cstring> header is needed for the string functions: strcpy_s(), strcat_s() and strlen(). The cctype header file is needed for the toupper() function.

I want to explain how I copied characters from the original string to a temporary string in reversed order.

First, I got the length of the original string, using the strlen() function.

length=strlen(aWord);

Then in the loop, I copied the last character of the original string to the first place of the temporary string and so on.

Let us examine the code in the loop.

for(i=0; i <length; i++)

temp[i]=aWord[length-(i+1)];

If an user enters the word 'Concatenation' then the word length will be 13. The index of the first character in a string is 0, then the index of the last character of the string will be 12. It means that the index of the last character is length -1.

A line of code that I placed in the loop is

temp[i]=aWord[length-(i+1)];

When i =0, temp[i] will refer to the first character of the temp string.

At the same time (when i =0) the aWord [length-(i+1)] will refer to the aWord[13 – (0 + 1)] character and it will be aWord[12] that is the last character of the 'Concatenation' string.

When i=1, the temp [1] will refer to the second character of the temp string and aWord [13-(1+1)] will refer to the second from the end character of the 'Concatenation' string.

That way, we can copy all characters in reversed order.

When we have copied all the characters from the original string to the temp string, we need to add null to the end of the temp string, because a string in C++ must be terminated with null.

The line of code temp[length]='\0'; will do the job.

The whole code is included in visual_studio_2017.zip.

```
#include "stdafx.h" #include <stdio.h>

#include <cctype>

#include <cstring>

#include <iostream>

int main()

{

    char more = 'Y';

    char prompt1[] = "\nEnter a word not more than 20 characters and press enter.\n";

    char prompt3[] = "\nDo you want to continue? Y/N\n";

    char aWord[20];

    char aCopy[40];
```

```
int length = 0;

char temp[20];

int i;

  while (toupper(more) == 'Y')

  {

  std::cout << prompt1;

  std::cin >> aWord;

  std::cout << "aWord=" << aWord << std::endl;

  strcpy_s(aCopy, aWord);

  std::cout << "aCopy=" << aCopy <<

  std::endl; length = strlen(aWord);

  std::cout << "length=" << length <<

  std::endl;

          //fill temp[] array with the word characters in opposite
order.

      for (i = 0; i <length; i++)

      temp[i] = aWord[length - (i + 1)];
```

```
        temp[length] = '\0';

        std::cout << "Temp=" << temp <<std::endl;

        strcat_s(aCopy, temp);

            std::cout << "aCopy after concatenation of temp=" <<
aCopy << std::endl;

        std::cout << prompt3;

        std::cin >> more;

    }

  return 0;

}
```

Output:

```
C:\amazon\book2017\cplus\cpluscode\cplus_new\strings\stringfunctions\Debug

Enter a word not more than 20 characters and press enter.
Computer
aWord=Computer
aCopy=Computer
length=8
Temp=retupmoC
aCopy after concatination of temp=ComputerretupmoC

Do you want to continue? Y/N
```

Figure String manipulation.

Lists

Let us imagine a puzzle. You have a row of boxes. Each box contains a card with one letter. You have to figure out the sequence of the letters, so that the letters compose a word.

T	C	O	N	E	L	Y	G	O	H
5	10	6	3	2	9	1	7	8	4

Figure A linked list

In the table above, you can see that each box has a number. You may guess that these numbers are the key to the puzzle. The first box has a letter T inside and number 5 on the front side. Take a card with the letter T and put it aside. The number 5 may point to the next letter. Count boxes. The fifth box has the letter 'E.' Take the card with the 'E' letter and place it next to T. You will get "TE." The box with the letter 'E' has number 2 on its side. So, take the card from the 2nd box and place it next to "TE." You will get "TEC."

The box with the letter 'C' has the number 10, so take the card from the 10th box. You will get "TECH." The box with the letter 'H' has number 4, so take the card from the 4th box. You got "TECHN." Continue following the numbers, and you will get the whole word: TECHNOLOGY.

That is how a linked list works. It is made of nodes. Each node has at least one variable that holds data (a text or number or object) and one variable (pointer) that holds the address of the next node. This system walks through the node list as you did in the puzzle. The pointer of the last node has null value, or it may point to the first node.

Then we have a closed linked list.

ADD A NODE

If you want to add a new node to the end of the linked list, you have to create a new node. Then point the pointer of the last node to the address of the new node and assign null to the new node pointer.

Figure Adding a node to the end of the linked list.

If you want to add a new node to the beginning of the linked list, you have to create a new node.

Point the pointer of the new node to the first node, and that is it.

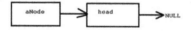

Figure Adding a node to the head of the linked list.

If you need to add a node in the middle of the linked list, you have to create a new node, and then break the chain: redirect the node (previous to the break), to a new node and point the pointer of the new node to the next node (the one after the break).

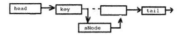

Figure Adding a node in the middle of the linked list.

DELETE A NODE

To delete a node with a certain key, you walk along with the list until you find the key. Then you assign the key node to the temp node. Then you point the node previous to the key node to the node next to the key node. See Figure 60. As a result, the temp key becomes isolated from the list. Now you can delete the temp.

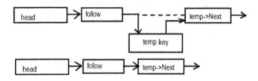

Figure Delete a node.

Below is a code for Node class. For simplicity sake, I created a node that holds an integer and node pointer to the next node. Both class member variables are declared as private. It is good programming practice not to use global variables, because private members cannot be seen from the outside of the class. We still need to set and to read these private member variables. The public functions set and will do the job.

CHAPTER 3:

Binary trees

B inary trees are one of the most useful of all the basic data structures and are by far the most interesting. They are the perfect example of how recursion and pointers can be used to do some very useful things.

One of the best techniques for creating lists of things is the linked list, but finding an element in the list can take a while. And, if you have a large amount of unstructured data, an array won't help much either. You can try sorting the array but, even so, inserting items into it will still be difficult. If you have an array that you want to keep sorted, inserting new elements will take a lot of shuffling! And trying to find things in a list as quickly as possible is quite important, especially in scenarios like these:

- You're building an MMORPG game and players need to be able to sign in quickly—that involves quickly looking players up

- You're building software to process credit cards and millions of transactions need to be handled hourly—credit card balances need to found very quickly

- You're using a low-power device, such as a tablet or smartphone, and showing your users an address book. You don't want your users to keep hanging because your data structure is slow.

This section will discuss the tools needed to overcome these problems and more.

The idea of the solution is to be able to store elements in a structure like a linked list, using pointers to help structure the memory, but in an easier way than the linked list. Doing this requires that the memory have more structure than a simple list.

So what does structuring data mean? When we started this journey, we only had arrays, but these never really gave us the ability to use data structures other than sequential lists. Linked lists use pointers to grow sequential lists incrementally but don't use the flexibility of the pointer to build more sophisticated structures.

What are these more sophisticated structures in memory? Structures that hold more than a single next node at any given time are a good example. But why would you want this? Simple. If you have two "next nodes," one can be used to represent elements that are more than the current element. This is called a binary tree.

These are named because there are always one or two branches from every node. Each of the next nodes is a child, and the node that links to the child is the parent node.

This is what a binary tree might look like:

10

6 14

5 8 11 18

In the tree, the left child on each of the elements is smaller than the element, and the right child is larger. 10 is the parent node for the whole tree, and the child nodes of 6 and 14 are both parent nodes to their own small trees, called subtrees.

Binary trees have one very important property: each child is an entire tree. Combine this with the rule of the left child being smaller and the right child being larger, and you have an easy way of defining algorithms that locate specific nodes in the tree.

First, look at the current node value. If it equals the search target, it's done. If it's more than the search target, go left; otherwise, go right. This works because each node to the left of the tree is less than the current mode value, and each on the right is more.

In an ideal world, your binary tree will be balanced with the exact same number of nodes on both sides. In such cases, every child tree is roughly 50 percent of the entire tree and, when you search the tree for a value, the search can eliminate 50 percent of the results each time it gets to a child node. So, if you had a tree of 1000 elements, 500 would be immediately eliminated. Search that tree again (it only has 50 elements now), and you can cut it by about 50 percent again. That way it doesn't take long to find the value you want.

So, how many times must a tree be subdivided before you get to one element? The answer to that is log2n (n is the number of elements the tree has). This is a small value, even if your tree is large—if your tree had, say, 32 billion elements, the value would be 32; almost 100 million times faster than a search of a linked list of four billion elements, where every single one has to be assessed.

If the tree isn't balanced, you won't be able to eliminate roughly half of the elements; worst case, each node only has one child and that makes the tree nothing more than a linked list with a few extra pointers, thus requiring you to search all elements.

So, when a tree is balanced approximately, it's much faster and easier to search for nodes than the same search on a linked list. This is because you can structure the memory of how you want it.

Implementing a Binary Tree

To implement a binary tree, begin by declaring the node structure:

Struct node

{

int key_value;

node *p_left;

node *p_right;

};

The node can store values as a simple integer, key_value, and has two child trees —p_left, and p_right.

There are some common functions that you want on your binary tree: inserting, searching, removing, and destroying:

node* insert (node* p_tree, int key);

node *search (node* p_tree, int key);

void destroyTree (node* p_tree);

node *remove (node* p_tree, int key);

Inserting

We'll use a recursive algorithm for inserting it into the tree. Recursion is fantastic for trees because there are two small trees for each tree; that makes the entire tree recursive by nature. The function takes a key and a tree that already exists (even an empty one) and returns a new tree that has the inserted value.

node* insert (node *p_tree, int key)

{

// base case--we have got to an empty tree and our new node

```
// needs to be inserted here

if ( p_tree == NULL )

{

node* p_new_tree = new node;

p_new_tree->p_left = NULL;

p_new_tree->p_right = NULL;

p_new_tree->key_value = key;

return p_new_tree;

}

// decide – left subtree or right subtree for the insertion

// depending on the what the node value is

if( key < p_tree->key_value )

{

// build a new tree from p_tree->left, and add in the key

// replace existing p_tree->left pointer with a pointer

// to new tree. Set the p_tree->p_left pointer

// in case p_tree->left is NULL. (If it isn't NULL,,
```

```
// p_tree->p_left won't change but it set it just

// to make sure.)

p_tree->p_left = insert( p_tree->p_left, key );

}

else

{

// Insertion into the right side is symmetric to the

// insertion in the left

p_tree->p_right = insert( p_tree->p_right, key );

}

return p_tree;

}
```

The basic logic here is this: if you have an empty tree, you create a new one. If not, the value for insertion goes to the left subtree if it's more than the current node, and the left subtree is then replaced with the new one. Otherwise, insert it into the right subtree and replace it.

When it comes to seeing it in action, build an empty tree into a tree with a couple of nodes. If the value 10 is inserted in the empty tree (NULL), immediately we will hit base case, and the result will be a tree of:

1

And both of the child trees will point to NULL.

Then insert 5 into the tree and make the following call:

insert(a tree with a parent , 5)

Because 5 is lower than 10, the call onto the left-subtree is recursive:

insert(NULL, 5)

insert(a tree with a parent , 5)

The call of

insert(NULL, 5)

creates and returns a new tree

5

When the returned tree is received, insert(,5) links the trees. In this example, 10's left child was NULL before. Therefore, the left child of 10 is established a new tree:

1

5

If we now add 7, we get:

insert(NULL, 7)

insert(a tree with a parent, 7)

insert(a tree with a parent , 7)

So, first off,

insert(NULL, 7)

will return a new tree:

7

And then

insert(a tree with a parent, 7)

will link to the subtree of 7 in this way:

5

7

Lastly, the tree gets returned to:

insert(a tree with a parent , 7)

And this will link it back:

10

5

7

Because there was already a pointer from 10 to the node with 5, it isn't really necessary to relink 10's left child to the tree with 5 as the parent, but it does eliminate one conditional check to see if the subtree is empty.

Destroying

This should also be a recursive function. Before deleting the current node, the algorithm destroys both of the subtrees that are at the current node.

```
void destroy_tree (node *p_tree)

{

if ( p_tree != NULL )

{

destroy_tree( p_tree->p_left );

destroy_tree( p_tree->p_right );

delete p_tree;

}

}
```

As a way of better understanding this, let's say that the value of the node was printed before the node was deleted:

```
void destroy_tree (node *p_tree)

{

if ( p_tree != NULL )

{

destroy_tree( p_tree->p_left );

destroy_tree( p_tree->p_right );

cout << "Deleting node: " << p_tree->key_value;

delete p_tree;

}

}
```

As you can see, the tree is deleted from the bottom up. Nodes 5 and 8 go first, then 6, before moving to the other side and deleting 11 and 18, followed by 14. Lastly, 10 will be deleted. The tree values aren't important; what matters is where the node is. In the following binary tree, rather than the node values, we use the order of deletion:

7

3 6

1 2 4 5

It can be helpful to walk through the code manually on a few trees, so you can see it much clearer.

Deleting from trees is a great example of a recursive algorithm that's not easy to do as an iterative implementation. First, you need a loop that can deal with both sides of the tree at the same time. You need to be able to delete a subtree while simultaneously tracking the next one, and that needs to be done for every level. With the stack, you can keep your place much more easily. The best way of visualizing this is to say that each stack frame will store the tree branch that has been deleted or destroyed already:

destroy_tree( )

destroy_tree( )—knows whether the subtree was the left or right

Each of the stack frames knows which bits of the tree have to be destroyed because it knows what point in the function execution should continue. When the first call to destroy the tree is made, the program is notified by the stack frame to continue executing when the second call is made to destroy_tree. When that second call is made, the program is told to continue with the delete tree. Because every function has a stack frame of its own, it can track the entire state of the tree's destruction at the current time, one tree level at a time.

To implement this in a non-recursive way would require having a data structure that retains the same amount and type of information. You could, for example, write a function that holds a linked list as a way of simulating the list. That linked list would have subtrees that were being destroyed and trees left for destruction. Then a loop-based algorithm could be written to add the subtrees to the list and remove them after they were destroyed fully. Basically, recursion lets you use the stack data structure built-in rather than needing to write your own.

CHAPTER 4:

Inheritance

Example:

```cpp
#include <iostream>

using namespace std;

// defining a simple student class with 2 members

class Student

{

public:

    int  studentID;

    string studentName;

// Function to display the members of the class

    void Display()

    {

        cout<<"Student ID "<<studentID<<endl;
```

```
        cout<<"Student Name "<<studentName;

    }

};

int main () {

Student stud1;

//Assigning values to the properties of the class

    stud1.studentID=1;

    stud1.studentName="John";

    stud1.Display();


    return 0;

}
```

With the above program:

- We have a class called 'Student' which has 2 members, one is 'studentID' and the other is called 'studentName'.
- We then define a member function called 'Display()' which outputs the 'studentID' and 'studentName' to the console.

- We can then call the member function from the object in the main program.

With this program, the output is as follows:

Student ID 1

Student Name John

So Then What is Inheritance?

Inheritance is a concept wherein we can define a class to inherit the properties and methods of another class. This helps in not having the need to define the class again or having the properties and methods defined again.

Let's say that we had a class called 'Person,' which had a property of 'Name' and a method of 'Display.' Then through inheritance, we can define a class called Student, which could inherit the Person class. The Student class would automatically get the ID member and the Display function. The Student class could then define its own additional members if required.

To define an inherited class, we use the following syntax.

Derived class:Base class

Here the 'Derived class' is the class that will inherit the properties of the other class, known as the 'Base class.'

So if we had a base class with a property and a function as shown below.

Base class

{

Public or protected:

Property1;

}

Then when we define the derived class from the base class, the derived class will have access to the property. Note that the property and function need to have the access modifier as public or protected. We will look at access modifiers in greater detail later on.

Derived class: Base Class

{

// No need to define property1, it will automatically inherit these.

}

Now let's look at a simple example of inheritance via code.

Example 2: The following program is used to showcase how to use a simple inherited class.

#include <iostream>

```cpp
using namespace std;

// Defining a simple Person class with a property of Name

class Person

{

public:

    string Name;

};

// Here we have the derived class. It defines another property of ID

class Student:public Person

{

public:

    int ID;

// Function to display both ID and Name. Since Name is available from the base class of Person, we are able to access it here.

 void Display()

    {

        cout<<"Student ID "<<ID<<endl;
```

```
    cout<<"Student Name "<<Name;
  }
};

int main () {

Student stud1;

  stud1.ID=1;

  stud1.Name="John";

  stud1.Display();

  return 0;

}
```

With the above program:

- We are defining a class called 'Person' that has one member called 'Name.'
- We then use inheritance to define the 'Student' class. Notice that we now define another property called 'ID.'
- In the 'Display' function, note that we can use the 'Name' property without the need for defining it in the 'Student' class again.

With this program, the output is as follows:

Student ID 1

Student Name John

Now we have seen how to use derived and base classes, which is also known as inheritance.

1.2 Functions in Derived Classes

We can also define functions that can be inherited from base classes. Let's see how we can achieve this.

If we, for instance, had a base class with a property and a function as shown below.

Base class

{

Public or protected:

Property1;

Fucntion1;

}

When we define the derived class from the base class, the derived class will have access to the property and the function as well. Note that the property and function need to have the access modifier as either public or protected.

Derived class: Base Class

{

// No need to define property1 and Function1, it will automatically inherit these.

}

Let's now look at an example where we can use functions in derived classes.

Example 3: The following program is used to showcase how to use an inherited class with functions.

#include <iostream>

using namespace std;

// Defining a simple Person class with a property of Name, ID, and also a function called Display.

class Person

{

public:

   string Name;

   int ID;

```cpp
    void Display()

    {

      cout<<"ID "<<ID<<endl;

      cout<<"Name "<<Name;

    }

};

// The Student class simply derives itself from the Person base class

class Student:public Person {

};

int main () {

// Since the derived class has access to the properties and functions of
the base class , these can be accessed via the Student object

Student stud1;

  stud1.ID=1;

  stud1.Name="John";

  stud1.Display();

  return 0;
```

}

With this program, the output is as follows:

ID 1

Name John

We can also redefine the Display function in the Student class. But if you look at the above example, you will notice that the Display function in the Person class has the display text as ID and Name. But suppose we wanted to have the display name as Student ID and Student name in the student class, we can redefine the Display function. Let's look at an example of this.

Example 4: The following program shows how to use an inherited class with redefined functions.

```
#include <iostream>

using namespace std;

class Person

{

public:

    string Name;

    int ID;
```

```cpp
void Display()

{

    cout<<"ID "<<ID<<endl;

    cout<<"Name "<<Name;

}

};

class Student:public Person {

public:

// Here we are redefining the Display function

void Display()

{

    cout<<"Student ID "<<ID<<endl;

    cout<<"Student Name "<<Name;

}

};

int main () {

Student stud1;
```

```
stud1.ID=1;

stud1.Name="John";

stud1.Display();

return 0;
}
```

With this program, the output is as follows:

Student ID 1

Student Name John

1.3 Multiple Inheritance

We can also make the derived class inherit from multiple base classes. This helps in getting more functionality out of multiple classes all at once.

Derived class: base class1, base class2… base classN

Here you just need to separate the base classes with a comma.

So if we had a base class with a property and a function as shown below.

Base class1

```
{
```

Public or protected:

Property1;

Fuction1;

}

And another base class as follows.

Base class2

{

Public or protected:

Property2;

Fucntion2;

}

Then when we define the derived class from both of the base classes, the derived class will have access to the property and the function of both classes.

Derived class: Base Class1, Base Class2

{

// No need to define property1, property2, and Function1, Fucntion2 it will automatically inherit these.

```
}
```

Again note that the property and function need to have the access modifier as either public or protected. Let's look at an example of multiple derived classes.

Example 5: The following program is used to showcase how to use multiple derived classes.

```
#include <iostream>

using namespace std;

// Defining the first base class of Person

class Person

{

public:

    string Name;

    int ID;

    void Display()

    {

        cout<<"ID"<<ID<<endl;

        cout<<"Name"<<Name;
```

```
}

};

// Defining the second base class of Marks

class Marks

{

public:

    int marks1,marks2;

    void Sum()

    {

        cout<<marks1+marks2;

    }

};
```

// The derived class inherits from both the Person and Marks base class.

```
class Student:public Person,public Marks {

public:

    void Display()
```

```
    {

        cout<<"Student ID "<<ID<<endl;

        cout<<"Student Name "<<Name<<endl;

    }

};

int main () {

Student stud1;

    stud1.ID=1;

    stud1.Name="John";

    stud1.Display();

    stud1.marks1=5;

    stud1.marks2=10;

    stud1.Sum();

    return 0;

}
```

With the above program:

- We are defining 2 base classes, one is called 'Person', and the other is called 'Marks.'
- The derived class 'Student' derives both classes and is able to use the members from both classes.

With this program, the output is as follows:

Student ID 1

Student Name John

15

1.4 Access Control

Class modifiers can be used to define the visibility of properties and methods in a class. Below are the various modifiers available.

- Private—With private, the properties and methods are only available to the class itself.
- Protected—With protected, the properties and methods are only available to the class itself and subclasses derived from that class.
- Public—With public, the properties and methods are available to all classes.

Let's say we had the following structure for a class.

Class classname

{

Private:

Property1;

Fucntion1;

}

Both 'property1' and 'function1' would not be accessible anywhere else except the class it is defined in. If you try to access any of these properties or functions from the main program, you will get a compile-time error.

Now let's define the class below, but this time we'll use the protected access modifier.

Class classname1

{

Protected:

Property1;

Fucntion1;

}

Now 'property1' and 'function1' are accessible from both the above class and any other class that derives from it.

So if we had the below-derived class definition, we would be able to access both 'property1' and 'fucntion1' in the derived class. But note that we will not be able to use these properties in any other non-derived class.

Class derivedclassname: classname1

{

}

Let' look at another example of access modifiers.

Example 6: The following program is used to showcase how to use access modifiers.

```
#include <iostream>

using namespace std;

class Person

{

public:

    int ID;

protected:

// Note that we are defining the Name property as protected
```

```cpp
string Name;

void Display()

{

    cout<<"ID "<<ID<<endl;

    cout<<"Name "<<Name;

}

// Note that we have defined the city property as private

private:

    string city;

};

class Student:public Person {

public:

    void Display()

    {

        cout<<"Student ID "<<ID<<endl;

        cout<<"Student Name "<<Name<<endl;

    }
```

```
};

int main () {

Student stud1;

    stud1.ID=1;

    stud1.Name="John";

    stud1.Display();

    return 0;

}
```

With this program, the output is as follows:

error: 'std::_cxx11::string Person::Name' is protected

Why are we getting this error? The 'person' class has 2 properties called ID and Name. The name has the protected access modifier, which means that it can only be accessed in the derived class. But we are trying to access it in the main class, which is wrong. Hence the correct way to implement this is as follows.

Example 7: The following program shows how to use access modifiers in the proper way.

```
#include <iostream>

using namespace std;
```

```cpp
class Person

{

public:

    int ID;

protected:

    string Name;

    void Display()

    {

        cout<<"ID "<<ID<<endl;

        cout<<"Name "<<Name;

    }

private:

    string city;

};

class Student:public Person {

public:
```

// We have now defined a function which can set the value of the protected property accordingly.

```cpp
void InputName(string pName)

{

  Name=pName;

}

void Display()

{

  cout<<"Student ID "<<ID<<endl;

  cout<<"Student Name "<<Name<<endl;

}

};

int main () {

Student stud1;

  stud1.ID=1;

  stud1.InputName("John");

  stud1.Display();
```

```
    return 0;

}
```

In the above program, we now correctly define a method called 'InputName' in the 'Student' class, which can access the protected 'Name' member.

With this program, the output is as follows:

Student ID 1

Student Name John

Now let's look at the same example and try to display the property called 'City,' which is defined in the 'Person' class.

Example 8: The following program shows a second example of how to use access modifiers the wrong way.

```
#include <iostream>

using namespace std;

class Person

{

public:

    int ID;
```

```
protected:

    string Name;

    void Display()

    {

        cout<<"ID "<<ID<<endl;

        cout<<"Name "<<Name;

    }

private:

    string city;

};

class Student:public Person {

public:

    void InputName(string pName)

    {

        Name=pName;

    }

    void Display()
```

```
{

    cout<<"Student ID "<<ID<<endl;
```

// Note that we are trying to use the private property in the derived class.

```
    cout<<"Student city "<<city<<endl;

    cout<<"Student Name "<<Name<<endl;

}

};

int main () {

Student stud1;

    stud1.ID=1;

    stud1.InputName("John");

    stud1.Display();

    return 0;

}
```

With this program, the output is as follows:

error: 'std::_cxx11::string Person::city' is private

Since the 'City' property is private, it cannot even be used in the derived class. We can only work with this property in the 'Person' class.

CHAPTER 5

Advanced Basics

Pointers

Pointers have been mentioned previously, and they are the memory address of a variable, this is much like a house address for a person. These can be passed around a parameter and allow the effects of passing by reference mentioned previously.

The program below will show the address of a variable:

```
#include <stdio.h>

int main()

{

int var;

printf("The address is: %x\n", &var);

return 0;

}
```

Output:

> The address is: 10ffa2c

Note: This will be different almost every time you run

Note the highlighted statement, the '&' (Reference Operator) is used to return the memory location of the variable and allows certain statements to access the data in that location. The "%x' is used because a memory location is in hexadecimal.

To create a pointer, we use the dereferencing operator (*), this will create a pointer variable that is designed to hold a memory locations address. Below is a program that creates a pointer and uses reference operator (&) to store another regular variable's address in the newly created pointer. The dereferencing operator (*) is also used to access or change the actual data in that memory location.

- Dereferencing operator (*) is used to create a pointer, it is also used when changing the actual value
- Referencing operator (&) is used when obtaining the memory location of a pointer

//Regular variable

int var = 10;

//Pointer

int* pointer;

//Storing of var memory location

pointer = &var;

//Pointer is now effecivly 'var' so

//things like this can happen

*pointer = 20;

printf("Var's value is now: %d", var);

Output:

>Var's value is now: 20

NULL pointers

When you create a pointer, is it initially not given anything to point at, this is dangerous because the pointer when created it references random memory, and changing this data in the memory location can crash the program. To prevent this, when we create a pointer we assign it to NULL like so:

int* pointer = NULL;

This means the pointer has an address of '0', this is a reserved memory location to identify a null pointer. A null pointer can be checked by an if statement:

if (pointer){}

This will succeed if the pointer isn't null.

Using pointers

Now some real-world uses of pointers are passing them as parameters and effectively passing them by reference. The example below will show the effect:

```
void Change_Value(int* reference)

{

//Changes the value in the memory location

*reference = 20;

}

int main()

{

//Creates pointer to variable

int var = 10;

int* pointer = &var;

printf("The value before call: %d\n", var);

//Method call

Change_Value(pointer);
```

//Prints new value

printf("The value after call: %d\n", var);

return 0;

}

Output:

>The value before call: 10

>The value after call: 20

This passes the memory location, not the value of the variable, meaning you have the location where you can make changes.

Note the parameter is int* this is the pointer type, so for an example of a pointer to a char would be char*.

Pointer Arithmetic

There are times when moving a pointer along to another memory location might be useful; this is where pointer arithmetic comes into use. If we were to execute say ptr++ and the ptr was an integer pointer it would now move 4bytes (Size of an int) along, and we were to run it again, another 4bytes etc. This can mean pointer (if pointing to valid array structures) can act much like an array can. An example is below:

int arrayInt[] = { 10, 20, 30 };

```
size_t arrayInt_Size = 3;

//Will point to the first array index

int* ptr = &arrayInt;

for (int i = 0; i < arrayInt_Size; i++)

{

//Remember, *ptr gets the value in the memory location

printf("Value of arrayInt[%d] = %d\n", i, *ptr);

ptr++;

}
```

Output:

>Value of arrayInt[0] = 10

>Value of arrayInt[1] = 20

>Value of arrayInt[2] = 30

This shows that a pointer to the first address of the array can be incremented along the addresses of the array (Remember each value of an array is stored in neighbouring memory locations)

You can do the opposite and decrement a pointer i.e. make the pointers value decrease.

There is also way to compare pointers using relational operators such as ==, < and >. The most common use for this is checking if two pointer point to the same location:

int value;

//Assigns ptr1 and prt2 the same value

int* ptr1 = &value;

int* ptr2 = &value;

//ptr3 is assigned another value

int* ptr3 = NULL;

if (ptr1 == ptr2)

{

printf("ptr1 and ptr2 are equal!\n");

}

if (!ptr1 == ptr3)

{

printf("ptr1 is not equal to ptr3\n");

}

This checks if the various pointers are equal. The same can be done with > and <.

Function pointers

Much like you can do with variables, you can also do the same with functions; below is a snippet of code that shows a function pointer being defined. Key sections will be highlighted:

```
void printAddition(int value1, int value2)

{

int result = value1 + value2;

printf("The result is: %d", result);

}

int main()

{

//Function pointer definition

//<retrunType>(*<Name>)(<Parameters>)

void(*functionPtr)(int, int);

functionPtr = &printAddition;

//Invoking call to pointer function
```

```
(*functionPtr)(100, 200);

return 0;

}
```

The basic structure for defining a function pointer is like so

`<Return_Type> (*<Name>) (<Parameters>)`

Where in this case:

`<Return_Type> = void`

`<Name> = functionPtr`

`<Parameters> = int, int`

This function pointer can now be passed as a parameter and used in situations where you would want to change the behaviour of code but with almost the same code.

An example could be dynamically choosing what operation a calculator should perform (Note: this is complex code and should be used a rough example, so don't worry if you don't fully understand)

```
void calculator(int value1, int value2, int(*opp)(int,int))

{

int result = (*opp)(value1, value2);
```

```
printf("The result from the operation: %d\n", result);

}

//Adds two values

int add(int num1, int num2)

{

return num1 + num2;

}

//Subtracts two values

int sub(int num1, int num2)

{

return num1 - num2;

}

int main()

{

calculator(10, 20, &add);

calculator(10, 20, &sub);

return 0;
```

}

Here what is happening we are passing the function 'add' and 'sub' as parameters for the function calculator, as you see from the highlight the function parameter is defined like it is above with the return type, name and parameters being defined, all that is passed into calculator is &add and &sub for the function pointers. The calculator function then goes on to invoke the pointer and passes in the values and returns the result.

Storage Classifications

In C each variable can be given a storage class that can define certain characteristics.

The classes are:

- Automatic variables
- Static variables
- Register variables
- External variables

Automatic variables

Every variable we have defined so far has been an automatic variable; they are created when a function is called and automatically destroyed when a function exits. These variables are also known as local variables.

auto int value;

Is the same as

int value;

Static variables

Static is used when you want to keep the variable from being destroyed when it goes out of scope; this variable will persist until the program is complete. The static variable is created only once throughout the lifetime of the program. Below is an example of a static variable in use:

```
void tick()

{

//This will run once

static int count = 0;

count++;

printf("The count is now: %d\n", count);

}

int main()

{

tick();

tick();
```

tick();

}

Output:

>The count is now: 1

>The count is now: 2

>The count is now: 3

The area highlighted section is the static definition and will only run once.

Register variables

The register is used to define a variable that is to be store in register memory opposed to regular memory, the benefits register memory has is it is much much quicker to access; however, there is only space for a few variables.

Defining a register variable is done like so:

register int value;

External variable

We touched on this before, but a global variable is a variable not defined in a scope and, therefore, can be used anywhere. An external variable Is a variable defined in a separate location like another file, and the extern keyword is used to signify that the variable is in another file. You would include another file as a reference by placing this at the top of your file:

#include "FileName.c"

This is to tell the program to reference this file as well. Note the files need to be in the same location.

Program 1 [File_2.c]

```
#include <stdio.h>

#include "C_TUT.c"

int main()

{

extern int globalValue;

printf("The global variable is: %d", globalValue);

}
```

Program 2 (It is small) [C_TUT.c]

```
#include <stdio.h>

int globalValue = 1032;
```

The Output of running File_2.c:

>The global variable is: 1032

This shows that the globalValue is referenced from C_TUT.c and used in another file by using the extern keyword.

We touched on recursion in the basic section of the tutorial, and again it's the definition of a function´s tasks with definition to itself. As promised, there are a few more examples of recursion explained below:

```c
int factorial(int x)

{

int r;

//Stopping condition

if (x == 1)

{

//Has a conclusion so looping stop

return 1;

}

else

{

//Recursive definition
```

```
return r = x * factorial(x - 1);

}

}

int main()

{

puts("Please enter a number: ");

//Reads in user input

int a, b;

scanf("%d", &a);

//Starts the execution

b = factorial(a);

printf("The factorial is: %d", b);

}
```

This is the world-famous example of recursion that is used to find a factorial of a number (3 factorial is 3x2x1). It works by the recursive return statement above; it stops by having a return statement without a recursive definition, i.e. when x = 1, the function just returns 1; this means the stack can unwind and find an answer. There is a flow diagram below:

Recursion

Recursion is a difficult concept and will only be lightly touched on here, and its real-world uses and functionality explained in the advanced section.

Recursion is a definition of a functions commands involving a reference to itself, yes very confusing, I know, but I use some examples to explain.

```
const int maxLoops = 5;

void Sequence(int previous, int now, size_t loopCount)

{

//Works out next value

int next = previous + now;

//Prints new value

printf("New value: %d\n", next);

//Increments counts

loopCount++;

//Stopping condition to make sure infinite looping doesn't occur

if (loopCount < maxLoops)

{
```

```
//Recursive call

Sequence(now, next, loopCount);

}

}

int main()

{

Sequence(1, 1, 0);

}
```

Output:

>New value: 2

>New value: 3

>New value: 5

>New value: 8

>New value: 13

There're a few things to note, the lack of iteration loops, recursion in its essence causes looping. The second thing to note if the if statement labelled 'stopping condition,' if recursive set-ups don't have conditions that stop them looping they will loop forever, so this is a crucial element for using recursion effectively.

We touched on recursion in the basic section of the tutorial, and again it's the definition of a function´s tasks with definition to itself. As promised, there are a few more examples of recursion explained below:

```
int factorial(int x)

{

int r;

//Stopping condition

if (x == 1)

{

//Has a conclusion so looping stop

return 1;

}

else

{

//Recursive  definition

return r = x * factorial(x - 1);
```

```
}

}

int main()

{

puts("Please enter a number: ");

//Reads in user input

int a, b;

scanf("%d", &a);

//Starts the execution

b = factorial(a);

printf("The factorial is: %d", b);

}
```

This is the world-famous example of recursion that is used to find a factorial of a number (3 factorial is 3x2x1). It works by the recursive return statement above; it stops by having a return statement without a recursive definition, i.e. when x = 1, the function just returns 1; this means the stack can unwind and find an answer.

There is a flow diagram below:

```
function factorial(3) {
    if (3 === 0)
        return 1;
    else {
        return x * factorial(3 - 1);        2* 3 = 6 is
    }                                       returned
}

let num = 3;
let result = factorial(3);

function factorial(2) {
    if (2 === 0)
        return 1;                           1* 2 = 2 is
    else {                                  returned
        return x * factorial(2 - 1);
    }
}

function factorial(1) {
    if (1 === 0)
        return 1;                           1* 1 = 1 is
    else {                                  returned
        return x * factorial(1 - 1);
    }
}
                                            1 is
function factorial(0) {                     returned
    if (3 === 0)
        return 1;
    else {
        return x * factorial(1 - 1);
    }
}
```

2

1

0

CHAPTER 6:

STL Containers and Iterators

Containers

Containers are the primary contribution of the STL, and they are for holding and accessing a sequence of objects. The STL provides different types of containers, such as vector, list, map, and hash tables. However, based on the characteristics of data arrangement, the STL containers are categorized into three major sections:

1. Sequence containers such as vector, fixed-size array, list, forward_list, and deque;
2. Associative containers:
a) Ordered (sorted) associative containers such as set, multiset, map, and multimap;
b) Unordered (unsorted) associative containers such as unordered_set, unordered_multiset, unordered_map and unordered_multimap; and
3. Container adapters such as stack, queue, and priority_queue.

In addition to these fully qualified containers, C++ provides three almost qualified containers, viz., string, built-in-array and valarray.

Each of the containers are sophisticated template classes with the default constructor, constructor from arguments, copy constructor, assignment operator, and definite destructor. Apart from that, most of the containers define its own iterator, and every container has its own operation member functions.

Container iterators

From those sections, we know that each container provides its own iterator and using that iterator operations are performed on the elements of the container.

Among the five categories of iterators, each container defines any one of the three categories, viz.,

Forward iterators:

- Can read;
- Can write;
- Can be repeated read/write at a single location;
- Can move forward (++), but cannot move backwards, thus the name forward iterator; and
- Is used in: unordered associative containers and forward list, which are for the best space-efficient storage.
- Bidirectional iterator:
- Is same as the forward iterator, but it can also move backwards (so, ++ as well as --), thus is named bidirectional; and

- Is used in containers: list, set, map, multiset, and multimap.

- Random access iterator:

- Is the same as the bidirectional iterator, but it can jump (+=N or –=N, where N is a whole number) instead of (+=1 or -=1, where +=1 is ++ and -=1 is --), thus is named random access iterator(jump iterator); and

- Is used in containers: vector, string, deque and array<T,N>.

Apart from helping the operations of STL algorithms in the containers, the iterators also help in executing internal operations (member functions) of the containers.

Some internal operations are common to all the sequence and associative containers, and they are:

O(1):

begin(), end(), cbegin(), cend(), rbegin()*, rend()*, crbegin()*, crend()*, empty(), swap(), size()†, max_size(), shrink_to_fit()‡, emplace() and emplace_back()*;

O(n):

Assignment operator: =,

Relational operators:

!=, ==, <††, <=††, >†† and >=††, and clear();

O (variable):

- Insert()†, erase()† and emplace()†(they are fast in node-based containers and slow in (middle of) contiguous-memory containers); and
- Constructors (usually, the composition of classes or
- Their default constructors have constant complexity, but all other constructors and destructors may have linear complexity).

Note:

a) The forward list and unordered associative containers use forward iterators so they do not have the reverse iterator operations: emplace back(), rbegin(), rend), crbegin() and crend().

b) The associative containers support reverse iterators, but they do not support emplace back. This is so because the associative containers keep their elements in a sorted order, so it does not accept the command emplace back (), which insist on placing the new element at the back of the container.

†The forward list:

1. Does not support the operator size();
2. Instead of insert(), erase() and emplace(), it provides insert after(), erase after() and emplace after();
3. Has special iterators before begin(), cbefore begin(), such that
- an operation in forward list:

- my_fwd_list.insert_after

- (my_fwd_list.before_begin(), inv_data.gold);

- is equivalent to the following operation in list:

- my_list.insert

- (my_list.begin(), inv_data.gold);

- Note:

- None of the containers can write or read beyond end(), i.e.,

- my_fwd_list.insert_after

- (my_fwd_list.end(), inv_data.gold); is an error!

‡ shrink to fit () requests the removal of unused memory capacity and it is applicable only to vector, deque and string.

†† The unorder containers do not support the relational operators: <, <=, > and >=.

In the above list of operators, and O stand for the complexity, In short, though complexity means the time and/or space complexity of the function, in containers it is the time complexity;

- O(1) stands for constant-time complexity;

- O(log n) stands for logarithm-time complexity;

- O(n) stands for linear-time complexity;

in comparison, O(n) > O(log n) > O(1), which means O(1) is the fastest operation; and caution: These are expected, or average complexity, and the Standard Library document quotes worst-case complexities for some of the operators.

There are a few containers which do not support iterators, and they are: container adapters, bitset, and valarray. Note: C++11 defines iterators begin () and end () for the valarray.

STL Iterators

Iterators, containers, and algorithms are components of the Standard Template Library written by Alexander Stepanov et al., of Hewlett-Packard in the early 1990s and subsequently merged and advanced in the Standard Library.

An iterator is an abstraction of a specialized pointer that dereferences over elements of a given container (such as vector, map, and user made container classes).

Each container class would contain member functions for generating iterators, for example, members begin (), and end () would return iterator for the first element, and for one after its last element, respectively.

The following figure depicts the relation between an iterator (*it) and its container (vector<int>data {1111, 1134, 1134, 1124, 1124, 1134, 1111, 1176, 1124, 1134, 1176}).

Then, the iterator can incorporate those elements of the container in algorithmic operations (such as sort, accumulate, and user made algorithm functions).

In other words, an iterator associates a container with an algorithm.

The most frequently used iterators are from begin () and end (). This is illustrated in the figure below:

As shown in the figure, both data [0] and data.begin() represent the same element, i.e., elem 1, but data[N] and data.end() represent a "no man land" and accessing this can cause a runtime error. However, the member function end () is very useful in making conditions in iterative statements.

The following code illustrates this fundamental property of iterators:

```
// iterators.cpp

#include "..\..\my_essentials.hpp"

void illustrate iterators()

{

int arr[] = {1111, 1134, 1134, 1124, 1124, 1134, 1111, 1176, 1124, 1134, 1176};

vector<int>data(arr, arr+ sizeof(arr)/sizeof(arr[0]) );
```

```
// vector<int>data2{1111, 1134, 1134, 1124, 1124, 1134, 1111, 1176,
1124, 1134, 1176}; // fine with gcc4.7.0

cout << "\n Illustration of iterators: \n"

        << "\n Given vector: data =\n\t( ";

for(auto element: data) // 'the range-based for' do not work with VC10.

        cout << element << "; ";

cout << ")\n\n Let us define an iterator, say *it for this vector.\n";

vector<int>::iterator it = data.begin();

/*

Note:

In STL containers, each container template class

defines its own iterator member class, so that

vector<int>::iterator is different from the

list <int>::iterator.

*/

cout << " Thus,\t\t*it = " << *it << " that is data[0]\n Iterators can
be incremented, i.e, ++it;\n";
```

++it;

cout << " After ++\t*it = " << *it << " that is data[1]\n Therefore, iterator *it dereferences through vector data.\n So, let us express the entire vector using the iterator: \n\t(";

for(auto it = data.begin(); it!=data.end(); ++it)

    cout << *it << "; ";

cout << ")\n";

cout << "\n Task: Since, this vector has repeated numbers,\n Can we keep only one copy of each number and remove the duplicates?\n Yes, we can!\n For that, we pass the iterator through three type of STL algorithms as shown below:\n";

cout << "\n Step.1 Sort in ascending order:\n";

sort(data.begin(), data.end());

cout << " After the iterator has passed through sort(): \n\t(";

for(auto element: data)

    cout << element << "; ";

cout << ")\n\n Step.2 Move the adjacent repeated elements to the left hand side:\n";

auto my_unique = unique(data.begin(), data.end());

cout << " After the iterator has passed through unique(): \n\t(";

for(auto element: data)

    cout << element << "; ";

/*

The function unique() has returned an iterator to

the identifier "my_unique" starting from which the

repeated elements are pushed up to one before the

end().

Note: The STL algorithms can displace the elements

but it cannot erase them, however each stl container

template class has a member function called

"erase()" operation for erasing the specified

elements.

In other words, iterators can modify elements in containers but not the containers themselves.

Therefore, to remove the duplicates, we apply the

operation erase() from the iterator "my unique" till

the end().

```
*/

cout << ")\n\n Step.3 Erase out those repeated elements:\n";

data.erase(my unique, data.end());

cout << " After the iterator has passed through erase() i.e., \n Final:\t(
";

for(auto element: data)

    cout << element << "; ";

cout << ")\n";

}

int main()

{

illustrate_iterators();

just_pause();

}
```

Output:

Illustration of iterators:

Given vector: data =

(1111; 1134; 1134; 1124; 1124; 1134; 1111; 1176; 1124; 1134; 1176;)

Let us define an iterator, say *it for this vector.

Thus,   *it = 1111 that is data[0].

Iterators can be incremented, i.e, ++it.

After ++   *it = 1134 that is data[1]

Therefore, iterator *it dereferences through vector data.

So, let us express the entire vector using the iterator:

(1111; 1134; 1134; 1124; 1124; 1134; 1111; 1176; 1124; 1134; 1176;)

Task: Since, this vector has repeated numbers,

Can we keep only one copy of each number and remove the duplicates?

Yes, we can!

For that, we pass the iterator through three types of STL algorithms as shown below:

Step.1 Sort in ascending order:

After the iterator has passed through sort():

(1111; 1111; 1124; 1124; 1124; 1134; 1134; 1134; 1134; 1176; 1176;)

Step.2 Move the adjacent repeated elements to the left hand side:

After the iterator has passed through unique():

(1111; 1124; 1134; 1176; 1124; 1134; 1134; 1134; 1134; 1176; 1176;)

Step.3 Erase out those repeated elements:

After the iterator has passed through erase() i.e.,

Final: (1111; 1124; 1134; 1176;)

The program presented above demonstrates the usefulness of iterators incorporating container data in algorithms.

As we saw, the iterators can be used for printing the contents of a container, so let us code a container-independent code in our header file "my_essentials.hpp". This is for easy printing of containers of one type name such as vector<T>, list<T>, set<T>, multiset<T>, deque<T> and fixed-size array<T,N>, but not for containers with two type names such as map<T1,T2> and unordered_multimap<T1,T2>.

```
//.........................................................

// Container independent code for printing out

// container with one typename

template<typename container>

void cout_container(const std::string& message, const container& data)
```

```
{

    std::cout << message << "{";

    if(data.empty()){

        std::cout << "NULL}"<<std::endl;

        return;

    }

    auto start = data.begin();

    auto end = data.end();

    while(true)

    {

        std::cout << *start;

        ++start;

        if(start != end)

            std::cout << ", ";

        else{

            std::cout <<'}' << std::endl;

            break;
```

```
        }

    }

}
```

//..

Let us add this template in the "my_essentials.hpp" and test the template with the following code.

Then, let us test this template:

```
// cout_containers.cpp

#include "..\..\my_essentials.hpp"

#include <array>

#include <vector>

#include <unordered_set>

#include <forward_list>

#include <set>

int main()

{

    // Let us define,
```

```cpp
// a fixed-size array

array<int,6> arr = {1,3,5,1,2,4};

cout_container("my array\t = ", arr);



// a vector

vector<int> vec(arr.begin(), arr.end());

cout_container("my vector\t = ", vec);



// a forward_list

forward_list<int>

    f_lis(arr.begin(), arr.end());

cout_container("my forward_list\t = ",f_lis);



// an unordered_set

unordered_set<int>

    u_set(arr.begin(), arr.end());

cout_container("my unordered_set = ", u_set);
```

```
// a set container

set<int>se(arr.begin(), arr.end());

cout_container("my set\t\t = ", se);

just_pause();

}
```

The output is:

my array   = {1, 3, 5, 1, 2, 4}

my vector   = {1, 3, 5, 1, 2, 4}

my forward_list = {1, 3, 5, 1, 2, 4}

my unordered_set = {1, 3, 5, 2, 4}

my set   = {1, 2, 3, 4, 5}

As we experimented with some applications of iterators, now we summarize their operations in the following table.

Iterators do not have a single definition, so not all iterators can support every operation mentioned above. Iterators are categorized into five kinds, viz.

Thus, with this primary discussion, we found that pointers and their property of dereferencing over different objects play a vital role to iterators and STL operations.

CHAPTER 7:

STL Algorithm

T he STL algorithms are found in <algorithms> header file, so we need to include it in our program. The algorithms can be classified as:

- Non-modifying algorithms: e.g. for each, count, search etc.
- Modifying algorithms: e.g copy, transform, etc.
- Removing algorithms: remove, remove if, etc.
- Mutating algorithms: reverse, rotate, etc.
- Sorting algorithms: sort, partial sort, etc.
- Sorted range algorithms: binary search, merge, etc.
- Numeric algorithms: accumulate, partial sum, inner product, etc.

The following example shows how to sort () function works on arrays.

Program 13.11: sorting of array using sort algorithm

#include <iostream>

#include <algorithm>

using namespace std;

```
int main()

{

    int a[ ] = {3,5,7,2,9};

    sort(a, a + 5);

    cout << "Sorted Array:" << endl;

    for (int i = 0; i <5; i++)

        cout << a[i] << " ";

    return 0;

}
```

Output:

Sorted Array:

2 3 5 7 9

In the example above, when we pass array name an as an argument, we are telling the function, to sort at the beginning of the array. If we wanted it to start the sort at the third element of the array, we can use, sort(a+3, a+5);

We have used a+5 for the second argument, which specifies that we want to sort to the last element in the array.

Now similar sort() function can work with vector container as shown in following program. This shows that STL algorithms are generic.

Program 13.12: Sorting of vector using sort algorithm

```
#include <iostream>

#include <algorithm>

#include <vector>

using namespace std;

int main()

{

    int a[ ] = {5,3,7,6,2,9};

    vector<int> v(a, a+6) ;

    sort(v.begin(), v.end());

    for (int i = 0; i != v.size(); i++)

        cout << v[i] << " ";
```

```
cout << endl;

return 0;

}
```

Output: 2 3 5 6 7 9

As you can see, the sorting function works almost the same as on an array. The first parameter in sort() accepts an iterator to the first element using begin() as it returns a iterator to the first element. So it will start sorting at the first element in the vector. Same way end() returns an iterator that points to 1 past the last element in the container. Note that sort function sorts up to but not including what we pass as the second parameter.

find() and count() algorithm

find() algorithm is helpful to find particular value from the container. count() is used to count how many times a particular value appears in container.

Program 13.13: Finding value from vector using find algorithm

```
#include <iostream>

#include <algorithm>

#include <vector>
```

```cpp
using namespace std;

int main()

{

vector<int> v;

for(int i = 0; i < 10; i++)

v.push_back(i);

int a = 5;

vector<int>::iterator it;

it = find(v.begin(),v.end(),a);

if(it != v.end()) {

cout << "found " << a<< endl;

}

else {

cout << "could not find " << a << endl;

}

int c = count(v.begin(), v.end(), 6);

    cout<<"Number of 6 stored in vector:" << c;
```

return 0;

}

Output: found 5

Number of 6 stored in vector: 1

- For each()

This algorithm applies a specified function object to each element in a container. Original values in container will not change, but it is used for display modified elements. It takes the first two arguments as the start and end range. The third argument is an address of a function object.

For example, for each() algorithm squares all elements of the array and displays them.

Program 13.14: To square all elements of array using for each algorithm

```cpp
#include <iostream>

#include <vector>

#include <algorithm>

using namespace std;

void square(int a)

{
```

```
    cout<<a*a<<endl;

}

int main()

{

int s[ ]={1,2,3,4};

for_each(s, s+4, square);

return 0;

}
```

Output:

1

4

9

16

CHAPTER 8:

Library Functions

Library functions and user-defined functions in C++

Learning objective

After completing this topic, you should be able to give a brief account of library functions and user-defined functions in C++.

1. Incorporation of library functions

The C++ programmer has access to a large selection of library functions.

You can use any function in the library by simply including the name of the header file that contains the appropriate function prototype.

Generally, library functions are specified in a pair of files.

The function definition is contained in a source file that usually has a .c or .cpp file extension.

Note

Usually, you are not supplied with the source code for library functions with a compiler.

Instead, you are supplied with precompiled object files that can be linked to your program.

The function prototype is contained in a header file, which may be distinguished by an .h, .hpp, or .hxx file extension.

Note

Header files also contain definitions of various data types and constants needed by those functions.

Though not mandatory, it's a good idea to organize your own functions in the same way as supplied library functions.

This allows you to use the functions in more than one program without having to respecify the code.

In order to call library functions in a program, you must specify the header file that contains the appropriate function prototype.

This is usually done at the beginning of a source file.

But it must be done before the function is used by the program.

Header files can be included in a program by using the #include preprocessor directive.

This tells the preprocessor to open the named header file and insert its contents where the #include statement appears.

#include <string>

#include "myfuncs.h"

You can name files in an #include statement in two ways, that is in double quotes or in angle brackets (<>).

Filenames in angle brackets tell the preprocessor to look through a search path specified in the environment.

#include <string>

#include "myfuncs.h"

Filenames in double quotes tell the preprocessor to search the current directory first, then the specified search path.

An error is reported if a file cannot be found.

#include <string>

#include "myfuncs.h"

The linker always searches for the compiled versions of any functions specified in an included header file.

Available files

The C standard library provides a collection of functions for performing common tasks such as:

- String handling
- Character and type conversion
- Mathematics
- Input and output

A wide variety of C++ library files are also available.

The ANSI standard for C++ libraries was ratified in 1998.

The iostream file is probably the most common and generic of all C++ library files.

Most C++ programs include this header file.

The iostream file provides a large range of input/output functions and other I/O stream information.

For example, this is where cin and cout data and functions are prototyped.

Note

C++ I/O occurs in streams of bytes, where a stream is simply a sequence of bytes.

There are many variations of C++ libraries available to programmers.

And these libraries originate from a number of sources.

For example, some libraries come with C++ application development software.

C++ function libraries may also be supplied by sources such as device driver manufacturers, and C++ programming web sites and bulletin boards.

Your best source of reference is usually the manuals and help files included with your C++ application development software.

There are also a number of reference books available, some of which cover specific compilers.

Use of library functions

To demonstrate the use of standard library functions, let's consider a program that does the following:

- Gets the absolute value of the number -55

```
#include <iostream>

using namespace std;

#include <cmath>

void main(void)
```

{

cout <<"The absolute value of -55 is "<<abs(-55)<< "\n";

- Calculates the square root of 100

calculates the square root of 100

cout <<"The square root of 100 is "<<sqrt(100.0)<< "\n";

- evaluates 10 to the power of 5

evaluates 10 to the power of 5

cout<<"10 to the power of 5 is"<<pow(10, 5)<< "\n";

The result of each calculation is output to the screen.

Note

This program uses no user-defined functions.

The standard math library contains functions to perform each of the three calculations required.

These are:

- abs()
- sqrt()
- pow()

pow()

```
#include <iostream>

using namespace std;

#include <cmath>

void main(void)

{

    cout <<"The absolute value of -55 is "<<abs(-55)<< "\n";

    cout <<"The square root of 100 is "<<sqrt(100.0)<< "\n";

    cout <<"10 to the power of 5 is "<<pow(10,5)<< "\n";

}
```

The first thing to decide when writing this program is which header files to include.

To call abs(), sqrt(), and pow(), you need to include the header file cmath in a preprocessor directive.

You also need to include the header file iostream so that cin and cout statements can be used.

```
#include <iostream>

using namespace std;

#include <cmath>
```

```
void main(void)

{

    cout <<"The absolute value of -55 is "<<abs(-55)<< "\n";

    cout <<"The square root of 100 is "<<sqrt(100.0)<< "\n";

    cout <<"10 to the power of 5 is "<<pow(10,5)<< "\n";

}
```

Note

The function abs() is also included in the stdlib.h header file.

Once you've completed the preprocessor directives, you can begin coding main().

```
#include <iostream>

using namespace std;

#include <cmath>

void main(void)

{

    cout <<"The absolute value of -55 is "<<abs(-55)<< "\n";

    cout <<"The square root of 100 is "<<sqrt(100.0)<< "\n";
```

```
cout <<"10 to the power of 5 is "<<pow(10,5)<< "\n";

}
```

The return value of each of the three functions is displayed directly on screen by three separate cout statements.

You can display a combination of constants, data types, and expression values in a cout statement, provided that each unique item is separated by the insertion operator (<<).

```
#include <iostream>

using namespace std;

#include <cmath>

void main(void)

{

    cout <<"The absolute value of -55 is "<<abs(-55)<< "\n";

    cout <<"The square root of 100 is "<<sqrt(100.0)<< "\n";

    cout <<"10 to the power of 5 is "<<pow(10,5)<< "\n";

}
```

In the first cout statement, the first value displayed is a constant string.

Then the return value of the math library function abs() is displayed through a call to the function.

```cpp
#include <iostream>

using namespace std;

#include <cmath>

void main(void)

{

    cout <<"The absolute value of -55 is "<<abs(-55)<< "\n";

    cout <<"The square root of 100 is "<<sqrt(100.0)<< "\n";

    cout <<"10 to the power of 5 is "<<pow(10,5)<< "\n";

}
```

The abs() function calculates the absolute value of the integer passed as its function parameter. And the function returns a value of type int.

In this example the argument is a constant, instead of a variable of type int.

```cpp
#include <iostream>

using namespace std;

#include <cmath>
```

```
void main(void)

{

  cout <<"The absolute value of -55 is "<<abs(-55)<< "\n";

  cout <<"The square root of 100 is "<<sqrt(100.0)<< "\n";

  cout <<"10 to the power of 5 is "<<pow(10,5)<< "\n";

}
```

When the cout statement is executed, the function is called, and the number 55 is displayed on screen.

```
#include <iostream>

using namespace std;

#include <cmath>

void main(void)

{

  cout <<"The absolute value of -55 is "<<abs(-55)<< "\n";

  cout <<"The square root of 100 is "<<sqrt(100.0)<< "\n";

  cout <<"10 to the power of 5 is "<<pow(10,5)<< "\n";

}
```

The next two lines of code perform function calls in the same way as the first line.

The function sqrt() accepts a single argument of type double and returns a value of type double.

In this example, the number 10 is displayed on screen.

```cpp
#include <iostream>

using namespace std;

#include <cmath>

void main(void)

{

    cout <<"The absolute value of -55 is "<<abs(-55)<< "\n";

    cout <<"The square root of 100 is "<<sqrt(100.0)<< "\n";

    cout <<"10 to the power of 5 is "<<pow(10,5)<< "\n";

}
```

Note

A domain error occurs if the argument is a negative number.

The library function pow() accepts two arguments of type double and returns a value of type double.

When the cout statement executes, the number 100000 is displayed.

```
#include <iostream>

using namespace std;

#include <cmath>

void main(void)

{

    cout <<"The absolute value of -55 is "<<abs(-55)<< "\n";

    cout <<"The square root of 100 is "<<sqrt(100.0)<< "\n";

    cout <<"10 to the power of 5 is "<<pow(10,5)<< "\n";

}
```

CHAPTER 9:

I/O

I/O basic

I/O basic knowledge

- Neither C++ nor C has built input and output in the language. They use functions(C) or other I/O obje cts (C++) in language library.

- C++ I/O class and head file

1. Iofs stand for three head files <iostream> <fstream> and <sstream>. <iostream> includes <ios> automatically. They are three main header file you should include in your C++ application.

2. Classes: iostream(streambuf), fstream(filebuf), stringstream(stringbuf) and four pre-defined object: cin, cout, clog and cerr

3. Clog is just like cerr, but it buffer its output.

4. C++ normally flushes the input buffer when you press enter. For output to the display, C++ program normally flushes the output buffer when you transmit a newline character, or reaches an input statement.

5. >> And << don't need to format string, C++ will automatically, convert it, it's better than printf and scanf in C language.

6. Through inheritance, fstream and cin(cout) share the same usage. All the knowledge can be used directly in fstream. I like it the most.

Input

Input basic knowledge

- For Input, you need to master one basic idea, two languages, and three data type.

- One basic idea: In order to make continuously input, you need to use while(inputMethod), When two things happens:

1. User want to end input(ctrl+D) or read the end of File;

2. Read fail (for example, cin>> int, but input letter 'a'),

InputMethod will return false. Then you need to use some flag or status to tell the difference between EOF and error inside of while loop.

- Two languages is c and c++, they use the different inputMethod. three data types are: number and word(no space in middle), character(white), and string(include space in middle)

- Two languages common used input method

- Number and non-white character word Character (including white-character) string(line)

C   scanf("%d %f %c %s",&i, &f,&c);   int   a   =   getchar();
fgets(stdin, char*p, n)

C++   cin>>i>>f>>c>>w; cin.get(char & c);

Ch = cin.get(); cin.get(char *p, n);

cin.getline(char *p, n);

getline(cin, string);

- In scanf, you need to specify exact data type when you read.
1. H: short int or short unsigned. Example: %hd or %hu.
2. I: a long int or long unsigned, or double (for %f conversions.) Example: %ld, %lu, or %lf.
3. L: The value to be parsed is a long for integer types or long double for float types. Example: %Ld, %Lu, or %Lf.
4. *: Tells scanf() do to the conversion specified, but not store it anywhere. This is what you use if you want scanf() to eat some data, but you don't want to store it anywhere; you don't give scanf() an argument for this conversion. Example: %*d.

- Scanf("%c" &c) will read any character, including whitespace character. If you want to scanf skip any whitespace, you can use space before %c.
1. While(true){
2. Scanf("%c",&c);
3. //scanf(" %c",&c);

4. Printf("you ␣ input: ␣%d" c);

5. }

Output:

When you input a(enter), output will be like you input: 97(a value) you input: 10(enter value)

- cin>>c will not read white character(tab, space , newline), If you want to read them from input buffer, You should use getchar() or cin.get(); If you want the user to input his or her name.

1. While(true){

2. Cin>>c;

3. Cout<<"you ␣ input:"<<c<<endl;

4. }

Output:

When you input " a(enter)" output will be like:you input: a. then cursor wait for here.

- Using cin>> or scanf will terminate the string after it reads the first space. The best way to handle this situation is to use the function to read a line;

- Read word and line:

1. Scanf(%s,char_array) //c

2. Cin>>char_array or ; //c++

3. Cin>> str;

4. //line

5. Gets(char_array) //c

6. Fgets(char_array, n , FILE *)

7. Cin.getline(char * ,int n)

8. Cin.get(char * ,int n)

9. Std::getline(istream& is, string& str)

Line 1: Read a word until reach white character.

Line 7: Recommend to use this for safety.

Line 9: C++ read and discard newline

Line 1: Not read newline

- Cin.read function has the same interface with cin.get, but it doesn't append a null character to input, It's not intend for keyboard input, but for binary format of file
- For C++, three get, two getline, other use >>;
- Difference between cin.get(char) and int = cin.get()

1. while(cin.get(c))

2. // use cin.get(char) in reading loop

3. cin.get() != '\n'

4. //use cin.get() return character to test sth.

5. cin.get()!= EOF

Line 7: When used in EOF, you have to use int. because EOF may not be expressed by char type

- Confused functions: cin.get and cin.getline are almost the same things.

Cin.get (char* s, streamsize n, char delim);

Cin.getline (char* s, streamsize n, char delim);

Istream& getline (istream& is, string& str);

1. For each line, if you don't know the max length, just use getline(cin, string). You don't need to input any length. (you can reserve length of string if you want to avoid allocation of memory)

2. cin.get() doesn't discard delim from input stream. However, cin.getline() will read and discard newline. (It's easy for you to remember, because, line is defined by newline character)

3. In cin.getline(char* s, int n) The failbit flag is set if the function extracts no characters(newline is a character), Or if the delimiting character is not found once (n-1) characters have already been written to s. Note that if the character that follows those (n-1) characters in the input sequence is precisely the delimiting character, it is also extracted and the failbit flag is not set.

4. In.cin.get(char* s , int n). The failbit flag is set only if the function extracts no characters.

5. cin.get(char* s, n) is more flexible than cin.getline. Because when it read to the array is full, It doesn't set failbit. At this time you can use gcount() or peek() to see if the next character is a new line. It's more customized than cin.getline();

Input Pattern

- It is a bad idea to test the stream on the outside and then read/write to it inside the body of the conditional/loop statement. This is because the act of reading may make the stream bad. It is usually better to do the read as part of the test.

while(!cin.fail()){ // that is bad programming style

cin>>i; //here may make stream fail().

..... //then i is not valid value

}

- If you just want to input, you don't want to know eof or deal with failbit. You can use below:

while(scanf("%d",&i) != 1)

while((int c = getchar())!=EOF)

while(fgets(line, sizeof(line), fp) != NULL)

//in c language, use these to exit loop!

while(cin>>input)

while(cin.get(p, 20))

while(getline(ifstream, string)) {

//in C++ language, use bool operator to exit loop.

//do some useful things. //input is right.

}

- If you want to know eof or deal with the error. You can use the below code. When you press enter, the read will end. When you input letter, it will get rid of this letter until you input number.
1. while(true) //use break to exit loop;
2. {
3.   cin>>i//or getline(ifstream, string);
4.   If(cin.eof()){ //If it's EOF
5.   cout<<"EOF ⌴ encountered"<<endl
6.   //break;
7.   }
8. If(cin.fail()) //deal with Invalide input
9. {
10. cin.clear(); //Important. clear state and buffer
11. while(cin.get()!='\n') //get rid rest of line,

12. continue ;

13. cout<<"please␣input␣a␣number"<<endl;

14. continue;

15. }

16. // input is right.do some useful things.

17. }

- In the previous example, why do we need to distinguish eof and fail? When fail happen, maybe there are invalid character in buffer. After clean the buffer, I can continue to read input from input buffer. Three methods to clean invalid character in the buffer.

```
cin.clear();    //Important. clear state and buffer
```

```
while(cin.get()!='\n')
```

```
continue ;      // method 1
```

```
while(!issapce(cin.get()))
```

```
continue; //method 2
```

```
basic_istream& ignore(streamsize _Count = 1, \
```

```
int_type _Delim = traits_type::eof()); //method 3
```

```
cin.ignore(5, 'a');
```

```
cin.ignore(numeric_limits<streamsize>::max(), '\n');
```

- You can use istream_iterator, It can save you some trouble to judge EOF.

1. Class A{

2. Private:

3. Int x,y;

4. Friend istream& operator>>(istream& in, A&);

5. Friend ostream& operator<<(ostream& in, const A&);

6. };

7. istream& operator>>(istream& in, A& a){

8. In>>a.x>>a.y;

9. return in;

10. }

11. Ostream& operator<<(ostream& out, const A& a){

12. Out<<a.x<< " ␣ " <<a.y;

13. Return out;

14. }

15. Vector<A> v;

16. Copy(istream_iterator<A>(cin), istream_iterator<A>(),

17. Back_inserter(v));

18. Copy(v.begin(), v.end(),ostream_iterator<A>(cout, "\n"));

- In summary, its better just use judgment to exit end loop. If you need to different specific action to take to deal with EOF or error. Use while(true), then use eof() of feof() fail() or clear() functions in c++ and c to deal with and break the loop;

- For cout, It can recognize type automatically, and It is extensible, you can redefine << operator so that cout can recognize you data type.
1. Class Foo{
2. Friend ostream & operator<<(ostream& s,const Foo &r);
1. 3.}
3. Ostream & operator<<(ostream& s, const Foo &r){
2. 6. S<<Foo.a<<Foo.b<<endl;
3. 7.}

- How to print pointer address in C and C++?

char* amount = "dozen";

cout<< amount ; //print "dozen" string

cout<<(void*) amount;//prints the address of pointer

printf("%p", (void*) p);

- Format is key point for Output. You need to know the common manipulator to control the output format.
- Number base manipulators: hex, oct and dec; Field widths: Width, fill, precision Setf()
- You don't need to know the details, just name of them. When you want to use them, go to reference website to look.

A detail format manipulators can be seen on C++ primer P1090. You need to include <iomanip>

- << is a bitwise left-shift operator in C language, but in C++, we overloaded it in ostream class, cout is an object of ostream,

- You can use cout<<flush to force flushing the output buffer

- cout.write can be used to output a string; It will output certain length string, even reach the end of string.

Other stream

File

- When you studied cin and cout very well, you will find that file operation is so easy. Just change cin or cout to your ifstream , ofstream or fstream object.

std::fstream ifs;

ifs.open ("test.txt", ios_base::in | ios_base::binary);

if(!ifs.is_open())

   exit(1);

char c = ifs.get();

// use all previous input methods

ifs.close();

- Only read ifsteam; only write ofsteam; write and read fstream.
- For ios_base::binary mode, use write() and read() function.
- For writing, pay attention to the difference between ios_base:: trunc and ios_base:: app
- Random access is used mostly on binary file. Because the position can be pinpointed exactly. For seekg() for input, and seekp() for output.(p is put, g is get) It moves the pointer. tellp() and tellg() function. It tells the position of pointer.

Buffer and string buffer

- Stringstream is a convenient way to manipulate strings like an independent I/O device. Sometimes it is very convenient to use stringstream to convert between strings and other numerical types. The usage of stringstream are much the same with iostream, so it is not a burden to learn.
- You need to build a stringstream from a string, or convert a stringstream back to a string.

1. stringstream outstr;
2. outstr<<"salary ⎵ value"<<123333.00<<endl;
3. string str = outstr.str() //change to string
4. istringstream Instr(str);

5. while(instr>>number)

6. cout<<number<<endl

7. char sentence []="Yan ⌣ is ⌣ 41 ⌣ years ⌣ old";

8. char str [20];

9. int i;

10. sscanf (sentence,"%s ⌣ %*s ⌣ %d", str, &i);

11. sprintf(...);

Line 1 to 3: Change number to a text.

Line 5 to 7: Change text to a number.

Line 9 to end: C language method. In line 12, you can see "*s", it means input will be ignored. So str = Yan, i = 41.

Manipulate stream

1. Peek return the next character from input without extracting from the input stream. For example, you want to read input up to the first newline or period.

char input[80];

int i = 0;

while((ch=cin.peek()) != '.' && ch != '\n')

  cin.get(input[i++];)

input[i] = '\0';

2. Gcount() method returns the number of characters read by the last unformatted extraction method. That means character read by the a get(), getline(), ignore(), or read(), but not extraction operator.

3. Putback() function inserts a character back in the input buffer.

CHAPTER 10

Memory and Resources

Memory Management

C++ programming language provides a lot of options to users when it comes to managing the memory used by an executing program. In this chapter, we shall be exploring some of these frequently used options. We would also introduce some modern techniques aimed at reducing the memory management problems that have plagued C++ projects in the past.

Memory Available to C++ Programs

Modern operating systems usually reserve a section of its memory for executing a program that allows the operating system to manage multiple program executions simultaneously. There are different operating systems which layout the memory of executing the program in different ways. However, the layout would include the following four sections.

- Code: The program's compiled executable instructions are held in the code section memory. While the program executes, the contents of the code section should never change. Also, during the program's executions, the code segment does not change as well.

- Data: Persistent variables and global variables are held in the data section of the memory as in static locals. Throughout the life span of the executing program is the variables of the data would exist. However, unless the data is a constant, the executing program may freely change their values. Although the values stored in the variables found in the data segment may change during the program's execution, the size of the data segment wouldn't change while the program is executing. It is so because the program's source code precisely defines the numbers of global and static local variables. It is also possible for the compiler to compute the exact size of the data segment.

- Heap: The section where the executing program obtains dynamic memory is called the heap. Using the new operator gets the memory from the heap, and the delete operator returns the previously allocated memory back to the heap. The size of the heap shrinks and fries during the program's execution as the program deallocates and allocates dynamic memory using the delete and new.

- Stack: Function parameters and local variables are always stored in the stack. Function parameters and local variables disappear when the function returns and appears when a function is called. The size of the stack also shrinks and grows during the program's execution as various functions execute.

Generally, operating systems limit the size of the stack. Deep recursion can consume a considerable amount of stack space. For example, let's consider an improperly written recursive function of one that omits the base case and thus exhibits an "infinite" recursion that would consume all the space that is available on the stack. A situation such as this is known as a stack overflow. Modern operating systems terminate any process that consumes a lot of the stack space. However, on some embedded systems, this stack overflow may go undetected. Typically, heap space is plentiful, and operating systems can use virtual memory to provide more space than it's available in real memory for an executing program. The extra space for the virtual memory comes from a disk drive, and the operating system shuttles data from the disk to real memory as needed by the executing program. Programs that make use of a virtual memory run a lot more slowly than programs that make use of little virtual memory.

Manual Memory Management

Frequent memory management issues with delete and new are the majorly difficult to find and fix the source of the logic error. Programmers have to adhere strictly to the following tenets:

- Everything you call new, it should always have an associated call to delete provided the allocated memory isn't longer needed. It may sound simple, but it isn't always clear when delete should be used, but the function below shows a memory leak:

```
void calc(int n) {

// ...

// Do some stuff

// ...

int *x = new int[n];

// ...

// Do some stuff with x

// ...

// Exit function without deleting x's memory

}
```

Provided a program calls on the calc function enough times, the program will eventually run out of memory. In the calc function, x is a local variable. In that light, x lives on the stack. So when a user uses a particular call to calc completes, the function's clean up code automatically releases the space helped by the variable x. Because all functions automatically manage the memory for their local and parameter variables. The problem with x is assigned via new to point to memory allocated from the heap and not the stack. Function executions manage to which x pointed is no deallocated automatically.

- Then operator delete should never be used to free up memory that has not been allocated from its previous call to new. The code fragment below illustrates one such example:

int list[10], *x = list; // x points to list

// ...

// Do some stuff

// ... delete [ ] x; // Logic error, attempt to deallocate x's memory

The space references by the pointer x were not allocated by the operator new, so the operator delete should not be used to attempt to free the memory. When you attempt to delete a memory that is not allocated with new, it results in an undefined behavior that proves a logic error.

- The operator delete must not be used to deallocate the same memory more than once. This case is common when two pointers refer to the same memory. Pointers like this are called aliases. The following code fragment below illustrates this situation better:

int *p = new int[10], *y = x; // y aliases x

// ...

// Do some stuff with x and/or y

// ...

delete [ ] x; // Free up x's memory

// ...

// Do some other stuff

// ...

delete [ ] y; // Logic error, y's memory already freed!

Since the pointer x and pointer y point to the same memory, then x and y are aliases of each other. If you deallocate a memory that is referenced by one of them, then the other memory is also deallocated since it is the same memory.

- When you deallocating previous memory with delete, they should never accessed. When you attempt to access deleted memory result, it would result in an undefined behaviors which represent a logical error.

int *list = new int[10];

// ... // Use list, then

// ... delete [ ] list;

// Deallocate list's memory

// ... // Sometime later

// ... int x = list[2]; // Logic error, but sometimes works!

The code fragment above illustrates how such a situation could arise. For the purpose of efficiency, the delete operator makes heap space as available without modifying the contents in the memory.

Resource Management

It is essential that programmers call clear internationally when they finish with a linked list object. Take a look at the following definition:

void x() {

IntList1 my_list; // Constructor called here

// Add some numbers to the list

my_list.insert(12);

my_list.insert(7);

my_list.insert(-14);

// Print the list

my_list.print();

} // Oops! Forgot to call my list.clear!

In the code above, the variable my list is local to function x. When the function x finishes executing the variable my list, it will go out of scope. At this stage, the space on the stack-allocated for the local IntList1 variable named my list is reclaimed. Although the list's head-allocated elements space remains, the only access the program can have to the memory is through my list.head, but my list no longer exists. This is a classic example of a memory leak. Observe that none of the classes we have designed so gat apart from the IntList1 have this problem. However, C++ offers a way out for class designers to specify actions that have to occur at the end of an object's lifespan. A constructor that executes a code at the beginning of an object's existence is known as a destructor. A destructor is a special method that executes immediately before the object stops existing. A destructor can also have the same name as its class with a tilde ~ prefix. Additionally, a destructor does not accept arguments. Code 9.2 shows how to add a destructor to a code and also ass the previously suggested optimization of the length and clear methods.

Code 9.2

```
// Code9.2

class Code9.2 {

// The nested private Node class from before

struct Node {

int data; // A data element of the list
```

Node *next; // The node that follows this one in the list

Node(int d); // Constructor

};

Node *head; // Points to the first item in the list

Node *tail; // Points to the last item in the list

int len; // The number of elements in the list

public:

// The constructor makes an initially empty list

IntList2();

// The destructor that reclaims the list's memory

~Code9.2(); // Inserts n onto the back of the list.

void insert(int n);

// Prints the contents of the linked list of integers.

void print() const;

// Returns the length of the linked list.

int length() const;

// Removes all the elements in the linked list.

```
void clear();

};
```

Conclusion

After taking you on a guide on ten of the must-know topics in C++, it is left to you now to develop your skills. And one thing with languages, be in English, French, or programming languages, practice makes perfect. The knowledge we've thought you in this book can be likened to learning the alphabet and some basic words in English. So, we'd advise you to practice with it more. Focus your mind on understanding why we use some statements; the result we want to obtain.

Go online, download all the necessary application that you find easy to work with, and if you'd have to pay for it, purchase it. And when you have everything all set and ready, pick up a project and learn. You could build your own little project, or you could pick an already made project and try to replicate it. If you ever get stuck anywhere, you can always go back, and view and the programmer made the project and proceeded. But always try to push yourself to your limit, think deep about it before checking.

It would also help you a great deal to pick up other really good books to get different perceptions about a section in C++ to broaden your understanding of it. Even though we can assure you of the quality of this book is sufficient to set you on the right path to becoming a success in C++, we would recommend you also read out other books on the programming language.

Also, you could consider picking a different language other than C++ to learn side by side with C++. Leaning a new language is an efficient way to get a more in-depth understanding of C++. A new language brings in better comprehension of the programming language in general. It also broadens your mentality of solving problems, which brings out the specificities of the main C++ language. And even though you may not use this new language codes in C++, it would expose you to proven ideas that you can transpose into C++. A programming language we would advise you to study alongside C++ is Haskell. You can also study Java because it is way closer to our everyday English than C++, and it would be easier for you to understand. You can also check out our book on Java.

Additionally, always try to stay up to date. Catch up with the modern C++ features like C++11, C++14, C++ 17, and a host of other new features in the standard library. Some of its latest features, like lambdas, is easy to grasp. All you need is a good resource and time, and in no time, you'd see yourself becoming a master in them. And so, why not take a cup of tea, find a nice relaxing spot where you find it easier to focus and get started. And just like the famous saying goes, "a journey of a thousand miles begins with a step." So, take that step today, and let us be that guild that will set you on the right path.

CYBERSECURITY

LEARN INFORMATION TECHNOLOGY SECURITY: HOW TO PROTECT YOUR ELECTRONIC DATA FROM HACKER ATTACKS WHILE YOU ARE BROWSING THE INTERNET WITH YOUR SMART DEVICES, PC OR TELEVISION

ALAN GRID

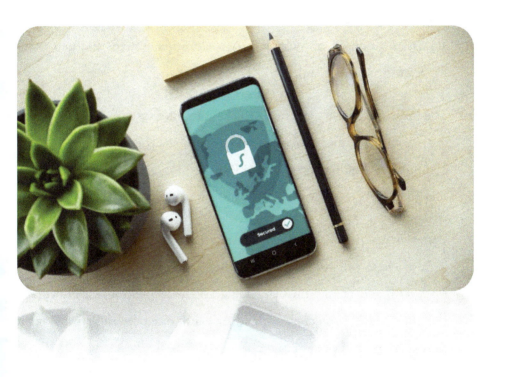

Introduction

Computer technology has evolved in unimaginable sophistication and innovation ever since its inception. The majority of the advancements, reach, and the power of the internet has aided the popularity of information technology. Today, almost any industry or individual uses computer systems and networks for some purpose or another.

The measures that are taken to protect computer systems, networks and devices against cyber-attacks are categorized as cybersecurity. Although computer technology has evolved leaps and bounds, the same can't be said about cybersecurity.

Cyber-attacks have become increasingly complex and deceptive, with highly skilled cyber-criminals dedicating enormous amounts of time, resources, and energy into launching serious cyber-attacks. However, the means for protecting individuals and organizations from such attacks have been slow to catch up.

Various security measures are discussed at length, including the proper use of passwords and PINs, creating routine back-ups, practicing caution when connecting to public networks, and much more. The discussion also includes how to put those countermeasures into effect without affecting one's lifestyle, productivity, and budget.

The internet has changed the way companies do business. Computers and networks have changed many processes of businesses from manufacturing, operations, communications to finance, distribution, marketing, and customer service. It is common to find the presence of the use of computer systems and the internet in almost all processes related to businesses in one way or another.

The advancements in computer technology, cheaper hardware, and the popularity of the internet have paved the way for the next big thing in technology: The Internet of Things. Objects that used to be "dumb" and needed human intervention have been made "smart" by giving such objects the ability to collect and transmit data and respond to remote commands. The Internet of Things is predicted to continue to grow rapidly while changing the daily lives of humans and the operations of businesses. IoT devices connect to the internet to perform their duties. As a result, they have been targeted by cyber-attacks with varying motives. The fact that IoT is a relatively novel technology means that IoT devices are yet to be equipped with cybersecurity measures that computers feature. Furthermore, IoT devices are used to carry out demanding duties, including access control and aiding in healthcare.

What is Cyber Security?

The protection of a computer system or network from the adverse effects such as theft or damages to the computer hardware, Software, data, or the services provided by those elements is known as cybersecurity. Cybersecurity is also known as Computer Security and IT

Security (Information Technology Security). The field of cybersecurity has fast evolved over the years due to the rapid increase in the use and reliance on the internet, computers, and wireless networks. The use of devices that are also prone to cyber-attacks such as smart mobile phones, smart televisions, and devices falling under the category of the "Internet of Things" (IoT) has also contributed to the need for the rapid evolution of cybersecurity. The technology and politics that surround the use of the internet, computers, networks, and smart devices are complex that pose many challenges to the world of cybersecurity.

Due to the fast-changing nature of technology and other factors, cybersecurity is always evolving. Cybersecurity approaches, tools, risk management methods, technologies, best practices, and training are always changing as a result. Threats to cybersecurity also advance with the evolution of technology and the use of devices, Software, and networks that are prone to those threats. Many organizations and even individuals put high levels of emphasis on cybersecurity to protect their valuable hardware, Software, data, services, and organizational objectives.

Cybersecurity has been a huge focus for businesses due to the risk of data breaches that can cripple them in many ways. Such breaches often lead to the loss of highly sensitive data that costs companies their revenues, competitive advantage, reputation, and consumer trust. A data breach is estimated to cost a company around $3.6 million, making cybersecurity a high priority for any business.

Cyber Attacks and Vulnerabilities

A weakness in the design, implementation, internal control, or the operations of a computer, hardware, smart device, Software, or a network results in the exposure to cyber-attacks. The Common Vulnerabilities and Exposures is a database that documents such known vulnerabilities to cyber threats. At least one active attack or an exploit that exists is called an exploitable vulnerability. Various manual and automated tools are used to identify vulnerabilities to cyber-attacks.

When it comes to computers and networks, attacks largely attempt to expose, disable, alter, steal, destroy, or gain access to the use of assets. Any such offensive maneuver that tries to target computer systems, networks, infrastructures, and personal devices can be called a cyber-attack. A cyber-attack can be carried out by an individual or a group with malicious intent putting hardware, data, and functionalities at risk.

Cyber-attacks can be categorized as cyber warfare or cyberterrorism, depending on the nature of the attack and its threat. Furthermore, cyber-attacks can be carried out by various societies and sovereign states operating in anonymity. During a cyberattack, susceptible systems and devices are hacked into while achieving the malicious intents of the attacker or the attackers. The scale of a cyberattack may also vary from a single computer, device, individual, or company is the primary target to infrastructures of entire nations.

Information Security Culture

The behavior of employees plays a key role in establishing cybersecurity in companies. Changes and improvements of a company's culture and practices can help employees effectively work towards achieving information security. Employees sometimes do not realize that they are an integral part of a company's effort towards achieving satisfactory levels of cybersecurity. Their actions may sometimes not align with the cybersecurity goals of a company as a result.

A company should continuously make improvements to its information security culture while making sure that employees understand the role they need to play. The process is never-ending with an ongoing cycle of change, evaluation, and maintenance. The five steps involved in managing a company's information security culture are pre-evaluation, strategic planning, operative planning, implementing, and post-evaluation.

Pre-evaluation brings awareness regarding the company's current information security culture and policy while highlighting behavior that might make it vulnerable against cyber threats. The next step in the process, which is strategic planning, then creates a program towards increasing awareness with a clear target to achieve as a company. Operative planning involves working towards a better culture by improving internal communication, security awareness, and training.

Implementing is a step that consists of four phases, which are the commitment of management, communication with employees, providing courses for employees, and the commitment of the employees. Managers first commit to implementing better information security practices within the company and then communicates the company's intentions to the employees. Then the employees are provided with education and training regarding information security.

Finally, the employees of the company committed to bringing about an improved and satisfactory information security culture. The final step, which is Post-Evaluation, assesses how well the planning and implementation went and identifies any areas that remain to be unresolved.

Systems That Are Vulnerable to Cyber-Attacks

The number of individuals, businesses, and organizations relying on computer systems has grown rapidly. It has resulted in increasing the number of systems that are at risk of cyber-attacks. Such vulnerable entities are scattered across various industries, with almost all industries out there being vulnerable at different levels.

Financial Systems

Computer systems belonging to financial institutions and regulators have a high risk of being targeted by hackers. The U.S. Securities and Exchange Commission, investment banks, and commercial banks are prime targets of hackers seeking illicit gains and market manipulation. Furthermore, any website or mobile application that store or accept credit card numbers, bank account information, and brokerage accounts are also under the risk of being hacked.

Hackers and hacker groups take a high interest in attacking the networks and websites of such institutions since they can enjoy immediate financial spoils by making purchases, transferring money, and selling acquired data to interested parties in the black market. ATMs and in-store payment systems have also been targeted by hackers who aim to gather customer PIN codes and account details.

Dark Web

The dark web sounds scary and almost sends shivers down the spine of most people. The dark web is well-known for harboring illegal activity that lots of people don't want to engage in. The question starts spinning in our heads that if the dark web is a place for illegal activity, then why does it exist in the first place and who allows it to run without any kind of restrictions. Is there any purpose behind the existence and flourishing of the dark web, or is the place being handled by a strong bunch of lot? There are three major parts of the internet known as the deep web, surface web, and dark web. Let me discuss each type individually and in detail.

The surface web consists of around ten percent of the entire internet, and it includes things such as Google and other search engines. You can use keywords to search for different things to read, sell, or buy. Then comes the deep web that is the place where you can store the information that is unavailable to most users. This includes things that you have protected by a password such as a bank account subscription services as well as certain medical information. A majority of the webspace consists of this type of information. The third spot belongs to the dark web that is not accessible by a standard internet user. You cannot access this webspace through Firefox, Opera, and Google Chrome, and it can have any kind of information. The word dark is attributed to this web space because of its limited accessibility.

You might be wondering if the dark web is completely illegal for a common user. Thankfully, the answer is no. Mere entering the dark web doesn't count as an illegal activity, but what you do in the dark web can be categorized as legal or illegal. You can access the dark web through Tor anonymous browser. You can download it just like Google Chrome and Firefox. The difference is that it works in a different manner. You have to travel through different overlay networks when you are using Tor or The Onion Router. Just like an onion, it has a number of layers to pass through. The speed of Tor is usually slower than other browsers. If you can get your hands on a Virtual Private Network, it is better to ensure maximum security.

To clear the longstanding confusion, Tor is not a dark web but a tool to access the dark web. Also, Tor can be used to access general webspace such as Google and Yahoo, and your travel through the surface web will be more secure. Rather than a place for illegal activities, the dark web is considered as a place for a high level of online privacy. You can buy illegal drugs through on the dark web and get them delivered to your postal address without giving anyone a hint to what was in the package. The ultimate objective to achieve by using dark web depends on what you need, whether you are ready to take the risk of committing an illegal act.

Residents of countries such as Iran where the government control over the internet is touching extreme levels, the dark web becomes a necessity. Residents from these countries access Facebook and Twitter through the dark web. They log into their onion versions that have been officially launched for users who are subjected to censorship.

CHAPTER 1:

Common Cyberattacks

C yberattacks are getting highly sophisticated as hackers are coming up with the latest and innovative methods to stage an attack and threaten the security of different computer networks. The attacks are getting so much sophisticated that they are getting tougher to detect. Consequently, the attacks are getting more lethal than they were ever before. Cybersecurity doesn't depend on the size of your organization. Whether you have a start-up business or a multimillion-dollar company, you should be able to be aware of how risky a cyberattack can be. The rise of cyberattacks gives room to the question of why do hackers attack a cyberspace? What is the motivation behind such heinous attacks? A general perception is that financial gain drives them to stage high profile cyberattacks on the computer systems of big corporations. Some also do that for espionage purposes. This chapter will shed light on the motivations that hackers have on their backs to penetrate an individual computer or an enterprise computer. Most of the time, the attack is a kind of breach that aims at infiltrating the credit and debit card details. This information is then sold on the dark web later on to bag heavy profit. The story doesn't end here. In a majority of cases, profit is just a smokescreen to hide something bigger and deeper.

Espionage is also linked to a breach of data of a corporation or an official website of a country. These kinds of attacks typically are aimed at retrieving information from the victim. There are lots of things that remain the same when it comes to espionage through a cyberattack, including monitoring of communication running on the cyberspace. There is another popular technique in espionage known as stealing secrets. Earlier on, this task came into the domain of individuals who physically penetrated the space and compromised certain assets that are found inside the organization. To give you a taste of how it all happened, I'll state an example from Hollywood. If you are a fan of Tom Cruise and his spy thrillers, you might for sure be acquainted with the character of Ethan, who was always on some kind of mission to infiltrate a facility and steal some important documents that could turn the tables on the bad guys. Spy is the word that they use for such kind of person. Nowadays, things are different. There is hardly anything left in the physical domain. The craft of stealing an important bunch of information is more about being electric. Computers have the capacity to consume billions of files that were once stored in the company's ledgers and on loads of papers.

Espionage

Espionage attacks are getting more sophisticated nowadays. Most of them are state-sponsored or are financed by the corporate sector. Some professional groups act as independent contractors to spy for profit. Espionage is considered as a secretive activity in which attackers formulate a plan to avoid detection and achieve their objectives of collecting important information about the targeted company or individual. Spies are the most persistent attackers who keep on working until they achieve their objective. They keep on trying a number of techniques until they accomplish their mission. Even if they are detected, they don't stop their activities and go on until the completion of the mission.

In most cases, the initial worker is indirect, such as a trusted third-party in the form of an employee who has access to the computer system you want to target. Once the attacker has access inside the system, he will have to move through the systems of the organization and also make his way to the data stores of the company. If you are running a financial consultancy firm, the most important data should be informed about your company's clients. Once the attacker has access to the documents, he will be in a position to blackmail you.

Profit

The second most common motivation of a hacker is financial gains. They aim at making heavy profits by the attack. The methods of profit-driven attackers vary. Usually, if the data stolen pertains to credit card and debit card details, it is understood that the objective of the cybercrime is financial gain. The information cybercriminals steal afterward sold on the dark web to make a hefty profit. This is the greatest motivator in today's world in which locating the net worth of everyone is so easy. The transparency in financial transactions and details makes money as the single most important objective of a cyberattack. Everyone needs money, and no shortage of cybercriminals wouldn't hesitate to share a pie from the money.

Different hackers use different types of methods that lead to some monetary gain. Cybercriminals use a wide range of methods using financial malware such as Dridex, Shifu, Carbanak, and Rovnix to siphon off loads of swag from the bank accounts of the victim. Another method to rob victims is to by using ransomware such as Tesla. Denial of service attacks (DDoS) is another profit-motivated attack that has become pretty top-notch in popularity over the past years.

Whether you are the owner of a consultancy firm or a retailer of clothes, you are at a high risk of a serious cyber threat if you conduct your transactions online. They are always after user and financial details that could lead him to the source of your finances as well as your customers' finances. If they loot you, you are devastated because you will not have precious capital to hold grounds. If they loot your customers, you will lose your hard-earned reputation in the market that is equally devastating for your business. In both ways, you are at great risk of losing your business. Attackers, at the height of rage, can use a malware that can target your point of sale (POS) systems.

Sometimes, profit alone is the sole objective of an attacker. For example, your company has secured a contract from the Pentagon to produce sophisticated weapons, and you are on your way to producing them. Hackers can target your company's database to compromise sensitive information that can be of strategic and police use of the attacker. The attacker can be a country that needs this strategic information to update her defense assets. It can be used by politicians to shape up their political campaigns. The chances are high that the state sponsors this kind of attack. Usually, states conduct this kind of classified mission through state-backed resources, but sometimes lack of resources can come in their way, and they have to outsource this kind of mission to experts. Let's take a look at the most breached industries across the world. Virtually all business is at a considerable risk of a cyberattack, but some industries seem to be more vulnerable to these cyberattacks than the rest of the lot. The type of data that these companies hold makes them more vulnerable to cyberattacks. The very first industry on the line is the health industry.

Health

The health sector tops the list of cyberattacks in the United States, and there are some valid reasons for that. The health sector carries personal information such as names, addresses, information about the income of people, social security numbers, and email IDs. Hackers break into the databases at hospitals and access this information to exploit it later on. Their mode of attack is to gain a kind of unauthorized access to medical programs and an effort to get prescription drugs. Most of the threat has its origins inside the organization while some of the attacks are due to some kind of human error such as leakage of information about a patient by an employee of the hospital. The employee might not have suspected that the information could be manipulated by an individual or an organization.

Public Sector

The second vulnerable sector is public administration. Public administration, such as government departments carry details about the employees, such as names, addresses, bank account numbers, and other personal information that can be compromised and misused if it comes in the hands of bad guys.

Another reason why hackers highly target the public sector is that it suffers from a lack of funding in the cybersecurity realm that makes it weak and a potential target of cybercriminals. Personal information of high-ups and confidential information is at the top of the list of a hacker's to-do chart. Confidential information can be sold on the dark web for a heavy price. It can also be sold to a state for bigger profits.

Financial Sector

The financial sector is another field that is most vulnerable to cyberattacks. Hackers relish at the personal information of the owners of hefty bank accounts. In addition, they can lay their hands on the credit card information of the clients of a finance firm.

Food Sector

The food industry is also in the line of industries that can be at great risk of cyberattacks. These businesses are quite vulnerable to certain breaches because they are always collecting credit card details of their customers, and their names and addresses.

Once stolen, a hacker can use this precious information to steal the identity of a customer and gain unauthorized access to bank accounts.

CHAPTER 2:

Cybersecurity

Types of Cybersecurity

Does it seem that everything now depends on computers as well as the internet? Entertainment, communication, transportation, medicine, shopping, etc. Even banking institutions operate the company online of theirs.

The realization that many the planet is dependent on the internet should encourage us to challenge ourselves.

- Simply just how much of the lifetime of mine is driven by the net?

- Simply just how much of the private info of mine is stored on the web?

- Simply just how much of the company of mine is accessible over networks?

- Simply just how much of my customers' information is accessible over networks?

With these a remarkable dependence on computer systems, neglecting the possibility of cybercrime in the company of yours is incredibly risky & likely bad for you, your business, your employees, together with the buyers of yours.

Without a feeling of security, the company of yours is operating at extremely high risk for cyber-attacks.

Below are numerous kinds of cybersecurity you need to become mindful of. This could help you construct a good foundation for an excellent security strategy.

1. Critical infrastructure security

Important infrastructure safety includes the cyber-physical methods which fashionable societies rely on.

Common examples of essential infrastructure:

- Power grid

- Drinking h2o purification

- Site visitors' lights

Going shopping centers hospitals having the infrastructure of an energy grid on the internet leads to it being prone to cyber-attacks.

Companies with responsibility for any essential infrastructures must do due diligence to realize the vulnerabilities and defend the company of theirs against them. The protection, in addition to the resilience of this essential infrastructure, is crucial to our society's wellbeing and safety.

Companies that are not responsible for the infrastructure that is vital that; however, rely on it for a portion of the company of theirs, should certainly develop a contingency plan by analyzing precisely how an assault on essential infrastructure they rely on might affect them.

2. Application security

You have to choose application protection as among the selection of should have security methods adopted to protect the devices of yours. Software safety uses Software and hardware treatments to tackle outdoors threats, which can form in the development stage of an application.

Apps are a great deal much more accessible over networks, resulting in the adoption of safeguard steps through the development phase to be an imperative stage of the endeavor.

Types of Application security:

Antivirus programs

Firewalls encryption exhibits: These helps to ensure that unauthorized access is stayed away from. Companies likewise could detect extremely vulnerable specifics assets and protect them by certain system security procedures put on these data sets.

3. Network security

As cybersecurity is all about outside threats, community security guards against unauthorized intrusion of the respective inner networks of yours due to malicious goal.

Community security guarantees which internal networks are protected by preserving the infrastructure and inhibiting access to it.

In order to enable you to far better management group security monitoring, security teams currently use machine learning to flag unusual guests, in addition, to alert to threats on time, which is genuine. Network administrators keep on applying policies and procedures to prevent unauthorized access, modification, and exploitation of the system. Common examples of community protection implementation:

- Extra logins

- Revolutionary passwords

- System security

- Antivirus programs

- Antispyware software

- Encryption

- Firewalls Monitored internet access

4. Cloud security

Enhanced cybersecurity is of all the main reasons the cloud is recording over.

Cloud protection is a software program-based protection tool which protects as well as monitors the info in the cloud materials of yours. Cloud providers are continually producing & utilizing brand new security tools to help enterprise users better secure information of theirs. The misconception flying about cloud computing is its less secure compared to standard tactics. People will probably believe that the information of yours is much safer when stored on physical methods as well as the servers you've and influence. Nevertheless, it has been established by cloud security that command does not mean security in addition to accessibility matters a lot more than the physical location of the information of yours. Alert's Logic Cloud Security Report found that on premises environment computer customers experience many more incidents than those of service provider environments.

The statement further finds that

Service provider environment customers experienced an average of 27.8 attacks. Cloud computing security is comparable to conventional on-premise information centers, simply without the time in addition to the expense of maintaining big data facilities, and also, the risk of security breaches is reduced.

4. Internet of things (IoT) security

IoT details several non-critical as well as crucial cyber actual physical strategies, like appliances, sensors, televisions, Wi-Fi routers, printers, and security cameras.

Based upon Bain & Company's prediction

The combined marketplaces of IoT will create approximately 1dolar1 520 billion in 2021; a lot more than double the 1dolar1 235 billion invested in 2017.

IoT's info center, analytics, consumer devices, networks, legacy embedded approaches & connectors will be the primary engineering of the IoT market.

IoT solutions are usually posted a vulnerable state and in addition, provide hardly any to no security patching. This poses unique security challenges for all those users.

5. Information security

This describes the shelter of information and data from theft, unauthorized access, breaches, etc. to uphold user privacy and also quit identity theft.

6. Disaster recovery

This requires preparing and strategizing to enable companies to recuperate from cybersecurity/IT disasters. This requires a risk assessment, analysis, prioritizing, and make catastrophe response in addition to recovery methods ready to go. This allows organizations to recuperate quicker from disasters and lower losses.

7. Website security

This is utilized to stop as well as protect websites from cybersecurity risks on the internet. Alternate website protection plans are planning to discuss the website's information source, applications, source codes, and files. Typically, there carries a frequent rise in the volume of data breaches on websites of the past few years, leading to identity thefts, downtime, financial losses, loss of track record in addition to brand image, etc. The main reason for this goes on to become the misconception amongst website owners that the site of theirs is protected by website hosting provider. So, offering them susceptible to cyber-attacks. A number of the primary key techniques and tools utilized for website security are site checking in addition to malware removal, website plan firewall, application security testing, etc.

8. Endpoint security

This allows organizations to protect the servers of theirs, mobile devices & workstations from remote and local cyber-attacks. Since products on a method are interconnected, it tends to make entry points for threats and vulnerabilities. Endpoint protection effectively secures the device by blocking attempts created accessing these entry points. File integrity monitoring, anti-malware software programs as well as antivirus, etc. Are big methods employed.

Types of Cyber Security tools

1. IBMQRadarAdvisor and Watson

This is undoubtedly the absolute best protection program used by companies. Watson, using artificial intelligence (AI), is self-learning and self-evolving telephone system. Just what it is able to be, prior to actually the chance is detected, it eliminates the section. The operating goes as such: IBM QRadar tracks the place. It gathers information and links online, offline, and within the unit with that code. It formulates a technique to add it next when an event is raised; it eliminates the chance. This is of all the absolute best web incidents? Kill security plans being used.

2. Wireshark

It is among the most popular community analyzer protocol. It assesses the vulnerable regions on the device in which the individual is working. Wireshark can collect or perhaps view the minutes of the info in addition to activities that are going on a product. The incoming and outgoing packets of info along with the protocol that's being employed in the transmission could be viewed. Just what it is able to be captures the lifestyle info and in addition, creates a traditional analysis sheet that should assist in tracking.

3. Cryptostopper

It is among the best tools on the net right now to prevent the ransomware or perhaps malware attacks on merchandise. What crypto stopper does is it finds the bots which are encrypting the documents along with deletes them. It creates a design or perhaps a deception way of the chance to latch it on by itself upon the device, when it latches itself; crypto stopper detects in addition to deletes that code. Cryptostopper makers have an inclination to produce a promise of a nine-second threat detection and also elimination challenge. It isolates the workstation along with the affected areas of the unit so that the ransomware cannot manage to affect progressively more areas.

4. N MAP

It is of all the countless primary and also open source utilities created for community securities. NMAP is not just great with very little but large networks too. It recognizes the hosts and the receiver on a product. Along with it, furthermore, it uses the distributions of operating systems. It's in a position to scan hundreds and thousands of devices on a process in one moment.

5. Burp Suite

It is another web scanning algorithm security program, which allows you to browse online uses. The main reason behind this specific gadget is checking and also penetrate the jeopardized approach. It checks the surfaces which might be influenced along with the sender along with destination's responses as well as requests for the risk. If any threat is found, it's in a position to either be quarantined or might be eliminated.

6. OpenVAS

A utility of Nessus, but fairly unique from Nessus and Metasploit though they do precisely the same, but unique. It is viewed as most likely the most stable, less loophole, and use of web security tools on the net at the next.

You are going to find two primary components of OpenVAS.

Scanner: It experiences the insecure areas as well as directs a compiled report of the majority of it with the supervisor of its.

Manager: It compiles the requests which are obtained from the scanner, and after that, it is able to make a report of all of this type of incidences.

7. Nessus

Nessus is but one additional unit which checks for malicious hackers. It goes through the pcs on the device for unauthorized hackers who try to make use of the info coming from the net. Generally, it is believed that Nessus scans for unauthorized access for 1200 times.

Apart from others, it doesn't make assumptions that distinct ports are simply set for web servers as Port 80 is set for Web Server only.

And also, it is an open-source unit, which provides an insecure patching assistance center, which further helps in giving achievable methods because of the affected areas.

8. Metasploit Framework

Created by Rapid7 in Boston, Massachusetts. It is considered the best open-source framework, which is utilized for checking vulnerabilities. It is a command shell as it works within UNIX; therefore owners are competent to work the hand of theirs along with automobile guidelines to take a look at along with run the scripts. Metasploit Framework has a couple of built-in, too as a few final party interfaces, which could be used to exploit the affected areas.

9. SolarWinds Mail Assure

It is a multi-functional application that addresses the vast majority of the email security issues. It is information from nearly 2 million domains, which is coming from 80 5 nations. It is the same made available as Software as a Service (SAAS). It is able to assist in the defense of the user's applications from spams, viruses, phishing, and malware.

There are plenty of other net protection tools out there that could help in eliminating the opportunity together with the above-mentioned list. They are as follows:

- Aircrack-ng

- Call Manager

- MailControl

CHAPTER 3:

Improving Your Security

Securing a Wireless Network

Therefore, it is crucial for people to learn how to protect their wireless networks to ensure their confidential information does not fall into the wrong hands.

This chapter will give a brief introduction to securing a personal wireless network and how to do it. For most of the examples, NETGEAR routers will be used. If users have a different router, keep in mind that some things will be different.

Encryption

Let us begin by discussing basic encryption. Encryption, when regarding data movement over a network, is the process by which plaintext is converted into a scrambled mixture of characters.

This decreases the probability that the information that was sent over an encrypted network is being used for malicious purposes.

As for encryption regarding wireless routers, it is the process by which an encrypted authentication key is produced every time the correct login credentials are entered, allowing access to the network. In simpler terms, every time a user logs in to a secured router, a unique key is generated, which allows access to that internet connection.

WPA

Wi-Fi Protected Access or WPA is a security tool that was developed to replace WEP security. There are two types: WPA and WPA2. The difference is that WPA2 is a newer, more secure version of WPA. Anytime users have to log in to a wireless network, whether it's at their house or at school, they are most likely, logging into a WPA/WPA2 encrypted network. These security features work by checking whether or not the login credentials entered are accurate, and if they are, an encrypted authentication key unique to that very login is generated. Once this key is generated, it is checked by the corresponding network, allowing the transmission of data to start, assuming the login credentials were a match. Now that we have seen the basics of WPA encryption, we will discuss some basic steps that can be taken to secure personal wireless networks.

Wireless router credentials

When a wireless router is first set up, it is very important that the default login credentials are changed. Most personal wireless routers come with a standard login username and password such as:

Username: admin

Password: password

Hackers know these default login credentials, meaning, it is crucial that they are changed right away. Using a lengthy password with a combination of characters, both upper and lower cases will give users reliably secure credentials.

Service Set Identifier

A Service Set Identifier (SSID) refers to the computer language for the name of a wireless network. For example, the University of Arizona's wireless network is known as 'UAWifi.' It is important to change the name of a personal network from the default, as hackers may target a wireless network with a default name, thinking it is less secure. To further improve security, SSID broadcasting can be turned off. This means that the network will not be visible to outsiders. It will still be there, and if the specific SSID is searched for, it can be found. However, anyone scanning for a network to connect to won't be able to see this hidden network. This is especially useful when you have neighbors who are trying to gain access to your personal network.

Media Access Control

Media Access Control (MAC) is a set of numbers used to identify a specific device. Every device, whether it's a computer, tablet, or phone has an unique MAC address. To better protect a network, the router can be set to only allow specific MAC addresses to connect to that network. This adds another layer of security to your network by only permitting specific devices to connect. While this is a useful security feature, it is important to at least mention that there are software programs available that allow hackers to fake MAC addresses, allowing them to pretend to be the same device that's on your network.

The last tip we have for securing a router is the most effective method of keeping personal networks secure, turn the router off.

If you're going on vacation or you simply won't be using their network for an extended period, turning off the router is the best way to avoid hackers from getting into the network. They cannot access something that is not powered on and transmitting data.

Securing Mobile Devices

This chapter will explain the security risks mobile devices face and how to better protect your data on mobile phones or tablets.

Security risks

There are three main security risks for mobile devices: physical theft, internet theft, and application permissions.

Physical theft

The physical theft of a device can allow a person to access the device and snoop through all personal information that was stored.

That could be anything from passwords, text messages, photos, emails, and so on.

Internet theft

This applies to any data stolen or seen while browsing the internet on a mobile device, whether it's on a wireless network or a mobile carrier service.

Application permissions

This is probably the biggest security threat to mobile device owners for one simple reason. People do not read what permissions an application has when downloading the app. Business Insider published a recent study which found that in 2017, 90% of consumers accepted legal terms and conditions without reading through them. This is where the security risks come into play.

The basics

Listed below are six methods that can be used to better protect mobile device security. These are up-to-date operating systems, app privileges, geo-tracking awareness, lock screens, Wi-Fi or Bluetooth safety, and internet browsing.

Operating systems

An operating system is the basis of a mobile device that manages all networks and Software. For example, Apple uses iOS, while Android uses Android OS. Maintaining up-to-date Software for all types of mobile operating systems aid in keeping a mobile device safer. As the developers of these operating systems learn of security flaws, they are patched, and an update is sent out worldwide. This is one of the easiest methods to protect yourself from upcoming malicious Software or security weaknesses.

Applications

We all love apps, whether they come from the Apple Store or the Google Play Store, but what most people do not know is the information these apps can access via a user's mobile phone. Most people never bother to read the fine print when they are downloading the new Candy Crush game or when they're updating their Instagram app. Therefore, phones are incredibly easy targets for hackers.

Many applications request far too much data from a phone, which may not even be related to the app's actual purpose. For example, in Candy Crush's license agreement under section 10, it clearly states that the developers may use any personal data collected in any way that follows their privacy policy. They also go on to state that if users link their account to a social media site, they will use all personal data available from those sites as well to identify the user.

Geo-tracking

Most mobile device users have absolutely no idea how frequently their locations are being pinged and stored in a company's servers. Many free applications available for download in the Apple Store or Google Play Store are not actually free. There is a growing trend among app developers to collect your location using your phone or tablet's GPS system, this is known as geo-tracking. This information is gathered in huge quantities and is bought by large business entities who utilize this data to study and accurately predict consumer behavior.

Advertisers are always looking for new ways to capture your attention so that you will buy their product. If an app developer collects GPS locations from an individual on a daily basis, he or she could look at it and say, "Wow, this person seems to drive by a certain store every day." This app developer then takes this information and sells it to the store that the individual in question drives by every day so that the individual can be targeted with advertisements. These advertisements could come in the form of emails or spam text messages. How can these stores know how to direct ads at specific individuals? The answer to this is that more than just the individual's location data can be used for marketing. This app developer could have permissions that he or she will gain access to the phone's personal information like contacts, emails, etc. This allows the app developer to not only sell an individual's daily transit routes, as well as the information needed for advertisers to reach them specifically.

Passwords

This is one of the easiest methods to protecting data on a mobile phone. A simple lock screen password can prevent someone from gaining access to your phone or tablet if it is stolen. Think about all the applications, text messages, emails, and photos that are on a person's phone or tablet. Then think about someone being able to access all that information without even needing a password.

Wi-Fi safety

To avoid hackers seeing information sent from a user's mobile device, the user needs to be careful when using Wi-Fi. According to Lawyers' Professional Indemnity Company (LAWPRO), here are some tips on how you can do this:

1. First and foremost, only use wireless networks that are known and trusted. Avoid public wireless networks altogether, if possible. Public networks are usually not secure, making it easy for someone on the same network to pick up the information you sent.

2. If using a public network is a must, login to a Virtual Private Network (VPN) to secure the data you are transmitting. A VPN works by sending encrypted data through a tunnel that is safe from being accessed by anyone on the same network.

3. Make sure the network being used is running some form of WPA encryption. Most home company networks run WPA2 encryption, unlike public networks which have no security at all.

4. If you're connected to a network that isn't your own, make sure that the device sharing settings are turned off to avoid unknown devices from connecting with yours. This creates a link between devices designed to share data easier. However, this is also an effortless way for a hacker to connect to the user's device.

Bluetooth safety

1. Most Bluetooth capable devices are shipped by the manufacturer in unprotected mode. Also known as 'discovery mode.' This mode allows the device to be seen by others, making it easier to connect with.

2. If you are not using your Bluetooth, make sure to turn it off to avoid any connections to other unwanted devices. Turning your Bluetooth off when it's not in use eliminates all chances of an attacker's device connecting to yours.

3. If possible, change your device settings, so it requires user confirmation before it pairs with another device. This eliminates the possibility of another device secretly connecting.

4. Do not connect to unknown devices. Only pair with devices that are known and trusted.

5. The maximum range of Bluetooth connections can differ based on the power of the device itself, and by setting the range to the lowest possible setting, the risk of an attacker reaching the device is reduced.

Internet browsing

1. Internet browsing can still be dangerous, even on an iPad. Here are a few dos and don'ts from the McAfee Security Advice Center when it comes to surfing the web on a mobile device:

2. Install antivirus software, if possible, to run scans on any downloaded content on your device.

3. Always look at the URL of the web pages you visit. Make sure that you check the https security feature.

4. Fake websites tend to have some errors ranging from the overall look of the page to improper grammar.

5. If the URL of the website you wanted to visit is known, enter it directly to avoid any possible fake copies of the website.

6. Avoid clicking on advertisements as these can lead to malicious websites designed to install dangerous Software on your device.

CHAPTER 4:

Enhancing Physical Security

Early Detection is the Game Changer

The Study on Global Megatrends in Cybersecurity, sponsored by Raytheon and independently conducted by Ponemon Institute, provides new insights into the most critical cyber-threat trends emerging over the next three years through the eyes of those on the frontline of cybersecurity.1

More than 1,110 senior information-technology practitioners around the world were surveyed. The study revealed key insights and predictions from the expert practitioners for the next three years, such as:

Cyber extortion and data breaches impacting shareholder value will increase.

- 67 percent said the risk of cyber extortion, such as ransomware, will increase in frequency and payout.

- 60 percent predicted state-sponsored attacks would become even worse.

- Only 41 percent said their organization would be able to minimize Internet of Things (IoT) risks.

The frequency of cyber extortion, nation-state attacks, and attacks against industrial controls were predicted to increase by double-digits.

- 19 percent said cyber extortion is very frequent today, while 42 percent said this threat would be very frequent over the next three years.

- 26 percent said nation-state attacks are very frequent today, while 45 percent said this would be very frequent over the next three years.

- 40 percent said attacks against industrial controls and supervisory control and data acquisition (SCADA) systems are very frequent today, while 54 percent said this would be very frequent over the next three years.

The loss or theft of data from unsecured Internet of Things (IoT) devices is likely to happen and is a significant cybersecurity challenge.

- 82 percent said it is very likely, likely, or somewhat likely that their organization will have a loss or theft of data caused by an unsecured IoT device or application.

- 80 percent said likelihood of a security incident related to an unsecured IoT device or application could be catastrophic.

In summary, Raytheon and Ponemon Institute's Study on Global Megatrends in Cybersecurity provides several predictions from cybersecurity practitioners across the globe, who are on the frontline defending against the cyber attackers daily. Among them, over the next three years, even with all of the increased spending on cybersecurity:

- Cyber extortion and data breaches will greatly increase in frequency. This trend will largely be driven by sophisticated state-sponsored cyber attackers or organized groups.

- IoT devices, in particular, are very susceptible and will be targets that will be exploited.

  So, it is not a question of IF, but WHEN the cyber attackers will break-in. And when the cyber attackers break-in, they will remain undetected for many months.

  The median or mean number of days the cyber attackers remain undetected varies based on the source. Examples are:

- Mandiant's M-Trends Report;

- Verizon's Data Breach Investigations Report;

- IBM and Ponemon Institute's Cost of a Data Breach Study.

One thing is certain, however. The cyber attackers are able to hide for many months, and the longer it takes to detect the cyber attackers, the more the cost the organization ends up suffering.

Based on a research into dozens and dozens of cases, I have identified signals in the Cyber Attack Chain that every organization should understand and look for. When researching the cases, it became evident that in each case, the cyber attackers took steps that fit into one of the steps as I have outlined in the Cyber Attack Chain. It was also clear that in each step, there were signals of the cyber attackers at work, but that these signals were not detected by the organization.

It is time for every organization to understand what the Cyber Attack Signals are, and implement them as part of their cybersecurity program. By doing so, they will transform the defense into offense and detect the cyber attackers early. A Cyber Attack Signal is a high-probability signal of cyber attackers at work, trying to hide and avoid detection, while performing one of the tasks in the Cyber Attack Chain. They are at work to accomplish their ultimate objective—the theft of data or intellectual property (IP) or other compromise, harm, or disruption. A Cyber Attack Signal focuses on cyber attackers' behavior. I have identified 15 Cyber Attack Signals that, as a minimum, every organization should focus its monitoring on. These Top 15 signals relate to cyber attackers' behavior. They are timely signals, before the cyberattack is executed, occurring at the intrusion, lateral movement, or command and control steps of the Cyber Attack Chain, and are, therefore, of greatest value. This is not an exhaustive list, and there will probably be other signals relevant to an organization based on its risk profile and its Crown Jewels that may indicate the cyber attackers at work. As such, each organization should tailor its list of Cyber Attack Signals for monitoring.

Intrusion

Patch window

This is the time period a vulnerability remains unpatched and also how attackers could exploit it, providing an alert about Crown Jewels possibly impacted, probable attack timeline, and expected attacker behavior.

Web shell

This is the attempted installation or installation of a web shell to a web server.

It would exploit server or application vulnerabilities or configuration weaknesses to make the intrusion.

Lateral movement

Abnormal logons

These are anomalies in logons compared to normal logon patterns.

Privileged users' behavior

These are anomalies in the behavior of privileged users (users with greater access levels and capabilities) compared to normal behavior.

WMI anomalies

This is an abnormal activity with Windows Management Instrumentation (WMI), a set of tools for system administrators to manage Windows systems locally and remotely.

Internal reconnaissance signals

These are anomalies in scripts or batch scripts running on email, web and file servers or domain controller or hosts, or scanning of servers and ports.

Malware signals

These are anomalies from normal behavior patterns in terms of users, files, processes, tasks, sources, and destinations to indicate initial malware installation or propagation.

Ransomware signals

This is anomalous activity to indicate initial ransomware installation or propagation, such as the installation of new .dll file or attempted communication with a TOR website (i.e., server on the TOR network, a service used to provide anonymity over the Internet.)

Malicious PowerShell

This is an abnormal activity with PowerShell, a scripting language for system administrators to automate tasks, such as odd characters (e.g., +

'$ %) added in the scripts, use of "powershell.exe" by abnormal users at unusual times or locations or scripts containing command parameters.

RDP signals

These are anomalies with Remote Desktop Protocol (RDP), which enables a user (e.g., as help-desk staff) to use a graphical interface to connect to another computer in a network, such as abnormal RDP users, source or destination logons.

SMB anomalies

These are anomalies with Server Message Block (SMB), a protocol in Microsoft Windows that enables remotely managing files, file sharing, printing, and directory share, among other functions in a network.

Unusual logs behavior

These are anomalies in event logs, such as event logs removed, stopped, or cleared with details (user details, date, time, type of log, the command executed, asset impacted, source, and destination).

Command and control

C&C communications

This is anomalous activity indicating attempted communication or communications with a command and control (C&C) server, such as a request to an unusual domain name or a one-off domain name, a request to the numeric IP address as the domain name for the host, requests to certain IP addresses or hosts with a certain frequency (hourly, daily or other).

ICMP packets

These are anomalies with Internet Control Message Protocol (ICMP) packets, such as abnormal size, frequency, source, or destination.

Hidden tunnels

These are anomalies of HTTP, HTTPS r DNS traffic compared to normal baseline patterns indicating communications with a C&C server using a tunnel designed to blend in with normal traffic.

CHAPTER 5:

Securing Your Small Business

Computer and Network Security

As the internet has evolved over the past decade, so have hackers. Network security has become one of the most crucial factors companies consider because of the continuous growth of computer networks.

Big corporations like Microsoft are constantly designing and building software products that need to be protected against hackers and foreign attackers because these are the kinds of people who will stop at nothing until they get what they want.

The more network security an individual has, the less chance there is of a hacker accessing their data and files.

Network security is the process by which measures are taken to prevent unauthorized access, misuse, or modification of information passed over a network. In other words, network security simply means that any computers accessing a private network are protected from any forms of cyber theft or manipulation.

Network security

There are three ways to better protect a network; these are intrusion detection systems, WPA/WPA2, which stands for 'Wireless Protected Access,' and Security Sockets Layer (SSL).

Intrusion Detection Systems

These systems are software pr0grams designed to protect networks. They are intended to monitor server channels and detect malicious programs being sent across these servers. There are two types of IDS systems. The first is known as an active IDS, this is a more secure software that not only monitors server channels, but it can also block and remove any malicious programs it detects. This type of IDS system doesn't need human involvement to protect a computer or network. The second kind of IDS is less protective in that it only monitors a server and alerts a user to a threat if one is found. These programs will not destroy or quarantine any malicious software.

Wireless Protected Access

Wireless protected access, also known as 'WPA,' is a form of network encryption. There are two types of this security system, WPA, and WPA2. Both are more secure than the traditional WEP security found on old routers, and WPA2 is the most secure. Most modern routers found in stores today offer WPA2 encryption levels. The reason why both security features are useful is because they make it more difficult for an attacker to get into a wireless network. WPA2 offers a higher and more complex security layer by using different key setups for network access. This means that WPA2 makes it harder for an attacker to crack a password for a wireless network.

Security Sockets Layer

A Security Sockets Layer (SSL) is a form of internet protection provided by encryption. Its purpose is to encrypt any data you send over a network to prevent anyone else on your network from seeing the actual information being transferred. SSLs are very important for anyone entering private information on a website. They work by verifying what is known as a website certificate. A certificate is what websites use to verify themselves. When you connect to a website, the server the website runs on sends you its certificate to verify its authenticity. A website can only acquire these certificates by applying for them, and they have to follow a strict set of security guidelines. So, to keep this from getting complicated, if a website has a credible website certificate using SSL, any information you send or receive from that site will be encrypted and safe from any possible attackers. Also, you can see if a website is secure by looking for the https in the URL at the top of your internet browser.

Computer security

Computer security, on the other hand, is the protection of data physically stored on a computer. This includes taking steps to prevent attacks under the triad of information security, also known as the CIA (confidentiality, integrity, and availability).

A few of the basic methods below pertain to computer security and will cover passwords, software updates, firewalls, anti-virus or malware programs, ad-blockers, email encryption, and data backups.

Having a good password

A good password consists of three basic qualities: Its length, the characters used, and the combination of upper- and lower-case letters. The longer a password is, the harder it is to break. Some hackers try to use algorithms in which they send massive amounts of combinations, hoping that one is a match to the secret password. By increasing the length of a password, its chances of being cracked decreases.

A mixture of letters and symbols, such as exclamation marks, help protect your password from being stolen. This also applies to add uppercase letters into your password. A password such as 'password1' is very weak in comparison to a password like 'PasSWord2018!' The combination of upper-case letters and symbols decreases the chances that a password can be hacked through brute force.

Another method you can use to create incredibly secure passwords is getting a program like 'LastPass' or 'Password Boss.' These programs randomly create a password that is incredibly secure. Using a program like this will provide a unique password for everything a person uses. This means that if a hacker can get into one of an individual's accounts, they will not have the password for the other programs or web services.

Software updates

Software updates are very important as they protect your computer or mobile device. Software updates are used to patch holes or bugs found in an operating system, and this will make your device more secure. Check your operating system often to see if a new update is available. Some operating software update automatically.

Firewalls

Firewalls are great protection for computers because they prevent unwanted data from getting to your computer. They monitor the flow of incoming data and run checks to see if the information that's about to be received by your computer is harmful or not. For example, anytime a user downloads something from a website, the firewall will scan the file in question and determine if it is malicious or not. Not all firewalls are the same. Most operating systems come with a built-in firewall, so there is hardly a reason to install additional firewalls. Also, these OS companies are constantly updating their security features to make them more reliable. Firewalls prevent unauthorized access to or from a private network.

Antivirus software

One of the most effective and common methods of dealing with malware is anti-malware Software. Programs such as Windows Essentials, McAfee, and Bitdefender allow a user to run scans on a system to search for infected files. If any files are found to be corrupted, these programs alert the operator, allowing him or her to remove the files in question.

This type of Software is also very useful as it can scan any downloaded items or email attachments before allowing the user to download them. This is a crucial protective barrier, as it prevents any malicious programs from installing itself on a device.

These types of Software can also analyze what kind of virus, worm, or Trojan has infected the computer in question.

This kind of protective Software will remove anything malicious automatically from the computer but will be unable to recognize threats such as ransomware or keyloggers.

Ad blockers

Most browsers have extensions that can be added to the browser, which blocks pesky advertisements. For example, the Google Chrome web store has a variety of additional extensions users can download and run while using the browser (not all being adblockers).

Chrome has an adblocker made specifically for the Chrome browsers, which limit the number of ads that pop up while you visit websites. Ad blockers can also be downloaded directly onto the computer's hard drive instead of a web browser.

Email encryption

Encryption protects emails by making the content of emails unreadable to any entity, besides the intended recipients. Popular email services such as Gmail have since added encryption of emails to their network. However, it only protects data that's on their servers. This means that data is still vulnerable while it bounces around on other internet networks unless users implement client-side encryption. Most methods that allow this are complicated processes that require exchanging certificates with everyone who will be receiving or sending emails with one another.

Fortunately, there is an alternative called Virtru that works with Gmail accounts as well as Outlook. This allows users real, client-side encryption without the prolonged process of exchanging certificates. Virtru is a plug-in that users can download onto their web browsers to freely send and accept emails from Outlook or Gmail accounts without any compatibility issues.

Data backups

Data backups are an important but overlooked aspect of computer security. By performing regular backups of all important data on a computer, the user protects themselves from the risk of a crash or virus and lose important data. Data backups typically upload data to an outside source, either to a cloud storage server, or a storage device.

Any data that isn't backed up can be completely lost if the computer hardware fails or data is corrupted. Like the old saying, "It is better to be safe than sorry."

Failed security

If both security types fail, what could be put at risk? The types of information hackers may attempt to steal are divided into two categories: personal and financial. Regarding personal information, a hacker could use it to create fake web accounts, social media accounts, or a new identity altogether. The rampancy of identity theft today is fueled by the enormous amounts of information that can be collected from the internet. According to the identity protection service LifeLock, in 2017, 16.7 million people were victims of identity theft, resulting in $16.8 billion being stolen. In 2016, 15.4 million people were victimized, resulting in a loss of $16.2 billion. Over the past three years, the number of people who are victims of identity theft increased by 3.6 million.

With financial information, it all comes down to the individual's money. A hacker can use the stolen financial information to make online purchases, apply for loans, or go as far as to file tax returns under the victim's name. It is of the highest importance that both types of information remain protected and accurate.

According to the USA government, there are several diverse types of identity theft that the general public could fall victim to:

Child ID theft

Child identity theft is a type of theft that can go hidden for many years until the child has grown into an adult. By then, the damage to their identity from the theft has already been inflicted.

Tax ID theft

This occurs when a social security number is stolen and used to file tax returns by anyone other than the owner of the SSN.

Medical ID theft

This type of theft occurs when someone steals another person's medical information or health insurance data for medical services, or by billing false charges to the policy holder's company.

Social ID theft

Known nowadays as a 'catfish,' this kind of theft happens when someone steals another person's name, photographs, and other personal information to create a fake social media account.

CHAPTER 6:

Malware

L et's imagine a scenario where a client presents a file, and they are unsure if it's malware and what capabilities it has.

Where does this malware fit in the kill chain?

Is it the initial patient zero machine that will go online and download more malware code? What is this malware's specimen capability?

Understanding what the malware is capable of is one of the main purposes of malware analysis or reverse engineering. You also have to ask: What is the attacker's intention?

If it's malware specifically for ransom, they are trying to encrypt for files and ask for money. If its purpose is to install other stolen PI data, then its intention is larger than just quick financial gain. Knowing the intention of the attacker helps you understand where else this malware is infecting your environment.

Types of Malware

Malware is a very general category, and there are few subtypes within it:

Ransomware

This malware is designed to freeze files and, as the name suggests, demand ransom from its victims in exchange for releasing the data; successful attackers realized that they could take it a step further by demanding money but not releasing the data. Instead, attackers demand another payment, and the cycle continues.

Paying up might seem like the only solution to dealing with ransomware, but the fact is, once you pay, the attackers will keep asking for more.

Adware

This is Software that downloads, gathers, and presents unwanted ads or data while redirecting searches to certain websites.

Bots

Bots are automatic scripts that take command of your system. Your computer is used as a "zombie" to carry out attacks online. Most of the time, you are not aware that your computer is carrying out these attacks.

Rootkits

When a system is compromised, rootkits are designed to hide the fact that you have malware. Rootkits enable malware to operate in the open by imitating normal files.

Spyware

Spyware transmits data from the hard drive without the target knowing about the information theft.

Remote Access Tool (RAT)

After your system is compromised, RAT helps attackers remain in your systems and networks. RAT helps criminals to obtain your keystrokes, take photos with your camera, and/or expand to other machines. One of the most dominant features of this type permits the malware to transfer all of this information from the victim to the attacker in a protected way, so you are not even conscious you are being spied on.

Viruses

A virus pushes a copy of itself into a device and becomes a part of another computer program. It can spread between computers, leaving infections as it travels.

Worms

Similar to viruses, worms self-replicate, but they don't need a host program or human to propagate. Worms utilize a vulnerability in the target system or make use of social engineering to fool users into executing the program.

CHAPTER 7:

Cyber attacks

Web Attacks

SQL Injection

SQL injection is also called as SQLI. SQL is a particular type of attack which uses malicious code for manipulating backend databases to attain data that was not wished-for display. Such data may consist of various items such as private customer details, private data of the company, and user lists.

SQLI can cause destructive effects on a business. An effective SQLI attack can result in the deletion of complete tables, unsanctioned inspecting of user lists, and in few cases, the attacker can attain administrative access to a database, making it extremely destructive for a business. While calculating the expected price of SQLI, we must take into consideration the loss of customer faith in personal case information of the customer, such as details of credit card details, addresses, and phone numbers are stolen. Even though SQLI can be employed to attack any SQL database, the criminals frequently target websites.

Cross-Site Scripting

Cross-site scripting (abbreviated as XSS) is a type of injection breach where the criminal transmits malign code into content from otherwise trustworthy websites. Such incidents take place when an uncertain source is permitted to attach its own (malign) code into different web applications, making the malign code bundled together with other content, which is then directed to the browser of the victim.

Attackers normally send malign code in the form of fragments of the JavaScript code implemented by the browser of the victim. The exploits consist of malign executable scripts in various languages such as HTML, Java, Flash, and Ajax. Cross-site scripting attacks can be extremely destructive; nonetheless, dealing with susceptibilities enabling such attacks is comparatively simple.

Distributed Denial-of-Service (DDoS) Attack

The aim of Denial-of-service (DDoS) is to shut down a service or network, making it unreachable to its intended users. The attackers attain their aim through crushing the victim with the traffic load or else flooding it with data, which activates a crash. In both circumstances, the DoS attack denies genuine users like account holders, and company employees.

The targets of DDoS attacks are often web servers of prestigious organizations like government and trade organizations, commerce, media companies, and banking. Even though such attacks don't lead to theft or loss of crucial data or other assets, still such attacks can cost the target loads of time and money to mitigate. DDoS is frequently employed in combination to divert from attacks of another network

Password Attack

A password attack is an effort to obtain or else decrypt the password of the user with maligned intentions. Different techniques are used by crackers such as dictionary attacks, password sniffers, and cracking programs in password attacks. Even though there are some defense mechanisms against such attacks, however normally, the method used is to inculcate a password policy which comprises a minimum length, distorted words, and frequent alterations.

The recovery of the password is generally carried out by the continual guessing of the password by using a computer algorithm. The computer repeatedly tries various combinations until the successful discovery of the password.

Eavesdropping Attack

These attacks initiate with the interference of network traffic. Another term used for Eavesdropping breach is sniffing or snooping. It is a type of a network security attack where the attacker attempts to steal the data send or received by computers, smartphones, or other digital devices. Eavesdropping attacks are hard to detect as they do not cause anomalous data transmissions.

Eavesdropping attacks aim at faded transmissions amid the server and the client, which allows the attacker to obtain network transmissions. Different network monitors such as sniffers on a server can be installed by the attacker to implement an eavesdropping attack and intercept data. Any device which is inside the transmission and reception network is a vulnerability point, including the initial as well as terminal devices. One method to guard against such attacks is having the information of devices connected to a specific network as well as information about software running on such devices.

Brute-Force and Dictionary Network Attacks

Brute-force and dictionary attacks are networking attacks in which an attacker tries to log into account of the user through systematically checking and exasperating all likely passwords until he finds the correct one.

The ordinary way to carry out this type of attack is through the front door, as we must have a technique of logging in. If we have the necessary credentials, we can enter as a normal user without arising doubtful logs, or tripping IDS signatures, or requiring an unpatched entry.

The meaning of brute-force is to overpower the system via repetition. During password hacking, the brute force needs dictionary software, which combines dictionary words with hundreds of diverse variations. This process is rather slow. Brute-force dictionary attacks can make 100 to 1000 attempts per minute.

After trying for numerous hours or even days, such attacks can finally crack any password. These attacks restate the significance of best practices of passwords, particularly on critical resources like routers, network switches, and servers.

Insider Threats

An attack doesn't need to be always performed by someone from outside an organization. At times, malicious attacks are carried out on a network or computer system by any individual sanctioned to access the system. Insiders executing such attacks have the advantage over outsider attackers as they have authorized system access. Moreover, they are most likely to understand network architecture and system policies.

Additionally, normally there is minor security against insider attacks as the focus of the majority of organizations is to defend themselves against external attacks. Insider threats can leave an impact on all elements of computer security. Such attacks can range from injecting Trojan viruses to thieving private information from a system or network.

Man-in-the-Middle (MITM) Attacks

Man-in-the-middle (abbreviated as MITM) attacks are a kind of cybersecurity breach permitting an attacker/cracker to eavesdrop a communication amid two bodies. The attack takes place amid two genuinely communicating parties, allowing the attacker to capture communication, which they otherwise should not be able to access. This gives such attackers the name "man-in-the-middle." The invader "listens" to the communication through capturing the public key message transmission and then retransmits the key message whereas switching the demanded key with his own.

The two communicating parties continue to communicate routinely, without having any idea that the person who is sending messages is an unknown criminal who is trying to alter and access the message prior to its transmission to the receiver. Therefore, the intruder in this way controls the whole communication.

AI-Powered Attacks

The idea of a computer program learning on its own, constructing knowledge, and becoming more sophisticated in this process sounds scary (Adams 2017). We can easily dismiss artificial intelligence as another tech buzzword. Nevertheless, at present, it is being used in routinely applications with the help of an algorithmic process known as machine learning. Machine learning software aims to train a computer system to carry out a specific task on its own. Computers are trained to complete tasks by repeatedly doing them, whereby getting knowledge about particular hindrances that could hamper them.

Hackers can make use of artificial intelligence to hack into various systems such as autonomous drones and vehicles, altering them into prospective weapons. AI makes several cyber-attacks like password cracking, and denial-of-service attacks, identity theft, automatic, more efficient and powerful. AI can even be used to injure or murder people, or cause them emotional distress or steal their money. Attacks on a larger scale can affect national security, cut power supplies to complete districts, and may shut down hospitals as well.

CHAPTER 8:

Cyberwar

Consider an employee's W-2 form. Before the 2000s, the information on this form had a nominal value that approached the price of the paper on which it was printed. There was no easy way to monetize a stolen W-2 form. Today, there is a thriving black market for personally identifiable information. As of 2017, the going price for a W-2 is between $4 and $20, depending on the income of the wage earner. That may not seem like much, but it represents a massive increase from the two-cent value of a printed W-2 decades ago. Stealing even a single W-2 makes sense when attackers operate from a country where $20 is a full day's wages. Stealing them by the hundreds or thousands using automated attacks against scores of unsuspecting and unprepared small businesses makes even more sense for criminals anywhere in the world.

Having established why hackers are coming for your data, let's look at the damage done when they strike. Continuing with the W-2 theft example, state and federal laws require employers to report cyber theft, also known as a data breach. Failing to disclose the breach opens the door to class-action lawsuits where juries can award unlimited damages to victims due to your negligence. Disclosing the breach helps shield you and the organization from claims of negligence and, in some cases, will prevent class-action suits. However, the organization will not be off the hook completely. Defending a non-class action lawsuit will cost tens of thousands of dollars, even if you win.

Additional costs include losses the employee will suffer if their identity is used to open credit in their name, drain their bank accounts, etc. Worse, the threat of identity theft will follow them forever. Related, indirect costs to the employer include replacing the employee if he or she quits and a reduction in morale among peer employees. It may become harder and more expensive to hire good talent, and customers hearing of the breach may look at competitors they believe are more vigilant.

A single stolen W-2 might net an attacker $20, but your organization and employees may be on the hook for tens or hundreds of thousands of dollars in damages. And this is just one example of how cyber-attacks wreak havoc on an organization. Black markets and cyber espionage make seemingly mundane data worth stealing and exploiting. Trade secrets, access to bank accounts, and private communication are very lucrative targets. Sometimes it is not your own data, but a client's data accessible through you or your employees that is the target.

Our highly connected, the digital world has ushered in a new era of cybercrime. One that is growing fast and changing constantly. Executives who stick their heads in the sand, try to keep a data breach

COMPUTER PROGRAMMING FOR BEGINNERS AND CYBERSECURITY

a secret, pass off cybersecurity as just an IT problem, or wait for government protection will pay a steep price.

Many executives in the 1990s were adamant that computers were a novel expense that would never add real value to their business models. The idea that they would elevate the discussion of computers to an executive-level was as absurd as typing their own email. Executives that clung to this view doomed their company to lose ground when competitors with forward-thinking executives raised technology to a boardroom discussion. Today cybersecurity is what computers were then. It is history, repeating itself, and we already know who wins. Organizations led by executives that are willing to buck old-school thinking and grapple with the Wild West of cybersecurity will come out on top.

Today, the outdated view is thinking that cybersecurity is a technical problem best delegated to information technology (IT) experts. It goes hand-in-hand with the idea that cybersecurity involves only preventing attacks by anticipating them and implementing as many deterrents as possible. In contrast, a modern view of cybersecurity recognizes that countering every possible attack to achieve perfect security is financially unfeasible. This new mindset also considers what happens when attacks occur, because they will. Astute executives realize that spending every dime on prevention is futile and take a more holistic view of the problem.

526 | P a g .

Finding the right balance among various preventive and preparatory measures is like building an investment portfolio of stocks, bonds, and real estate. The right mix depends on what the external markets are doing and your appetite for taking risks. As time goes on, the markets will change, and your life circumstances change. Allocations in your portfolio adjust accordingly. This book is a guide to making investments in cybersecurity that reflect the external threat landscape, internal business strategy, and the organization's appetite for risk.

Despite having excellent cybersecurity teams and multi-million-dollar budgets, large companies have learned that cybersecurity is a business problem that must be managed from the top. They have realized that outsourcing and delegation only go so far when building a comprehensive cybersecurity plan and keeping it up to date as internal and external circumstances change. For the foreseeable future, the management of cybersecurity as a business problem will rest upon the shoulders of top management. Unless you embrace this new role, your organization will be a cybersecurity have-not in a time where data privacy and security are of increasing concern among clients and suppliers.

What happens if you do not step up to the plate? Well, according to a 2017 report, nearly one-quarter of small businesses that suffered a ransomware attack were forced to immediately stop their operations. How long can your organization survive if revenue-generating operations stopped abruptly while payroll and other expenses continued? What will long-term damage be done to your clients' perception of your organization's ability to offer uninterrupted service?

Savvy competitors simply wait for your market share to open up as a result of your inattention. On the flip side, effective management of cybersecurity is necessary just to stay on par with forward-thinking competitors. Having a comprehensive cybersecurity plan in place can position your company to survive the same attacks that will bankrupt (or severely disrupt) your peers. When that happens, you can pick up their market share and grow your company.

Another reason to take cybersecurity seriously at the executive level is that larger, cyber-savvy companies are often direct, or indirect, clients who take the security of their supply chain very seriously. Studies show that as many as 63 percent of data breaches are linked to a third-party because weak downstream suppliers make great back doors into otherwise secure systems. In response to this, the NIST Cybersecurity Framework (a technical implementation guide) was recently revised to add emphasis to supply chain scrutiny, and an executive order from the White House drove this same point home for government agencies. The government, their downstream contractors, and large private sector companies will begin culling lax suppliers and awarding business to those who demonstrate they take cybersecurity seriously. Nimble executives who address cybersecurity at their core will have an advantage—one that differentiates a company from its competitors and may command a premium. If you insist that your plate is full just managing what you already have, you will miss the opportunity to rise above your competitors, just like the old-school executives who refused to see technology as anything more than an expense.

Consumers have also become quite sensitive to cybersecurity, and it is reflected in their buying habits. Forward-thinking executives can capitalize on this trend too. A prominent example was Apple's stance on personal privacy when the FBI demanded they decrypt an iPhone used in a terrorist event. Playing up their investments in encryption and demonstrating loyalty to a client even in the worst of times helped solidify consumer trust in Apple products. We would never advocate brinksmanship with the FBI, but Apple's response was a brilliant way to gain confidence among consumers. Learning to manage cybersecurity from a business perspective means you can spot and leverage opportunities like this too.

CHAPTER 9:

Ethical Hacking

When it comes to security, being a hacker is one of the most commonly used terms. It appears everywhere, and even the entertainment industry and many authors often use it in their movies, books, TV shows, and other media forms.

Therefore, the word "hacker" is usually seen as a bad profession and always associated with dark or real criminal activity. So, when people hear that someone is involved in hacking, they immediately see that person as someone who has no good intentions.

They are usually presented as "operators from the shadows," even antisocial. On the other hand, they are also seen as a social activist.

This label became especially popular after a few things like WikiLeaks. Many hackers were involved in obtaining many important documents from governments, politicians, and companies that showed information that was very different from the information given to the public.

Organized groups such as Anonymous or Lizard Squad have also had a huge impact on the hacking experience in recent years.

Examples: Mischief or Criminal?

- Hacking is by no means a phenomenon that has appeared overnight. It existed in various forms and evolved all the way from the 1960s. However, it was never tackled as a criminal activity at first. We'll look at some cases that will take a closer look at some of the attacks, and generic examples that have gradually changed that picture.

- Access services or resources that you do not have permission to use. This is usually called stealing usernames and passwords. In some cases, obtaining this information without permission is considered a cybercrime, even if you do not use it or as accounts of friends or family members.

- There is a form of digital offense called network intrusion that is also considered a cybercrime. In essence, as with ordinary offenses, this means that you went somewhere without permission to enter (or in this case, access). So, in case someone gets access to a system or group of systems without permission, we can say that the person violated the network and thereby committed cybercrime. However, some network intrusions can take place without using hacker tools. Sometimes logging in to guest accounts without prior permission can be seen as cybercrime.

- One of the most complex yet simplest forms of hacking is to go after the most vulnerable element in the system—people. This type of cybercrime is known as social engineering, and we say it can be simple because the person is a much more accessible part of the system than any other, and it's easier to deal with. However, people can provide clues that are difficult to understand, whether spoken or not, making it difficult for the hacker to get the information they need.

- The issue of posting or sending illegal material has generally become difficult to address, especially in the past decade. Social media received a lot of attention, and many other internet-related services increased in use and popularity. This allowed many illegal materials to move from one place to another in the shortest possible time, allowing it to spread very quickly

- Fraud is also common, especially on the internet, and is also considered a cybercrime. Like the original term, fraud in cyberspace also means that a party or parties have usually been misled for financial gain or harm.

What does it mean to be an ethical hacker?

All the things we mentioned earlier in this chapter referred to hackers in general. The real goal, however, is to learn how to be an ethical hacker and explore the skills you should have. Ethical hackers are people who are usually employed by organizations to test their security. They usually work through direct employment or through temporary contracts. The key is that they use the same skills as all other hackers, but there is one big difference: they are allowed to attack the system directly from the system owner. In addition, an ethical hacker means that you reveal the weaknesses of the system you have evaluated (because every system in the world has them) only to the owner and no one else. In addition, organizations or individuals hiring ethical hackers use very strict contracts that specify which parts of the system are authorized for an attack and which are prohibited. The role of an ethical hacker also depends on the job to which he or she is entitled, i.e., the needs of the employer. Today, some organizations have permanent staff teams, and their job is to conduct ethical hacking activities. Hackers can be divided into 5 categories. Keep in mind that this format may vary, but we can say these are the most common:

- The first category is also referred to as "Script Kiddies." These hackers usually have no training or do, but very limited. They know how to use just some of the basic hacking tools and techniques, and since they are not competent enough, they may sometimes not fully understand their activities or the consequences of their work.

- The second category concerns hackers known as "White Hat hackers." They attack the computer system, but they are the good guys, which means they don't harm their work. These types of hackers are usually ethical hackers, but they can also be pentesters.

- "Gray Hat Hackers" are the third hacker category. As their name suggests, they are between good and bad, but their final decision is to choose the right side. Still, these types of hacker's struggle to gain trust because they can be suspicious.

- The fourth category we mention in this section is referred to as the "Black Hat Hackers." This category refers to the hackers we mentioned earlier in this chapter. These people usually work on the 'other side' of the law and are usually associated with criminal activities.

- Last but not least are the "Suicide hackers." They are called that because their goal is to prove the point, which is why they want to take out their target. These hackers don't have to worry about getting caught, because their goal is not to hide, but to prove, so that they are easier to find.

Responsibilities of an Ethical Hacker

The most important thing that an ethical hacker should learn and never forget is that he or she should always have permission for any kind of system attack. The ethical code that you, as an ethical hacker, must implement in every task says that no network or system should be tested or targeted if you do not own it or if you do not have permission to do so. Otherwise, you may be found guilty of multiple crimes that may have occurred in the meantime. First, it can hurt your career, and second, if it's something really serious, it can even threaten your freedom.

The smartest thing is to get a contract from your employer the moment you test or attack the required target. The contract is a written authorization, but you should keep in mind that you should only examine the parts of the system specified in that contract. So, if your employer wants to give you permission to hack additional parts of the system or remove authorization for some, he should first change the contract and you shouldn't continue working until you get the new permit. Note that the only thing that distinguishes an ethical hacker from the cybercriminal is the contract. Therefore, you should always pay special attention to the vocabulary related to privacy and confidentiality issues, as it often happens that you come across intimate information from your client, both business and personal.

That's one more reason why your contract should include who you can talk to about the things you found while researching the system and who are forbidden from hearing updates from you. In general, customers usually want to be the only people who know everything you eventually find out.

An organization known as the EC Council (International Council of Electronic Commerce Consultants) is one of the most important organizations when it comes to regulating these issues. According to them, an ethical hacker should keep all information obtained on the job private and treat it as confidential. This is indicated in particular for the customer's personal information, which means that you are not allowed to transfer, give, sell, collect or do any of the customer's information, such as social security number, etc. -mail address, home address, unique identification, name, and so on. The only way you can give this type of information to a third party is by having written permission from your employer (client). While some may argue about the distinction between hackers and ethical hackers, the division is quite simple: hackers are separated by their intentions. This means that those who plan to harm and use their skills to access data without permission are labeled as black hats, while those who work with their client's permission are considered white hat hackers. Naming these two categories of "the bad" and "the good" can be controversial, so we'll try to follow these expressions in the following way:

- Black hats usually operate outside the law, which means they do not have permission from the person called "the customer" to consent to their activities.

On the contrary, white hats have permission and permission from the person called "client," and they even keep the information they have between client and white hats only.

Gray hats, on the other hand, enter both areas and use both types of action in different periods.

Hacktivists are a category of hackers that we have not mentioned before. They belong to the movement known as Hacktivism, which refers to action's hackers use to influence the general public by promoting a particular political agenda. So far, hacktivists have been involved with agencies, large companies, and governments.

Hacker Ethics and Code of Conduct

Like any other profession, hacking has its Code of Conduct that establishes rules that can help customers (individuals or organizations) evaluate whether the person who interacts with their networks and computer systems is generally reliable. The organization that implemented this Code has already been identified and is known as the EC Council. Obtaining a CEH reference from the EC Council means that you fully understand the expectations you must meet. We've provided some parts of the code, so make sure you read it and get familiar with it.

- Information you gain during your professional work should be kept confidential and private (especially personal information)

- Unless you have your customer's permission, you may not give, transfer or sell the customer's home address, name, or other unique identifying information.

- You must protect the intellectual property, yours and others, by using skills that you have acquired yourself so that all benefits go to the original creator.

- Be sure to disclose to authorize personnel any danger that you suspect may be from the Internet community, electronic transactions, or other hardware and software indicators.

- Make sure that the services you provide are within your area of expertise so that you work honestly while aware of any limitations that may be a result of your education or experience.

- You may only work on projects for which you are qualified and carry out tasks that match your training, education, and work experience skills.

- You must not knowingly use software that has been obtained illegally or has been stored unethically.

- You may not participate in financial practices that may be considered misleading, such as double billing, bribery, etc.

- Make sure you use the customer's property properly, without exceeding the limits set in your contract.

- You must disclose a potential conflict of interest to all parties involved, especially if that conflict cannot be avoided.

- Make sure that you manage the entire project you are working on, including promotion and risk disclosure activities.

CHAPTER 10:

Mistakes Made in Cybersecurity

S tolen information and data will not lead to the end of the business. It is not a great sign for the business either. Studies and research indicate that a data breach in an organization's network can lead to a loss of $15.4 million, and the amount increases each year. People do not want to lose their money because of some issues or vulnerabilities in the system, do they? Indeed, businesses and organizations cannot make mistakes. These mistakes can lead to the loss of data, but a large organization is bound to make such mistakes. What the organization must do is to learn from those mistakes. You cannot expect your organization to do the exact thing repeatedly only because the outcome may change at one point. This chapter covers the different mistakes organizations make. You must protect your organization from making such mistakes during these times.

Failing to Map Data

Every organization must focus on understanding how and where the data flows. It should also look at where the data is saved. Remember, data is the livelihood of your company. It is only when you assess and identify the flow of data that you can see where it must be protected.

You must know if the data is flowing out of your organization and who it is shared with. When you have visibility, you will know what ends the hacker can attack. You will also know where you can catch the hacker.

Neglecting Security Testing

Vulnerabilities will reside across the database, systems, applications, and network. These vulnerabilities now extend to various devices like the IoT or Internet of Things and smartphones. Organizations must test these devices and connections regularly to scan for any vulnerabilities. You can also perform some penetration tests to learn about the vulnerabilities. Remember, you cannot guess the vulnerabilities, and will only find them when you test them.

Concentrating on Wrong Aspects

It is true that prevention is not an anachronism. As technology advances, so make the threats against it. Remember, a hacker will find a way to enter the border. A firewall will not always protect your systems if you have an employee who does not know what he is doing. Once a hacker is inside the system, he can acquire privileged information. He can also pretend to be an employee of the organization. Hackers can evade any security scans for a long time. If you have better visibility, you can find a hacker and reduce the chances of data leaks.

Forgetting the Basics

Often, it is the simple things you can use to overcome and threats to the system. You must train all your employees. Help them understand the type of password they must use. They must perform the right actions as well. It is only when this happens that you can maintain the network components properly and minimize the risk of data loss. You can also find ways to configure the data to prevent any changes adequately.

Avoiding Training

Remember to train your employees to know what they must do to prevent any attacks. The most common form of hack is a social engineering attack. The hacker will send information from a malicious source and mask the information to seem legit. He can then use the information the employee feeds into the website, and attack the configuration of the system and network. Make sure to train your staff about protecting their systems and how to identify social engineering attacks.

Security Monitoring

Most businesses cannot set up their security operations center or center of excellence since they lack the budget. This does not mean you cannot monitor the security of the systems and network. You must investigate the network and look for any threats or vulnerabilities.

You can use these methods to minimize the effect of an attack on the data and security.

Avoiding Vendor Risk Assessments

From earlier, you know vendor risks are the reasons for numerous data breaches. Hackers can enter the organization's systems through the vendor's application or network. Therefore, you must have a plan to help you assess the risks in third-party systems. You can also read the reports they share about their systems to learn more about their security.

Ignoring Shadow IT

Remember, the end-points in any network are often connected to other networks, and this makes it hard to control the flow of data through the network. Most employees access shadow devices and applications from their laptops and desktops. The IT department in most organizations does not support the use of such applications. If you do not know how to stop it, you must find a way to hide it. You can block these applications and websites.

It is not only about Malware

Most hackers use malware to establish their presence in a system or network. Once they are inside the network or system, they will use different strategies to perform the hack and move through your network. So, you need to find hack into the system in a legitimate way and perform the hack to detect any vulnerabilities.

Breaches won't Happen

This is one of the biggest mistakes most companies make. Some organizations do not protect their business and network since they believe cybercriminals do show mercy. This is never going to happen. Cybercriminals will attack any company, regardless of its size. You must prepare your defenses and identify the response to an attack. This will help you minimize the damage and react faster to any threats if the day does come.

Forgetting about the Management

You must understand that security must mature over time, and this is one of the primary objectives of an information security professional. In some instances where businesses have reached high levels of maturity, security is a part of the organization's culture. You must obtain permissions and approvals from the management before you investigate any attacks or the systems.

Doing it on Your Own

Regardless of whether you own a small business or are a part of a larger organization that lacks security skills, you must find someone to help you with testing your network and systems. Hire an ethical hacker to test the networks and systems. You can also partner with security service providers. Alternatively, you can speak to your management and hire the right professionals, or you can train the employees in your firm. You must avoid making these mistakes if you want to improve the security of your organization's systems and networks.

Tips to Keep Your Organization Secure

In this chapter, we will look at some tips to help you protect your organization from being a victim. Speak to the IT professionals and other stakeholders in the business to learn more about what you can do to prevent any cyber-attacks.

Creating an Information Security Policy

Every business must have a clearly defined security policy. This policy should provide information on the processes and actions every employee in the organization must follow. You must enforce this policy and train employees to perform the right actions. Remember to include the following in your information security policy:

- Best Practices for encryption

- Password requirements

- Usage of devices

- Email access

COMPUTER PROGRAMMING FOR BEGINNERS AND CYBERSECURITY

You must update this policy frequently, and let every employee in the organization know about the changes made to the policy.

Educating Employees

This is a very important aspect to consider. If you have a security policy, but your employees do not know what they must do, then it is a lost cause. Help your employees understand the different protocols they must perform. You need to have the training and let people know what they must do. This is one of the easiest ways to protect data.

Using Secure Passwords

Remember, passwords are important to maintain cybersecurity. Instruct your employees to choose passwords that are difficult for a hacker to guess. You must avoid the usage of dates and names in your password since hackers can easily connect you with those words. You must also instruct them to change passwords regularly. You can also use a multi-factor authentication system to add an extra layer of protection to the accounts.

Ensure Software is Updated

If you have outdated software in your systems, it can lead to a security risk. You should always update the software with the latest patches. For example, if you use the Windows Operating System, you must allow the updates to run so that you can cover any vulnerabilities or gaps.

Secure the Network

You must use firewalls to protect the network used in the system. Make sure to use encryption, so you make it harder for a hacker or any other user to access the data.

You must be careful when you use Wi-Fi since most hackers target those connections. Let employees know they should not use public Wi-Fi.

Ask them to use VPN connections to secure the transmission of data. Make sure to protect the router using a strong password.

Back-Up the Data

Regardless of how vigilant you are, a hacker can choose to target your system or network. Store the data on a disk in the event of such an attack. Let the system store the data automatically in a secure place. You could also store the data in a separate data center.

Control Access

You must ensure to maintain some control over the devices used by employees as well. Employees must be careful about the information on their screen, and should never leave it unlocked. If they leave their station or desk for a minute, they must log out of that system. Since anyone can walk away with a laptop, employees should be told never to leave it unattended. Since more business is conducted on tablets and smartphones, hackers target these devices.

Employees must secure their data on the phone and protect their phones using a password. They must report the loss or theft of the device promptly.

Cybersecurity Training

Organizations can always reduce the risk of cyber-attacks by training their employees. They can use Target Solutions Cybersecurity Training for employees. This training material will provide dynamic courses to check the user's knowledge about cybersecurity.

CHAPTER 11:

Economic Impact of Cybersecurity

The Business of Cybersecurity

F unding higher levels of cybersecurity is part of the business problem executives must address. Small and medium businesses often operate on razor-thin margins. Therefore, it is important to ensure every cybersecurity dollar is spent wisely. Failure to do so not only leaves gaps in security, but overspending can destroy a competitive edge on cost. When allocating funds, it is important to decide which cybersecurity expenses are treated as a cost of goods sold and which to consider as investments for improving profits and winning market share. It is the same problem executives faced during the rise of computers and the Internet decades ago: "Is this newfangled stuff to be treated as an expense or an investment?" We argue that it is both and will help you understand both perspectives.

It is particularly hard for busy leaders of small companies to prioritize risk management planning. They want to jump to the part where they buy cybersecurity solutions and get back to running their business as quickly as possible. Taking time to think about strategy, for a small company, seems like a waste of time when there are customers waiting to be served. But nothing could be further from the truth, and we also understand that it can be daunting to think about cybersecurity when everything is so technical. We use the terms strategy and tactical to identify those areas that need your attention and which to consider delegating or outsourcing.

Before we dive into our step-by-step explanation of your role, let's examine several of the contributions and benefits to executive involvement. Most of these functions are impossible to outsource because they require expertise and authority that only top management possesses. That doesn't mean you cannot use tools and advisors to help you along the way; it just means you cannot relinquish responsibility for them.

Stating and controlling direction. Goal setting starts at the top and reflects the needs of the business. Goals and objectives provide context for tactical planning, and communicating them clearly to a diverse team of expert tactical advisors keep everyone focu5sed, and on the same page.

Allocating budget. Business owners understand that cybersecurity measures will cost time and money, and as an executive, it is your responsibility to decide where the money will go. Your IT guru recommends a new firewall. Then your insurance agent recommends adding a cyber insurance policy. If you buy both (and you should buy both), how do you divide up the limited budget between all the possible solutions? If cybersecurity is relegated to just a tactical IT problem, you will have a fantastic firewall but no protection when a hacker finds their way around it.

Authorizing company-wide policies. Whether it's enforcing bring-your-own-device policies or using strong passwords, someone should be in control of what's being done and how well policies are being followed. The ability to authorize new cybersecurity measures comes from the top in any organization. The people-driven aspects of cybersecurity are absolutely a business problem that you, as the top manager, need to oversee.

Maintaining compliance. Once authorized, policies and procedures must be carried out. Failure to do so will be construed as negligence, which leads to prosecution and regulatory fines. Cyber insurance, citing "failure to follow" exclusions, will also deny coverage if you fail to maintain your own security standards. Your authority and your ability to develop a culture of compliance are critical to avoiding these catastrophic mistakes.

Empathy in a crisis. When a data breach happens, despite every effort to prevent it, clients and employees will be more forgiving if they believe top management was paying attention and making an effort. Even when responsibility for a breach can be traced to an individual or external actor, clients and employees want to know that you were being vigilant.

Justify spending. The return on investment for cybersecurity is obscured. It is hard to measure how bad things could have been if you did not invest in something that prevents or reduces loss, but that does not mean it is impossible. Risk management tools and techniques that have been adapted to cybersecurity can rationalize spending. Whether you report to yourself or another stakeholder in the company, you can invest with confidence when you can articulate the value.

We will not go deeply into tactical details that can be delegated to staff and vendors, although we will explain what they are and how they get used so you can manage them effectively.

Bonus: How to Stop Identity Theft on Facebook and Other Social Media

Sharing is a core value of social media and a key reason for the wild growth and success of companies such as Facebook, Twitter, YouTube, and LinkedIn. For some of us, it's fun to post comments, articles, photos, and videos for our friends and social media followers. Many people participate passively, watching, and reading others' posts but rarely sharing their own. Never have humans had such open and easy access to tell their personal stories or share their ideas, experiences, and feelings.

But like much about the Internet, all this sharing can draw unwanted and dangerous attention. You don't want the "bad guys" watching you. And any social media platform you use potentially connects you to mind-boggling numbers of people. Over a billion people worldwide have a Facebook account2, 307 million people actively use Twitter3, and the number of Instagram users exceeds 500 million. 4 That's why you must exercise complete control over your digital life, and you do that on social media by keeping a sharp eye on your privacy settings. Nearly all social media sites let you control who sees your information. When you review your privacy controls regularly, you ensure that you have the strongest security in place.

Who Can See Your Profile?

Social media networks continue to grow and allow you to connect with family, friends, colleagues, and classmates, but sharing without thinking about who sees your information just invites trouble.

We often ask people we meet if they've checked their social media privacy settings lately—many have no idea. That usually means the public can view their open profiles—posts, photos, likes, friends, and other activities. You may be OK with that openness, but you should be concerned. Scammers can "scrape" or copy your profile, learn more about you, and use that information to perpetrate any variety of scams, frauds, and hacks. For example, say you post a photo of your dog in your backyard and write a caption such as "Look at Buddy soaking up the sun." A scammer who reads that post now has a good chance of answering the password reset question on your email account if you selected: "What's your pet's name?" An open profile gives hackers the important details they need to hack your life—whether it's seizing your email account, assuming your identity in credit-card fraud, or cracking your bank account. 5 Strong privacy settings block hackers from seeing your profiles.

Know Your Privacy Settings and Your Friends

You can still enjoy social media and maintain good security; you just need to strike the right balance by knowing how privacy settings work at different sites. A simple Google search on a website's name and "privacy settings" will get you started. All social media sites will give you some measure of control over who sees your profile and activities. Your biggest decision will be selecting a security level that allows you to share with friends while keeping your privacy. Thankfully, it won't involve much effort.

In addition to beefing up your privacy settings, you'll also need to review your "friends" to make sure you still want them to see your social media activities. For example, should the friend of a friend know when you are on vacation because they can see your photos? It's important to remember that your posts have a larger audience than you realize. Also, social media companies frequently change their privacy policies and default settings. Pay attention to privacy updates you receive from Facebook and other sites: They're not just "fine print" and often contain important changes that need your attention if you want to keep strong privacy on social media. We think most people should follow this rule: Do not leave your profile open for everyone to see. A study by antivirus firm Norton found that four in every ten social media users have suffered fraud.6 Open profiles essentially hand over your personal information to scammers and hackers without much effort. Don't make their job easy. Think twice about what you share and with whom—a key rule to hack-proofing your life.

Conclusion

The United States has complained that Russian hackers had meddled with the 2016 presidential elections. It was a major incident. Russian hackers hacked into Democratic National Committee and published some pretty confidential emails during the 2016 presidential elections in the United States. This episode produced quite a stir in the legislative corridors of the United States. The power and impact of cybersecurity were revisited, and the importance of cybersecurity was elevated, and for the first time, cybersecurity was seen through the context of international relations. The incident was not normal as it had the potential to push the two countries into a kind of conflict. The level of the attack was unprecedented in nature, not only in the United States but also across the globe. People had started seeing cybersecurity from a different lens. The incident of Sony Pictures started spinning before the eyes of lots of people who responded with mixed sentiments. Some of them showed a bit of surprise, and others showed extreme concern, while a few showed no reaction at all.

The United States had accused a state of cyberattack in the past in the wake of the attack on Sony Picture Entertainment, but the scale and the impact of this attack were unprecedented. It meant that anyone with a computer could change the course of an election of the most powerful country in the world. But for seasoned cybersecurity experts, this development is not news. Since the advent of the internet back in the mid-1990s, the cyberspace has witnessed some pretty amazing growth that filled the pockets of millions of people due to rapid commercialization but also pushed people into the depths of the crisis. Cybersecurity has now climbed up the ladder and has reached the heads of the state who have started seeing the security of the world in a different way. Scholars of international relations see this new discipline as a subfield of security studies with a special focus on the implications of technology for international security. This takes into account its effects on the sovereignty, power, and world governance.

Cybersecurity has gained considerable attention for the past few years on the back of the fact that the attacker is usually not known. This creates a lot of confusion and suspicion that are very unhealthy for a peaceful international environment. Large nations sometimes use proxies to wage cyberattacks and afterward label them as a rogue to avoid direct confrontation with the power they are dealing with. We have seen this in the North Koran attack on Sony Pictures. North Korea denounced the attack by appreciated their deed as patriotic. Similarly, when the Russian hackers meddled in the US elections, Vladimir Putin, the Russian president, denies any involvement of the state in the attack but added to the tail of his speech that some patriotic minded Russian hackers might have committed that deed. He appeared to have been appreciating what the hackers had done to the country that had a long history of enmity with Russia.

Had Putin claimed the attack, there would have been an all-out war between the two superpowers of the world. Cybersecurity is playing a crucial role in international relations because the threat of nuclear war and the mutual assured destruction as a result of the war have negatively affected the world's strategic scenario. Humans, by nature, cannot live without a contest. Physical war is not possible as the threat of nuclear war keeps looming over the participants of the war. We can see this in the subcontinent where India and Pakistan, the two nuclear powers, have made the subcontinent a nuclear flashpoint in the area. Despite the fact that the possibility of a conflict remains high, the idea of a hot war is not usually pursued by the two countries. So, if countries must go into a conflict, they choose the cyber realm to fight each other. Cyberwarfare is an advanced mode of cold wars. I have quoted the example of a scenario in which India responded with a hacking attack after the Pulwama attack. Similarly, North Korea attacked Sony Pictures through a cyber-security breach because it didn't have the power to confront the United States, and also it had to give a befitting response to Sony Pictures for making the movie that was a spoof of an assassination attempt on Kim Jong-un.

Cybersecurity issues are becoming more lethal day by day, and it remains doubtful that it will help improve international relations. Up till now, it has shown great potential in complicating and destroying international relations.

This book has explained all the necessary details on the subject of cybersecurity. You have learned what the basics of cybersecurity are. You have also learned what the general motivations are behind an act of cybercriminal. I have discussed in detail was social engineering is and how it is used by malicious hackers to infiltrate a facility. Then I moved on to explain cyber terrorism, its types, and its adverse effects on the modern world, such as the relations between countries and the general peace of the country.